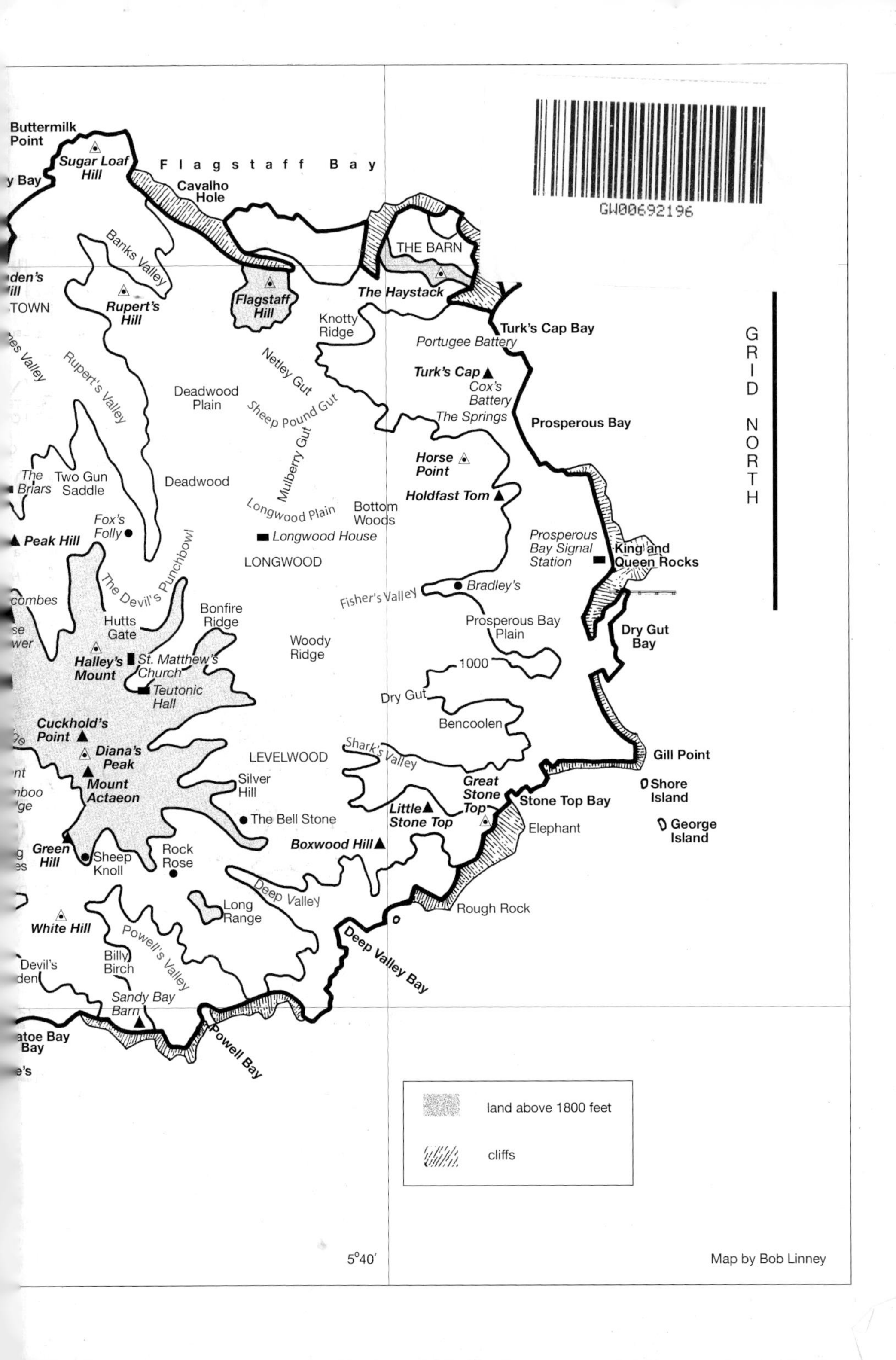
GW00692196
Buttermilk Point
Sugar Loaf Hill
Flagstaff Bay
Cavalho Hole
THE BARN
Banks Valley
Flagstaff Hill
The Haystack
Rupert's Hill
TOWN
Knotty Ridge
Turk's Cap Bay
Portugee Battery
Rupert's Valley
Netley Gut
Turk's Cap
Cox's Battery
Deadwood Plain
Sheep Pound Gut
The Springs
Prosperous Bay
Mulberry Gut
Horse Point
The Briars
Two Gun Saddle
Deadwood
Holdfast Tom
Longwood Plain
Bottom Woods
Fox's Folly
Peak Hill
Longwood House
Prosperous Bay Signal Station
King and Queen Rocks
The Devil's Punchbowl
LONGWOOD
Bradley's
Fisher's Valley
Bonfire Ridge
Hutts Gate
Prosperous Bay Plain
Dry Gut Bay
Woody Ridge
Halley's Mount
St. Matthew's Church
1000
Teutonic Hall
Dry Gut
Bencoolen
Cuckhold's Point
Diana's Peak
LEVELWOOD
Shark's Valley
Gill Point
Mount Actaeon
Silver Hill
Great Stone Top
Shore Island
Stone Top Bay
Little Stone Top
The Bell Stone
Elephant
George Island
Green Hill
Sheep Knoll
Rock Rose
Boxwood Hill
Deep Valley
Long Range
Rough Rock
White Hill
Powell's Valley
Deep Valley Bay
Billy Birch
Sandy Bay Barn
Powell Bay
GRID NORTH
land above 1800 feet
cliffs
5°40′
Map by Bob Linney

# ST HELENA

## ONE MAN'S ISLAND

by

Ian Baker

First published in Great Britain in 2004

by

WILTON 65
Hernes Keep, Winkfield, Windsor, Berkshire SL4 4SY



ISBN 0 947828 14 1

For Basil and Barbara

## ACKNOWLEDGEMENTS

I have been most fortunate over four decades to have the friendship of Basil and Barbara George; I owe them a special debt of gratitude, for without their continuous support and encouragement I probably wouldn't have written this book. They were sources of information of all kinds on any and everything, and Basil was a marvellous companion for many walks, Holdfast Tom for example could never have been recorded without him. I am grateful too, to their family, Kevin and Joey, and Emma and Anthony, for hospitality, friendship and help in so many ways.

I would like to record the friendship, hospitality and help of all kinds over the years from Maurice and Maisie Thomas; from Lynton and Christina and earlier generations of the Peters family; from Gary and Sandra Stevens, especially to Gary for those visits to the Asses Ears; and Pat Williams.

Nick Thorpe has been a great help over several years with provision of all kinds of information, much of it archival, hospitality and support. Clive Stewart and Edward Thorpe were excellent walking companions on my last visit, and their support, occasionally physical, and wide ranging interests were greatly appreciated.

I am grateful to Maureen Stevens, formerly of the St Helena Archives, for helping me find material I would otherwise have missed. Use of the St Helena Archives, the Jamestown Library, the British Library (especially the former India Office Library), and the Natural History Museum Library, are gratefully acknowledged.

I am most grateful to John Price for encouragement, and particularly for his reading of, comments on, and corrections to, the draft manuscript.

For the publication of the book I am indebted to Pamela

Lawrence, Chief Education Officer of the island, for her support, especially through the Revolving Book Fund. I am grateful too, to Diana Holderness of WILTON 65 for unflagging encouragement and patience.

Special thanks go to my wife who put up with my three long absences on the island, and whose patience through my endless talking about this extraordinary island never faltered.

I end with my gratitude to the many islanders, from all walks of life, who made me feel at home, and directly or indirectly exposed me to the fascination of all aspects of their island - I hope they will forgive me the errors, lapses, omissions, and my obsession with the geological intricacies of so many of St Helena's wilder places.

# INTRODUCTION

*St Helena : Probably the best known of all the solitary islands in the world.*

Whitaker's Almanack

Islands are special places. They are finite, complete. They are remote. They are of the sea, and because of that, their land has added value. I like islands, I always have. As a child, when the incoming tide surrounded my sandcastle I was happy - for a few moments I had my own island.

Increasingly we find it difficult to handle the complexity that we have let the world around us become. But an island is an entity, it is perhaps manageable, we can see its limits. We may even feel we can understand it. An island can begin to show its hidden corners, some of its magic, perhaps even reveal some of its skeletons. An island can become part of you, though perhaps not you part of it.

An island's remoteness gives you the chance to find time. Its everyday rapidly becomes your everyday, and makes you gear yourself to its different values and priorities. Things you might normally term insignificant become worth looking at, waiting for, watching; they become important. An island allows you to stop and stare, to look anew at things with which you're familiar, and to find the things with which you aren't. It gives you chances to look more closely at yourself.

And what about St Helena? Well, Whitaker's is some kind of a start. But it's on pretty thin ice, a generalisation like that. What about Pitcairn, or Easter Island? Better might be: *probably the island most featured on quiz shows*. How regularly do you hear, "Who died on St Helena on May 5th, 1821?" or "On which island was Napoleon exiled after the Battle of Waterloo?" Fletcher

Christian does appear occasionally, so do the great stone idols, but St Helena is very much the front runner.

*Solitary island*? There's no denying that. Continental coasts are 1200 miles to the east, and nearly 2000 to the west. Its nearest neighbour, an even smaller island, is over 700 miles away. It is this isolation, as much as anything, that has given St Helena much of its distinctive character.

*Best known*? Presumably because of Napoleon and his death, which would put it in the same sort of category as Boot Hill, or perhaps, to be fair, Missolonghi. It's not as though Napoleon's mortal remains are actually there. But Napoleon apart, what does anyone know about it as a place, a real island? Does anyone for example know where it is? Even the most popular T-shirt on the island asks, **Where on Earth *Is* St Helena Island.**

If I told you it was a tropical island, with long white beaches and palm trees by the turquoise sea, pirates' treasure, that sort of thing, would you believe it? It's easily enough pictured, isn't it? Well, it's certainly tropical, but it's got none of the rest. It's a great rocky island, with the waves pounding black boulder beaches, and high cliffs which hide its verdant rugged interior.

And it's got mist-swept high ridges, and deserts where it never rains, and forest from before the beginning of time, and pillars and towers and columns of rocks, sculpted into shapes of heaven and hell side by side, and delightful country houses and cattle. All of that on an island not even half the size of the Isle of Wight, the same size as Walt Disney World, or Greater Manchester.

It's got waves called *rollers,* the height of houses, and it's got more history than a handful of museums, all on your doorstep. Napoleon was only one of the birds of passage. What about Cavendish, William Dampier and his painted prince, Captain Cook, Charles Darwin, Captain Bligh, Edmond Halley, Wellington, Mason and Dixon, Chief Dinizulu, the real William Hickey? You name them, and they were all there.

St Helena is a glorious backwater, its people and its plants and its history brought in from all over the world. You can walk in biblical deserts in the morning; swim in rock pools with rainbow fish, before eating a few grilled for lunch. Then in the afternoon, sip tea on lawns surrounded by roses and dahlias, and after dinner, chat in the moonlight beneath banks of night-flowering Cereus. And you can do all that on foot.

This is a book about different bits of St Helena. There are bits of history, because that is so wrapped into its present. There are bits of Napoleon, and some of the other people, famous or infamous, from all corners of history's closets, front and back pages, who stopped by the island for one reason or other. And there's some of its many ghosts.

There are bits about its geography, because nothing else available tells you much about the wonders of the island. There are bits about its flora, which is one of the most extraordinary aspects of its natural history. Much of its original, unique flora was marooned there ten million years ago. Then over the last five hundred years, hundreds and hundreds of plants and flowers and trees were brought in by travellers from every corner of the globe, turning it into a sort of glorious botanic left luggage office.

There's something about its geology, because no other volcano in the world is quite like it, with elements as remarkable as its flora. There are bits of the Saints, with their origins in Britain, Europe, Africa, Madagascar, India, the East Indies, and China, to name but a few. A population like that almost makes it a gazetteer in its own right.

So it's a mixture of a book. And it's very personal, because that's the way the island affects you. As much as anything it's a sort of love story, of one man and his forty year fascination for the life of this island in all its remarkable diversity.

Few places on the planet offer such diverse variations. To be honest, I think that so much, in such a manageable area, has to be unique. I had difficulties in knowing not only where to start, but how to continue, and certainly where to finish. So many things are interwoven, often apparently quite illogically.

Remember this is one man's island, one man's views, feelings, beliefs, understandings. I apologise now to the islanders, for bits I've got wrong, or misrepresented, for bits I've forgotten, or left out intentionally. But in the picture of things this doesn't concern me unduly. Most island stories have differences depending on who tells them, even the many and varied histories offer radically different accounts of the same events. So if you disagree, or find another view, so much the better, it adds to the value of the island.

It's an odd sort of travel book too, because it's as much about time, as it is about place. It's an island where time's several dimensions are threaded with those of its diversities of place. A visit to St Helena is a visit into them all.

# CONTENTS

# PHOTOGRAPHS

## Plates 1 to 16 between pages 88 & 89

**Plate 20**

Top: Endemic Tree Ferns (*Dicksonia arborescens*)and Black Cabbage Trees

Btm: Endemic Black Cabbage Tree (*Melanodendron integrifolium)*

**Plate 21**

Top: High Hill and area round Blue Hill

Btm: Broad Bottom

**Plate 22**

Top left: Luffkins and rim of Sandy Bay

Top right: Lot and Sandy Bay Baptist chapel

Btm: Mount Pleasant

**Plate 23**

Top:Frightus Rock, Asses Ears, Man o' War Roost, Lot's Wife

Btm: Sandy Bay Beach from Horse's Head

**Plate 24**

Top: Battery below the Baptist chapel

Btm: Fortifications at Horse's Head

**Plate 25**

Top: Sandy Bay:Lot and Riding Stones Hill

Btm: Lot and Lot's Wife

**Plate 26**

Top: Centre of the volcano from Lot's Wife's Ponds

Btm: Man o' War Roost and inland cliffs

**Plate 27**

Top left: Lot's Wife's Ponds towards the Asses Ears

Top right: The back of Frightus Rock with Gary Stevens

Btm: Frightus Rock

**Plate 28**

Endemic Old Father Live Forever (*Pelargonium cotyledonis*)

**Plate 29**

Top left: Endemic Salad Plant (*Hypertelis acida*)
Top right: Speery Island and Manati Bay from Botley's Lay
Btm: Regrowth of endemic Scrubwoods (*Commidendrum rugosum*)

**Plate 30**

Top left: Black Rocks, coast below Castle Rock Plain
Top right: Man and Horse cliffs from Manati Bay
Btm: Sandy Bay Barn and southern coast from Sharks Bench

**Plate 31**

Top: Castle Rock and Speery Island
Btm: Man and Horse towards High Hill

**Plate 32**

Top: Endemic Baby's Toes (*Hydrodea cryptantha*)
Btm: Calcite stalactites, Manati Bay towards Devil's Hole

# CHAPTER 1

## WHERE ON EARTH *IS* ST HELENA?

*It is impossible to approach and see this singular island, for the first time, without wondering how the deuce it got there.*
Lieutenant James Prior, frigate *Nisus,* January 31st, 1812

It was the 21st day of May, 1502.

"Land!" Or more exactly its equivalent in Portuguese, croaked the voice of the half-dead lookout. "Land!"

Through the faceless swell of the South Atlantic, almost in disbelief, three little ships made for the grey smudge on the north-western horizon. The commander of the fleet was Admiral Joao da Nova, one of that handful of Portugal's intrepid seamen who were the astronauts of their time. The three ships anchored in a small bay, beneath the dark towering cliffs of the lee coast of the island.

After months at sea, the flotilla, returning home from India, had gained another temporary reprise. What was left of their water was foetid, the food rotten. The crew, weakened with scurvy, dysentery, malnutrition and whatever else, landed to find a stream of pure water. There were fish and sea birds, and no doubt some of the greenery that covered the island was edible. What a gift from God.

It was the feast day, in the Eastern Orthodox calendar, of Saint Helena, mother of Constantine, the first Christian Emperor of the Roman Empire. From the timbers of the smallest vessel, which had sadly sailed its last, da Nova and the grateful Portuguese built a chapel to thank the God that had saved them, and brought them to this special place.

The Portuguese had discovered St Helena.

It was the last week of April, 1964. I was in the tiny balance room at College, talking with a fellow inmate, Ian Ridley. Finals were a month away. A member of staff came in, his large frame filling the doorway and what little space was left of the room.

"You guys still working? I don't believe it." Pause. "What are you going to do when you graduate?" Pause. "Assuming you graduate."

We mumbled. We muttered. We'd like to stay on and do research, hopefully into volcanic rocks, we hazarded.

He stood for a while, he may have been thinking, he may have nodded off. But he spoke, "Baker. How'd you like to go to St Helena?"

"St Helena? Yes, great. Marvellous."

"Do what you want, just collect me all the phonolites, they're interesting, OK?" Pause, while I nodded my head. "Ridley, you want to go to Tenerife?"

"Great, yes. Fantastic."

"Good," and he walked off. And that was it. Things were so much simpler in the Stone Age.

"Well that's all right, then," said Ridley, "Where's St Helena?"

"I haven't a clue, but it's bound to be a long way away, and that suits me." I stood up, "I'm going to the library to find out."

Ridley, always pragmatic, added, "Better look up phonolite while you're at it."

I had heard about St Helena.

It was the first week of December, 1995. I was driving down to Chichester to leave my car, and the first snow was dusting the hills. It piped the skeletons of the trees, bringing out a third dimension in the flat grey monotone. The snow gave a feeling of Christmas as a child, like the pictures on Christmas cards. You expected to see robins, and sheltering, chilled rabbits. An occasional deer would have been perfectly in keeping. The sun didn't quite break through, it was just a bright, more or less circular patch of pale yellow sky.

I left the car, and returned to London by train. There were delays. There were frozen points, there were signal failures, there were automatic barrier failures. I got back home, and as the day wore on, there were snow warnings on television, and photos of

Kent looking a little like Siberia. The wonders of modern technology, of civilisation, and an inch or two of snow had seized up the M25. Two thousand cars were abandoned. The ancient ritual of Britons, masochists to the well loved perversities of the elements, confronting their annual nuclear winter, had begun.

Television continued its accounts of the difficulties of high technology facing up to the primitive deceptions of winter. Some authorities had started salting and gritting, others hadn't got the money to start. Even those that had started, might have insufficient money, or insufficient grit, or salt, or vehicles, or God alone knew what else, to continue. They warned, preemptive first strike, that the cost of this blizzard could well force them to curtail, or stop altogether, other road maintainance.

Here we were in the late twentieth century, on the edge of the new millenium, and early flakes of snow were bringing the transportation systems of western civilisation into chaos, threatening carnage on the roads. Here was I all set to return to St Helena, and in spite of this terrifying TV drama, people still wondered why I wanted to spend winter on a Godforsaken island they saw as some erstwhile Napoleonic penal colony.

After that near monosyllabic exchange in the balance room in 1964, I spent four months on the island, and returned for five more in 65/66, studying the geology. It was a different world, and I loved it, its liveliness and its incredible peace, its people, its history and its spectacular scenery. All of it collected on a dead volcano only 47 square miles in area, thousands of miles from anywhere.

Saint Helena had found me. I'd been hooked. And over the years, a bit like malaria, it had kept coming back. And now so was I.

I'd decided to go back for a variety of reasons. I wanted to see the island again, see how it had changed. But the main one was to 'walk' over it again. I'd covered the island doing the geology, and had loved the extreme diversity of its scenery, and the solitude. It's a small island, but you can get away from everything except nature itself. There are so few people, especially in the more remote areas (and that's pretty well most of the island), that you can be completely alone, if you want to be. Or you can go with people, if you want. Or tell people where you're going, so the isolation can be somehow shared, if that helps.

The variations in scenery are so great, and where man has been, the historical bits and pieces so intermingled, that you can decide exactly in what kind of world, almost in what kind of era, you want to spend the day. Desert or Alpine, cliffs or pastures, ancient forest or fishing rocks? You name it, and the choice is yours, and all at walking distance from the house, more or less. How about that? That's why I was going back.

So in '95/'96 I spent another four months on the island, and when I got home I thought that that was that, I must have got it out of my system. I'd re-visited this island from my past, seen it again, walked it again. So, I'd been there, done that, several times. By now, I thought I should have been *on* the T-shirt.

But it wasn't as simple as that. I'd been surprised in '95 when I'd found the island even better than I'd remembered. Almost without conscious thinking within a matter of months, I'd phoned Falmouth to book for another four months, in '98/'99. And the same thing happened again! Wonderful visit, and *that* will definitely be my last visit, I decided. Six months later and I'd booked again for 2003/04. Maybe I should get a season ticket.

St Helena lies in the middle of the South Atlantic, sixteen degrees south of the Equator. It has an area of 47 square miles, with maximum dimensions of approximately ten and a half by six and a half miles. It lies in the SE Trade Winds, and is cooled by the Benguela Current, so although in the tropics, it enjoys a subtropical to temperate climate. It can rain at almost any time of the year, but broadly April to October is cooler and wetter; November to March warmer and drier.

There are steep cliffs round most of the island, from 600 to over 1500 feet in height. From the cliff tops, the land rises more gently towards the central high ground at about 2700 ft. The outer fringes are largely barren, and above about 1500 ft most of the ground is agricultural, pasture or woodland. A small area of endemic flora is preserved in a National Park at the very apex of the island.

St Helena is a British Overseas Territory, with a Governor,

presiding over an elected local Council of 12 members. The islands of Ascension (700 miles north), the Tristan da Cunha group (1500 miles south), and Gough Island (300 miles south-west of Tristan), are dependencies of the island. Full British Citizenship was withdrawn from the islanders thirty years ago, but after a long struggle it was restored in 2002. The population of around 5000, having held fairly steady for decades (largely because of migration for off-shore work on Ascension and the Falklands), has in the last two years dropped to about 3800.

The island was settled by the British in 1659. In 1673 it was briefly captured by the Dutch, but later in the same year was reclaimed with naval intervention. From 1659 the island was administered by the Honourable East India Company (HEIC or just the EIC), with a temporary break for Napoleon, until 1834, when it became dependent on the Crown.

Fishing, mainly of tuna, is the principal industry, though employing only a relatively small number of people. A large part of the work force is employed on Ascension and in the Falklands. So a significant part of the island's income is derived from this offshore labour. Some money comes from the granting of fishing licenses, and an extremely modest income comes from the sale of stamps and first day covers. Nearly half of the island's annual budget comes from a grant from the British Government.

Those are the bare facts by way of background, but what exactly have I fallen for? The T-shirt asks '*Where* on Earth ...', but more difficult as a starter, and certainly as interesting, is '*Why* on Earth is St Helena Island?'

We could start with *What* is St Helena? It is a volcanic island, and that helps a little with *Why*?

For several hundred million years, the continents of the world as we think of them, were joined together in one huge super-continent. Then about a hundred million years ago, two 'western' masses started separating from the enormous 'eastern' block. These two masses were North and South America (as we know them), and the splits were the start of the Atlantic Ocean.

The Earth's surface is made up of a number of rigid *plates*,

50 miles or so thick, this is the Earth's crust. These huge plates, which can be land or ocean or both, are driven by a process known as *plate tectonics*. Heat in the Mantle generates convection currents on a colossal scale. This motion moves the plates which essentially 'float' on it. If the plates are forced apart, molten material is injected into the gap, or rift, between them.

Well, the Atlantic was being opened up. Vast quantities of molten material were forced between the plates, gradually pushing them apart on either side. The Americas were moved westerly, the rest, Eurasia and Africa, were moved east. The zone along which the Earth's surface was splitting was the mid-Atlantic Rift, buried beneath the newly forming ocean.

So the mid-Atlantic Rift was a hot zone with molten material continuously pushed into it. If in places the heat source was maintained, then a submarine volcano would develop. And exceptionally, very exceptionally, the heat source, now within the plate itself, continued, and the volcano grew and grew, bursting out of its ocean depths as an island volcano was born.

Such islands were rare events. From the Arctic to the Antarctic associated with the mid-Atlantic Rift you have: Iceland and the Azores, straddling the Rift, and in the south Atlantic, Ascension, St Helena, the Tristan group, Gough, and Bouvet in the deep south.

These islands are rare for two reasons: the magma source has to stay with the island, for millions of years, as the conveyor belt of plate tectonics moves it away. And they have to grow through immense depths of water. The great volcanic pile of St Helena is higher than Mt Blanc before it breaks the water's surface. Although only ten miles at its longest at the surface, the base of St Helena three miles down is more than eighty miles across.

I don't want to bog you down with geological numbers, but it took millions of years for St Helena to rise above the ocean's surface, to erupt spectacularly, a sort of giant beacon in the south Atlantic, for a few million more. Seven or eight million years ago the eruptions ceased. So whereas Tristan da Cunha erupted in 1961, and Ascension is probably only dormant, St Helena as a volcano is very, very dead. That's why its so interesting. Those million years after activity ceased have allowed the waves and the elements to carve and gouge the simple shape of a vigorous young volcano into the wonder that is the elderly island today.

So that's *why* on Earth is Saint Helena. And what fascinates me is what time has done to it. What Nature has done to it, the elements, and then of course Man. All of these have interacted to create the story of St Helena, and I just walk through its many different parts trying to capture some of that story.

# CHAPTER 2

## GETTING THERE

*The 12th of May in the morning, betimes,we discovered the island of St Helena; whereat there was great joy in the ship, as if we had been in Heaven.*
John Huyghen van Linschoten in 1589, after 132 days at sea without sight of land

Small though it may be, it's a lot easier to find the island today, and it doesn't take as long as it did early on. For a start, it's marked on the maps. And of course you can reach it by telephone, radio, fax, and e-mail. So you can ask them where they are. But there are still logistic difficulties to physically getting there. St Helena is one of few populated islands without an airport, indeed without an airstrip. So you don't find it in holiday brochures.

But one shipping company knows how to get there. For me in the nineties it was Curnow Shipping Limited in Falmouth, but now it's Andrew Weir Shipping Limited, at 2 Royal Mint Court, London EC3. As Managing Agents of the St Helena Shipping Line, they run the only commercial vessel which calls at the island, the RMS *Saint Helena.* In 1502 da Nova had three ships when he arrived, two when he left. Half a millenium later, there's only a single ship going to and from the island.

The 'RMS', as the vessel is called, serves St Helena for passengers, cargo and mail. The one exception is fuel oil, which arrives by tanker. But unless it grows on the island, swims round it, or falls from the sky onto it, everything you eat, wear, drink, travel in, live in, on or under, is brought by the RMS. Quite literally the island's lifeline, it is part of the island and her people. Custom built for the island, weighing in at 6767 tonnes, the RMS carries 128 passengers and 1500 tonnes of cargo. It was launched on Hallowe'en 1989, by Prince Andrew, Duke of York (there is a strong connection between the island and Dukes of York), and was delivered a year later.

The schedule for the sailings of the RMS is currently under review. For a trial period after September 2004 the RMS will operate only in the South Atlantic. Cape Town will be its main base for regular sailings, via Walvis Bay, to and from St Helena, and regular shuttles to and from Ascension. We must await the outcome of the year's trial to see if an annual call to Tristan will be reinstated. The intricasies of flights to and from Ascension, Johannesburg, Walvis Bay and Cape Town are now serious elements in sorting out a composite itinerary.

It was easier for me. I sailed from the UK in '95, '98 and '03, and that voyage in '95, after the thirty year gap, would set the scene. The RMS ensures that you get there in style, most probably heavier than when you departed. In today's world, it is a special style, as different as the island she is named after, and the people she serves.

I'd decided to go all the way by sea. I was nostalgic for the '60s, and the Union Castle sailings from Southampton. I wanted to remember the feeling of the remoteness of the island from Britain, indeed from anywhere. Sailing for fourteen days at fifteen knots covers a lot of water. It is a reminder of the island's isolation, that the Atlantic is a great ocean, and also that when you do eventually arrive, it's going to be all that way, and time, back again.

In December '95 the M4 hadn't been struck by the whiteout affecting the south-east, and the Queen Alexandra Dock at Cardiff was only cold. It was also broad, grey and almost empty. 'D' berth was the regular home in Wales of the RMS, and its equivalent of a terminal building had the atmosphere of a country bus station, casual, everybody apparently knowing everybody else. Friendly Welshmen take charge of the luggage, and point out that everyone has disappeared into the cafeteria. It's noisy, packed with Saints, mainly seeing off other Saints.

Embarkation starts at 1400, and more than three quarters of the people aren't going. Walk across the deserted dock, and welcome to a new world. Step off the gangway, and the ship envelops you. This will be your total environment for a fortnight, ninety of us on this particular run. Then there are the Captain and officers, British and St Helenian, and a crew of 36 Saint Helenian petty officers and ratings. The RMS becomes your world, and it will break you in gently for the island, nearly five thousand miles away.

It's a question of acclimatizing to a life of total relaxation, or stupor, or lethargy, or bliss. You choose. You're looked after 24 hours a day, fed and watered, entertained or left to your own devices. The most difficult decision is what you're going to eat. There's food and drinks fifteen or sixteen hours a day. Bars, restaurants, corridors with old island prints, lounges and paintings of bizarre island scenery, a shop, library, tiny swimmimg pool, a doctor, laundrette. The only thing missing is a palm tree to sit under, but a quick word with the Pursar and they'll knock one of those out.

So it's up gangway, through the lock, quietly away from the lights of Cardiff, and into the river. In '95 it was a gentle run down the Channel, and a quiet Bay of Biscay. In '98, it was force nine before we left the Bristol Channel, building erratically to force eleven in the Bay. But that's another story. After a decent night's sleep, and you've felt the ship beginning to move around a bit, a daily pattern begins.

If you asked for bed tea, it appears to the specified minute with *The Ocean Mail*, the ship's daily newspaper, presenting a panoply of activities for the day. Breakfast has more courses than the average state banquet. Lunches are cold and light in the sea lounge, hot and more substantial in the dining room. To keep you going, there's morning beef tea and coffee, afternoon tea and sandwiches. Dinners are early for those with children, later for the less calorifically challenged. More coffee and liqueurs with the evening's entertainment, and the bars stay open late. Perhaps they've done a deal with the marketting arm of Weight Watchers.

The Bay of Biscay is cold and lively. The Captain's cocktail party is warm and livelier. By now everyone at least recognises everyone else. The passengers form groups and sub-groups, even no groups, ill-defined, well-defined, reserved or amicable, with a closeness that allows you to join in or fall out, perfectly balanced, the choice is yours, nobody intrudes, nobody interferes.

The majority of the passengers are St Helenians of all ages, from many walks of life. There are more people of St Helenian origin in Britain than there are on the island. So the RMS has people going back after 20 or 30 years in the UK, some even 45 years away. Some are married to Brits, and children from a few months to some in their 20s have never seen the home of one or other, or both, of their parents. People are friendly, and most talk easily, and you slowly absorb stories of the island, of cooking, fishing, the climate, fruit flies or building a house. You cover a lot of ground in fourteen days

As the temperature begins to rise, deck quoits begin for the energetic. Someone sees a whale. There are videos to doze through after lunch. And in the pre-dawn of Day 5 we tie up in Tenerife for nine hours. With the Canaries, and generally most of the rougher weather, behind, dolphins disturb the vast mirror surface of the ocean, under a wall to wall pale blue sky. Out of sight of the African coast a weary merlin hitches a ride for a few miles before so elegantly flying off homewards. Later there are the steady lights of Dakar behind the bobbing lanterns of fishing boats.

As time wears on and the temperature rises, the atmosphere on board stays tranquil, but beneath the surface are darker currents. Who is going as what to the Fancy Dress? Are some of the quiz teams being helped by people in the audience? Is she standing on the right line for darts? Is it American or English dictionaries for Scrabble? Deck quoits is a problem, now that the ship is rock steady. There are no excuses for inept throws. St Helenians can be highly competitive. The skittles tournament is highly charged, and hilariously funny, depending on your outlook, but take care to stick with players of the same frame of mind.

There are 'Keep fit' sessions for passengers, videos powering the energetic forward, but attendance drops, leaving the most energetic sitting back, humming to the music. The officers keep fit playing deck tennis, and the Saints win the cricket match, passengers *v* crew. It was only to be expected, most of the twenty two players are Saints. The swimming pool is filled, but add a few bodies and it starts to overflow.

There are visits, to the bridge, the galley, and the engine rooms. There are more quizzes, frog racing, and a Casino night with cards almost buried under 10p coins. There is an excellent bar-b-que (in case we were in need of a square meal), dances, and clay pigeon shooting, though not necesarily in that order, or indeed juxtaposed. One loses track of events, and time, in the middle of the ocean.

But be prepared for an exhausting Day 10. This is the celebration of Crossing the Line, and the Captain and officers, as King Neptune and a supporting cast from Hell, entertain the assembled masses. It is the initiation of a handful of young press-ganged volunteers, crossing the Equator for the first time.

Afterwards, the volunteers wash off their body massages of kippers, selected offal, syrup, flour, eggs and unspeakable kitchen accessories, in the pool, now the colour and texture of Brown Windsor soup. Watch out for the chef's special at dinner. Watch out for other things too, for the dull roar of the dining room is punctuated with shrieks, perchance of delight, from improbable figures dressed as fairies or lightbulbs, witches or Belisha beacons. Geriatrics in tutus and six year olds with beards and hooks for hands, need to be fed.

After the Equator and the Fancy Dress Ball, the harsh reality of the world returns as, under a grey sky, the dull smudge of Ascension Island grows darker. It is a little sad, that after 4000 miles at sea, the welcome is flat, no evocative colours, no hint of the romance of this southern ocean. It looks a bit like the description by John Fryer, en route home from India in 1682, *another meer wart in the sea.*

The high central mass of Green Mountain is grey, its peak hidden in clouds. The only colour is provided by stretches of white beach sand, and guano spattered rocky shores. The sea, like the island, like the sky, is grey. Closer in, the impression is of a high-tech slag-heap. Satellite dishes, aerials, and white spheres of indeterminate content, dot a landscape of pyramidal cinder cones and craggy lava flows. Unlike St Helena, volcanically decidedly deceased, Ascension Island, very close to the mid-Atlantic Ridge, is dormant, it isn't yet dead.

So it seems a sad welcome. Another romantic pin prick of history and geography, and it's nailed to the floor of the ocean by high-tech screws of communication systems. But, this really is where the Americans track the long range ballistic missiles they fire from Florida. This really was the Earth receiving station for NASA's Apollo Project. On that fateful day in July 1969, so I'm told, "One small step for man, one giant leap for mankind" came from Neil Armstrong to the waiting world, courtesy of the NASA Tracking Station in the Devil's Ashpit, Ascension Island, dependency of St Helena. On such a flat grey day, just remember that.

There is to be a whistle-stop tour of the island, first 'colonised' by the Royal Marines in 1815, helping to guard the august personage of Napoleon Bonaparte, stashed 700 miles away on St Helena. The sea is crystal clear, full of not the long promised sharks, but small black fish which aren't even piranas. St Helenians help you ashore, and it's into Main Street, Georgetown, and a mixture of bright slashes of bougainvillea, the Expats Club, corrugated roofs, and a delightful church. Beyond the tortured low ground of slaggy lava flows and cinder cones, the remnant of the older volcano rises.

But after so many days at sea it is land, though your legs still think it is moving, and it is after all a sort of first gateway to St Helena. Geoff Shallcross, the Chief Pursar, an RMS and island legend in his own time, is driving our minibus. A young St Helenian WPC is driving the other. We have only two hours ashore, so Ascension is a series of disjointed images delivered in Geoff's inimitable style, a sort of collage of past, present and future of man. Grand though he may think he is with all his technology and concrete, what dominates, almost overwhelms, are the products of the volcano.

The landscape is lunar, great waves of the rubble of lava flows, and red-brown ash cones. There are feral donkeys, and land crabs clicking across the road. There are rows of barracks, the vast landing strip, fuel tanks, power lines, tracking dishes, and cars. Today the island is temporary home for 1200 or so people, more than 500 St Helenians, British at the BBC, with Cable and Wireless, with the RAF, and Americans with NASA, USAF and whatever.

This is very much a working island, not a holiday resort. Anyone not working is in transit, and better believe it. While the authorities are happiest if you don't stop at all, they are modestly pleased if you move on very quickly for some other island, "Have a nice transit."

The gigantic air strip started life more modestly in the Second World War, when it served an essential role in the delivery of aircraft from North America into various theatres of war, a stepping stone between Recife and Senegal. "Miss Ascension, your wife gets a pension," was the Canadian pilots' slogan as they flew the war machines towards it. Now the huge airstrip is big enough to land the Space Shuttle in an emergency, and it's a quick refuelling stopover for RAF flights heading to and from the Falklands.

The road zig-zags up Green Mountain, home of the island's water supply. Suddenly it is lush, with bamboos, eucalyptus and brilliant flowers, and through the mists, a cowshed with the Royal Marine crest lurches towards the vehicle. It is cool and soft, with the smell of rain and earth, you can almost hear the plants growing. What a delight after the ragged rock desert below, bananas, hibiscus, pig pens, cabbages and bignonia and datura. It is a different island, a totally different world, 2000 feet up in the sky. Now romance has come, maybe this is what the South Atlantic is all about.

Ascension has been a break in the sea, the wind and the sky. Its confusion of times is good preparation in that way, for St Helena. Back on board, Green Mountain is cut off by the cloud base, curtains of drifting rain cover all but the strongest features. There are navigation lights on the volcanic cones, whether for ships or space ships it doesn't matter. It is nearly dark as the RMS pulls away, and the human features of the island disappear in the grey-scape of sea and land and sky.

Time passes faster after Ascension. Games reach climactic finals, knuckles white for quoits or Scrabble, brows furrowed pegging out in crib, eyes closed for the ladies' darts, pencils snapping before the next quiz question. But there is a true undercurrent of excitement with the St Helenians, and the video on St Helena is standing room only. After that, the last evening has a party atmosphere, great fun, great spirit, everybody's going home.

Next day, around mid-day, thirty miles or so 'out', the outline of the island is visible, one end like a broken femur with its rounded hip-joint. Here is the *Black Rock*, with broken clouds settled over its top. It is longer and more solid than Ascension, there are vague signs of valleys and hills, ridge tops appear and disappear in drifting clouds of mist. Lunch is eaten quickly, and the features of the island grow clearer, the precipitous cliffs all round, jagged valleys climbing to the high ground of the green interior.

You can tell it's volcanic, from some way out you could see the layered lavas of the cliffs, much like those on Tenerife. You can see red and yellow bands of ash between the black basalt flows. With the eye of faith you can even see relic cinder cones like those on Ascension. The big difference with St Helena is that it is so much older. It's over seven million years since its volcanoes last erupted, and erosion has so dramatically carved and cut into them.

People look out for landmarks, but there is some confusion. It is one thing knowing every detail of the island when you live on it, it is very different looking at it from the sea, where all the geometry has changed. But nobody is really bothering about such fine detail, the cliffs are coming closer. It all looks so good. Yes, some of that joy of 1589 is there, even after a mere fourteen days at sea. People seem pretty happy with their thoughts of home, as much as with Heaven.

# CHAPTER 3

## LANDFALL AT LAST

*And whereas the said island hath bin found by experience to be very necessary and comodious for our loving subjects the said Governour and Company of Merchants trading into the East-Indies, for refreshing of their servants and people in their returnes homewards, being often then weak and decayed in their health by reason of their long voyages under their hott clymes.*
Charter re-issued by King Charles II, 16th December, 1673

I was excited about returning after so long. Two spells, nine months all told, on the island when I was in my early twenties, had made a big impression on me. Thirty years have diluted the memories, and no doubt exaggerated the better bits, so I'm also apprehensive about what I'll find. I'd kept in touch, admittedly more off than on, with St Helenian friends living on the island and in Britain. But I had only the vaguest ideas of how the island had changed.

In the '60s it had been a poor island, wages were low and its sole industry was New Zealand flax. There were half a dozen or more flax mills, but in 1966 it had all stopped, stone dead. The British Post Office was partly to blame, it was said, using rubber bands instead of twine.

The education system had been good, and medical provision seemed adequate. But you still saw people, adults and children, going barefoot, and children's clothes were often darned and handed down. Families were often large, and a population balance was maintained by the exit of young, and some not so young, people to work on Ascension or in the UK. When admission to work in the UK was greatly restricted around 1970, I hadn't been the only one to wonder what would happen with the population.

One thing that had been pretty well completed in the '60s, was the fencing of pastures, and the eradication of goats which had been allowed to roam wild since the 16th Century. Most of the endemic vegetation had been destroyed by goats and man. The contrast between the vegetated land, and the barren outer fringes, had been dramatic.Although there were then 500 cars on the island, it seemed as though almost everybody walked. Flax and other agricultural labourers going to work, children going to school, people going to one or other of the many churches, country women and their donkeys going to Saturday's market in town. Some country people rarely went into town, some only for boat days, some only on special days, one of the parades perhaps, or Christmas Eve.

I had stayed for my first season in town, in the Consulate Hotel. Most of the dozen or so others staying there were ex-pats, retired British and southern Africans. Ex-pats were allowed to settle on the island then, and could own property.Tourists were rare. Regular Union Castle ships called about once a month for a day, north or south bound, and that was long enough ashore for the majority. Souls like me, interested in specific elements of the island, were unusual, some Belgian entomologists, an occasional agricultural, or water consultant, surveyors for the planned Diplomatic Wireless Station.

A year later, I had the Consulate as a base again, but I brought a tent. I needed more time on the geology of the outlying areas, so I camped, or stayed elsewhere, and had my evening meal with island families. I developed a particular affection for the outlying areas.

I used to get back into town on Friday evenings, staggering into the Consulate for a reviving G and T, presented to me in a half pint mug by Mrs Moyce, her grin just visible above the bar. Saturday was a lively day. Well, after six days in a tent or ruin up country, anything involving people was pretty wild. Black puddings to help the beers go down at lunch time, and Cheese collecting for the Salvation Army during the evening session. But Sunday morning was no time for hangovers, off out again with a week's assorted stores, to the end of the road to be met by the donkey, and small boy in charge, that had dropped all my rocks there on Friday.

Electricity was pretty well restricted to town and Longwood. The island's telephone exchange was a community information installation. It was by the road at the top of Ladder Hill, opposite the old barracks. The operator could watch the road as she worked, and with no more than a couple of dozen telephones on the island, there was time enough for watching.

The Consulate had a telephone, but you didn't dial a number, although I swear there was a cyclostyled list pinned on the wall. You picked up the phone and waited. And after a brief chat with the operator, she asked you who you wanted. Not a number or a house, that was unnecessary, and wasting of valuable time. Mr So and So? No, he's just gone by, I'll call him in twenty minutes when he gets to the office. Well, Mr So and So, then? Not today lovey, he's gone fishing. Or whatever.

So it wasn't just the geology that had given me my fascination with the island. Yes, of course it was the rugged and lonely places, the silences and the wild shorelines, filling every working day. But it was those evening meals, talking with island people. It was bottle lanterns guttering in the Trade winds, stories of ghosts and ghostly places, it was the depths of the night sky, its stars barely out of reach, and the searing brilliance of cloud free days. I had a lot of memories to go back to.

Now it's 1995, and the RMS moves ahead very slowly, under the cliffs and into the Road in James Bay, and there is the running clatter of the anchor chain. The mouth of the V-shaped valley is dwarfed by the dark, towering cliffs, higher than Beachy Head. The Saints aren't daunted, they're home, already calling to boatmen. Lighters are in place, ready to start disembarking people, offloading luggage and cargo. A high speed rubber police boat powers off along the shore. That's new. Along one side of the bay, beneath a low overhang of cliff, is the wharf, with its collection of containers, buildings and cranes. That big crane's new, too.

There's a road along the top of the sea wall, with cars and crowds of people, and tops of trees behind, rising from a moat, and then the high Castle wall. Through an archway, are the houses of Jamestown and part of Main Street And the church now has a tower. What happened to the spire? Jacob's Ladder rises up the side of Ladder Hill, and a Union Jack flies from the flagstaff at the top.

There are traces of stone walls on one side, zig-zagging up to the barren ridge top. Far above, at the head of the valley, the promise of the verdant interior to the island we had seen from the sea, is just a hint beyond these brown barren rocks. There is sunshine and patches of cloud.

St Helenians aren't over demonstrative. You might see an occasional moist eye, but lumps in throats aren't visible. Nearly five thousand miles from Britain, they've come home to their island. I hadn't come home, but after thirty years, I had a lump in my throat. I'd come back, and it felt good.

The RMS is but one in an almost endless line of ships that have anchored in the Road. *Endeavour* with Captain Cook, the *Beagle* with Darwin, *Northumberland* bringing Napoleon, the *Erebus* and *Terror* of the first British voyage of scientific exploration into the Antarctic, they all anchored here. The Dutch, the Portuguese, the French, all anchored here. Cavendish and Dampier called here, Lancaster and Captain Bligh, but not with the *Bounty*. Whalers paused here briefly, and Joshua Slocum, the first man to sail single-handed round the globe, he anchored the *Spray* here, on his way home in 1898.

Edmond Halley spent more than a year here in 1676-7, and Wellington, then merely Major-General Sir Arthur Wellesley, stopped by in 1805 and nearly drowned. Chief Dinizulu, son of Cetawayo, and his entourage, landed in 1890, and 6000 Boer prisoners of war disembarked and re-embarked between 1900 and 1903. For 350 years, ships in their thousands dropped anchor in the Road. St Helena was one of the great ocean roadhouses.

Watching from the deck, waiting, the stark backdrop of cliffs softens as a gentle shower drifts, like lace curtains, down the valley from the high interior. It has always been like this on boat day. You are part of the scenario of expectancy when a ship comes to land, part of the unbroken history that for St Helena is as much its past as its present. Lying in the Road, this panoply of the island's history is as real as the drizzle, no more than a refreshing waft of cool air.

A launch takes you across the bay to the steps, at the end of the wharf. Fishing boats are tied to buoys, and depending on the time of year, there will be other vessels in the bay, ocean-going yachts from the Cape or America, Sydney or the Mediterranean, an ocean-going tug, the island's own flotilla of miscellanea. A strange piece of iron-work is the stern stearing gear of the *Papanui,* the boatman points out. It burnt out and sank in 1911, you can sort that one out when you find the plaque on the Library wall.

The launch slips alongside. Two broad sea-washed steps, a couple of ropes hanging, to steady yourself, and the boatman hands you ashore onto a 'landing,' and another dozen steps to the top of the wharf. On a good day, you don't notice the waves trundling round the headland with the Needle's Eye, and the blue-green water foaming slightly. It's just a quick two-step, and you're ashore. It's different on rough days, but that can wait too, the arrival is usually so smooth the only thing you notice is its novelty.

These days, a mini-bus takes you along the narrow wharf, and drops you, a hundred yards on, at Customs and the baggage hall, to seek out what is yours, from the piles, more or less alphabetically arranged.

I'm in no hurry. I was coming back, and I'd waited so long there was no need to rush. Not much point in rushing anyway, your baggage will still be there in the morning. Things move at a certain speed, and it's not as if you have a connection to catch. A few islanders are allowed through the low wharf gates, to meet the arrivals, and some of us can recognise each other, somewhat hesitatingly after so long. You know time has been passing all right, when the Customs officers look like schoolgirls. School girls! They were all stern men, in the olden days.

Basil had been there to meet me, Basil George. Basil had helped me find people who would feed me when I'd been camping, and had come out with me a few times in the field. His wife, Barbara, had been a newly arrived VSO when I was there first. And would I go for dinner when I'd dropped my stuff where I was staying? The Georges would be a mainstay for my return, and Basil, who had just retired as the first local Director of Education, was great company on a lot of my walking. Enormous fount of hospitality and information, and laughter, Basil and Barbara.

Chalk on your bags and out of the gates to the Seaside, the

stretch of road along the top of the seawall. Lines of cars, a melée of people, a massive bastion with cannon, the moat filled with trees and soft dust, and the South Atlantic thumping into the base of the new sea wall. The castle wall rises beyond the moat, and there's a huge new swimming pool. Wasn't that a tennis court in my time? And the 'Honeymoon chair' under a canopy of bougainvillea, that's still there.

The seaside continues round the little bay, past a new pub, Donny's, under the cliffs of its other side, but a road leads over a bridge, crossing the moat, past the Mule yard, through the archway into the main square of Jamestown, a square befitting the capital of one of Britain's oldest former colonies.

On the right are two large warehouse-like buildings, and a gap between them to the foot of that unbelievable set of seven hundred steps, 699 if you're a purist, with skinny iron handrails. This is Jacob's concrete Ladder, straight as a die, almost, up the steep lava-stepped side of the valley to Ladder Hill. In the corner, is the island's prison, though you're hardly aware of it, sheltered behind a tree, next door to St James' Church, with its spire removed before it fell down.

On your left is The Castle, its archway with the coat of arms of the Honourable East India Company. Then another archway, and a police station, on the corner of the low court house, imposing on its terrace of trees, cannon, and more broad steps. Gardens and great trees beyond, and in front, Main Street rises broadly up the slope of the valley floor, its colourwashed houses with sash windows.

It's a Georgian town. Forget the tarmac and the cars, and you could have stepped back two hundred years. The town is narrow, apparently just this strip of buildings along the bottom of the valley. The houses lie with their fronts to the street, their backs against the valley's brown rock and dust sides. The pavements are busy with people, and their clothes are present day, but the focus on time or date, even place, is a soft one.

It all sounds so grand, but it is all quite small, compact. It is simple, with an old world grace. It has character this place, it has undoubted class. Welcome to Jamestown. Welcome indeed to

Saint Helena.

Jamestown isn't an English town, it's a colonial town. But it's very much an *English* colonial town. And it's informal, like a small market town, which it also is. It's odd, even though you can hear the waves thumping, it doesn't really have the atmosphere of a seaside town, certainly not of a port, for the sea and the wharf are hidden beyond the wall. Once through the arch, the presence of the sea quickly becomes secondary. No, Jamestown is a remarkable little town, friendly, homely, yet it never ceases to surprise, any more than it never ceases to relax you.

In the olden days, when the Union Castle steamers stopped for a few hours, on their runs from Southampton to Capetown, this was the time to grab, or be grabbed by, a taxi and go for a rapid tour of the island. Most visitors on the RMS have a bit more time, staying for a week, while she does the shuttle run back to Ascension. Only a few of us are staying longer.

But in those days, that taxi ride was what you saw of the island. And perhaps an introduction, a quick tour, is what you need on arrival, for almost anything you might have imagined from the ship coming in is likely to be totally different in reality. Whatever you thought those high cliffs, grim as the walls of a prison fortress, might be protecting, cannot match up to what the next three hours will reveal.

So, living in the past, take a taxi, or today, take your place in Corker's open-topped bus, and keep your eyes and mind wide open. St Helena has an excellent road network for an island so small and so rugged. The roads are of necessity narrow, and of necessity wind about a great deal. But watch the scenery, don't watch the road, the driver does that.

Colin Corker's charabanc started life as a '30s, or thereabouts, Chevrolet truck, and has been sort of custom-cobbled into an open bus of considerable, but ill-defined, character. It starts from Corker's Garage, though the building on the side hardly constitutes a workshop. It was the ticket office and snacks stall of what used to be the *Paramount* cinema, which is now a food warehouse. Buildings in town, indeed on the island in general, go in for a lot of recycling.

The charabanc trundles up Main Street, stops at the Consulate Hotel, opposite the Post Office, the erstwhile Officers' Mess, to fill any vacant seats. Twenty yards further on, at the lovely Canister building, with peepul trees and beautiful bay windows, it bears left up Napoleon Street.

Twenty or so houses later, the road has become Side Path, a narrow roadway clinging to the side of the valley. It is out of town, rising rapidly above it, leaving it spread along the valley floor below. On the opposite side of the valley, the stone walls lining the roads, old and new, display their graffiti of 'Welcome Prince Andrew'. In the '60s it was 'Welcome Duke of Edinburgh,' and there were even bits left from 1947 of 'Long Live King George'. Very loyal people, the St Helenians.

The road side is rocks and rubble, sparsely sprinkled with aloes and prickly pear, but far below, the floor of James Valley is green, the town has become country gardens. Rearing above its other side, on top of a mighty cliff wall, is High Knoll, a fortress with more character at a distance than close to. In the head of the valley is the Heart-shaped Waterfall, but no water, and the road passes above The Briars, where Napoleon spent two months, and the satellite dishes and high tech bric-à- brac of Cable and Wireless. Zig-zagging on, it clears James Valley, leaving the toy town behind, the tiny RMS surrounded with its ant-like launches.

Quite abruptly there are bright flowers, growing like weeds. Round another bend in fir trees, and high above the road is Alarm House. This area was one of the first developed, with its alarm gun and observation post. Before the driver's even mentioned the ghostly redcoats, hung for mutiny in whenever, you've stopped on the edge of The Devil's Punch Bowl, and a grassy track, with a sign pointing to '*La tombe de Napoleon.*'

But onwards, turn left at St Matthew's Church, and along a narrow ridge, on the other side of the Punch Bowl. Then a tight right through Longwood Gate, down an avenue, a central street with cottages, heading for an open 'village' green. This is Longwood, the largest concentration of population outside Jamestown, and Half Tree Hollow on the hilltop above it. It was here that Napoleon and his entourage lived for five and a half years, until he died in 1821. The charabanc stops for the essential visit to Longwood House.

Back into the bus, back through Longwood, turn left again at Hutts Gate, heading straight towards the rugged green centre of the island with its three peaks. Much of the green is New Zealand flax, a memorial to the flax industry that died. Up on the top, and less shiny than the flax in the sun and wind, are the remnants of the island's bizarre endemic flora, including tree ferns and cabbage trees.

The road round the island sticks pretty well to the 1500 feet contour. It zig-zags round the east, sometimes in flax, sometimes in pines or eucalyptus or odd pastures, it goes up one long side of a valley, turns a hairpin, then back the other side, onto a ridge and hairpins into the next valley. There are colour-washed stone cottages, and new pleasantly compatible single storey houses, with gardens. Below the road, the outer rim of the island stretches to the cliff tops, varyingly barren, rocky, and colourful.

Above the road it is green, and the Peaks keep disappearing and reappearing, playing hide and seek with the flax, ridges and hills. Woody Ridge, Levelwood, Silver Hill, and seawards the valleys are steeper and steeper, narrowing almost into gorges. One ridge has the ruins of a colonial house, Rock Rose, and another has the brooding bulk of what looks like an enormous malevolent slug, straddling its crest.

Pause at Green Hill, for here the island falls spectacularly away from the central peaks, into the rocky desolation of Sandy Bay, the eroded core of the island's larger volcano. It is a painter's dream, this vast ampitheatre. Rich green headwaters curtaining round the rim, and a barren multicoloured panorama beneath, scattered with jagged rock pinnacles like Lot and Lot's Wife.

The bus wiggles its way round Sandy Bay, a district, a geographic entity, quarter of the the island. As you move, the whole scene, or collage of scenes, keeps changing. Rocks and ridges and cottages, hedges threaded with morning glory, plumbago, or bougainvillea, disappear, sometimes they reappear, and sometimes they are gone for ever. What is planted intentionally, what is wild, are impossible to separate.

Then over the ridge, and the road drops onto the north-western part of the island, away from the wild splendours of one side, to the splendours of rolling pastures with cattle and sheep, old houses half hidden in their trees. Past the Cathedral, the turning to the Boer cemetery, and back into thick pine woods to visit the Governor's residence, Plantation House.

There is a final flat stretch, running towards the fort on a hill, and views over the centre of the island, now like sun-drenched Welsh borders and a hint of rugged Mediterranean. Then, with a vengeance, it is back into the outer barren fringe of the island, dropping through Half Tree Hollow, with more houses now in its rock and dustscape than in Jamestown.

Past the Salvation Army, St Andrews, Jehovah's Witnesses, and the vast brand new gleaming New Apostolic church. Towards the cliff tops and shining ocean, Ladder Hill Fort and more military history than you can catch up with, even if the charabanc had stopped. Heavy WW II guns, crests on walls, military arches, and at the top of Jacob's Ladder it turns, leaving more islands spinning round your head than you can remember.

Down the other brown rubble and black rock side of James Valley, the charabanc's back in town. Clank round the corner of St John's Church, China Lane nearly as broad as it is long, the hospital, Roman Catholic church, more hints of trees and gardens and a school off right, a dog-leg passing the market, and stop by the Post Office to buy stamps.

Or you can get postcards in The Ark or The Star, The Canister, C and M's or The Emporium. Grab a snack or lunch or a drink, in one of several hostelries, The White Horse or The Standard, Wellington House or the Consulate in Main Street, or Ann's, in the Public Gardens. Try them all if you fancy a hundred yard stroll.

You've made it. That was the island, and its kaleidoscope of scenery from all over the world. What you could see from the road was only part of it, and all of that was rushed, and you're left with the thought that St Helena crams in more scenery and more history than most average sized countries. And you haven't talked to any of the residents yet, or walked in the country, or gone fishing (some good game fishing in season), or lost yourself in the Archives, gone scuba diving (quite a number of wrecks from over the centuries, and an energetic diving club), or climbed anywhere, or whatever else.

Getting around the island is simple, lots of very reasonably priced taxis, and lots of wonderful walking. You've seen something of the ruggedness, and a lot of the walking can be strenuous, some of it can be close on impossible, but that's for later. But there is also an extraordinary range of walks, or drives and a wander, for those less maniacally energetic, some memorable half or whole days out. One of the greatest treasures of the island is walking and effortlessly finding something new, something totally unexpected.

So, enough for the moment, you've just got back. Time to let some of it settle down round you, let some of it sink in. Find your accomodation for a start, or drop down to Donny's on the seaside and watch the sunset, wondering what might lie in store tomorrow. You can get quite tired planning what you can fit into your time, but there are plenty of places for a stimulating rest, spot of liquid refurbishment, and plenty of people always willing to help.

# CHAPTER 4

## AND WHO EXACTLY LIVES HERE?

*The people of St Helena are English by race, environment and upbringing. English is the only language spoken; and although they are now of mixed origin, they are by virtue of the Royal Charter of 1673 "free denizens of England."*

G.C.Kitching, Government Secretary,1937

It was my first night back, and I waited quietly, listening to the sounds gradually bringing the town back. Street lights are on all night now, eroding some of its secrecy. After midnight, there is distant music and a car or two coming down Napoleon Street, turning to go up towards the hospital. Until two o'clock there are a few young people, dressed brightly and casually, lots of laughter. Then there is soft silence, disturbed only by fairy terns muttering in the peepul tree outside my window, or wandering cats announcing somewhat randomly their lusts.

The church clock strikes its regular path through the night, and distant cockerels go off stridently at any hour. It is a foolish hen who thinks this means the day, or anything else, is about to begin. By four, the bakery has started working.

Soon after five, the mynas, the real time-keepers of the day, start their repetitive declarations, and are joined by other birds not wanting to be left out of the early morning performance.

At six, the sky is lightening and the street lights have gone out. On the opposite side of the valley, the lavas on top of Ladder Hill turn golden, and aloes are picked out a stark green in the sharpness of the first full sunlight. Slowly the gold drops down the side, down the Ladder, towards the houses of the valley floor. It will be a good hour and a half, before the sun arrives, here at the bottom.

At seven, the road sweepers start. Steady brush, brush, brush, and irregular punctuations of beer cans, rolling down the pavements, into the protective silence of the gutters. ‘Chew Chew’ or ‘Chuck ‘n Chew’, one or other of the personalised waste disposal trucks, collects the offerings. Sitting on the shop steps, schoolchildren wait for their buses. Once they’ve gone, mini-buses deliver the shop girls, to wait on the steps, for the shops to let them in. A steady run of traffic is coming down Ladder Hill, The Castle rush hour is on.

The sunlight now illuminates the roof tops of the houses. If you don’t live in rugged scenery, it is a surprise to have to wait so long after that first sign of dawn, for the first full flush of sunshine to touch you. But with the final brilliant bursting of the sun from the top of Munden’s, Main Street is light flooded, and the shops can open. The steady day in Jamestown settles down.

You’ve watched all the people to-ing and fro-ing for the start of the new day. And there were the Saints on the RMS, and the lighter and boat crews, and then the people as you went to wherever you’re staying. So you’ve seen a good number of the St Helenians who live on the island. In such a relatively small population, one thing that sticks out is that there seem very few common distinguishing features.

So who are the Saints? Well, that’s easy, or it’s not so easy. They’ve been British since May 1659, when the first small band landed with Captain Dutton. The only people to settle the island have been the British. There were serious, some would say unwarranted, some would say offensive, hiccups, in the interpretation of this, with the Immigration Act of 1971, and the Nationality Act of 1981. Then in 2002, coinciding with the 500th Anniversary of the discovery of the island by the Portuguese, St Helena became a British Overseas Territory and islanders could again receive British passports with full rights of entry and abode.

But if you’re interested in the people who live, and have lived for 350 years, so far from anywhere, that is almost academic. What isn’t, is where they came from. I’ve been interested in that for years, and on New Year’s Eve, a few days after I’d come back, I was thinking about it again. I’d been invited to a dance, in the old mess hall at Cable and Wireless, a lovely building that shortly after, though not as a direct result of the dance I might add, was sadly declared unsafe.

St Helenians enjoy their dances, and this was a good one. The music was loud and steady, that distinctive island thump - thump - thump laid over what eventually I recognized as *Mull of Kintyre*. It takes a while to re-acclimatize to the live music, especially the sound levels. Even if you dance cheek to cheek, or mouth to ear, there's no chance of conversation, assuming anyone might be interested in talking, that is.

The senior Brooks Brother (rhythm guitar and vocals) stands four square, a pint and a cigarette ever present - maybe he's got three arms? He and the group hammer out the Beatles, Frank Sinatra, Country and Western, and Second World War army songs, all with equal panache and the same steady beat. The atmosphere is friendly, non-stop noise. The Governor and his wife arrive as someone's guests, but leave before the dancing is too heavily entrenched. Liquids flow steadily and cheerfully, the dinner was good, the buffet queue animated.

'Black tie' it had said on the invitation, but that's what it always says. Most men are in DJs, but there are suits, a couple of T-shirts, and one lovely red blazer. Women's couture is pretty catholic, too. Some of the younger are in delicious little black numbers that affect bystanders' jaws. One had about as much material in it as a cummerbund, but the wearer certainly did an awful lot with it. There are floral frocks for the older, trouser suits for the better shaking of the leg. There are shining satins, there are skirts full of petticoats, some are backless, some are slit and slinky, most are close fitting.

There are at least 200 people there, so it's a decent representation of diverse physiologies. There are some who would go unnoticed in a west country Tesco's, or at a point to point. There are some, very few, who would not be out of place in a street market in Freetown or Accra. A lot could certainly blend into crowds in Bombay. And one young woman would have stopped the traffic in Bangkok, she was so beautiful, even by Thai standards.

It would be impossible to define a 'typical' St Helenian. But they might just fall into two very broadly-defined categories. Those with a range of physical characteristics and a skin colour ranging from European, and all that that entails, to a mid, almost reddish, or coppery, brown, or bronze, difficult to pin down, Indian. And a second broad grouping, of those with physiological features associated with West Africans and all that that entails. It doesn't help the concept of neat definitions that a number might be fitted into either of these rather artificial categories.

To get a clearer, or perhaps murkier, view, we need a quick skim through two centuries of history up to Melliss's book of 1875. The first settlers, from 1659, were from England. After the reclamation of the island from the Dutch troops in 1673, more English settlers arrived in dribs and drabs, rather than in any orchestrated immigration programme. That a specific group arrived after the Fire of London, is questionable, although there was an issue of stamps to commemorate them. Records also show that a lot of settlers, especially women, in the first decades left the island again. So the early population was male dominated, and stayed fairly small.

From the very beginning, hard work in the new settlement could only be undertaken with additional help from slaves. Dutton had been instructed by the Company's Court of Directors to collect five or six *blacks or negroes,* men or women, at the Cape Verdes, on his way down in 1659. It's not clear if he did, but the next ship out from England for Madras, was instructed to pick up ten or so *blacks* from the Guinea coast, and drop them off for the new settlement.

The terms *black* and *native*, as used by Europeans in the seventeenth and eighteenth, even nineteenth, centuries, were interchangeable *Black* did not necessarily mean *negro*, it referred to those of Asian origin, just as easily as to those of African origin. *Black* was a local inhabitant, a *native*, of any country, of any shade of skin from olive to ebony.

There was nothing on St Helena like the slave system of plantations of the Caribbean. Settlers had one or two slaves, or at most a handful, to work alongside them, and to work as well, whether or not the settler had a wife, in the house, cooking, washing, scrubbing. Slaves were part of the individual settler's investment into his property, part of his personal assets. The Company had their own slaves, on a larger scale than settlers individually, but collectively rarely more than 10% of the total slave population.

The Honourable East India Company ran St Helena, and the bulk of their trading and ports of call were *east* of the island. The Company had very little to do with the African mainland, especially the west African coast, partly because they had no trading interests, partly because sailing along that coast cost too much time.

St Helena was the principal stop for fleets *returning* from India, and the East. So although in the early years there are records of slaves from west Africa, the majority were collected in Madagascar, with some from further east. In the seventeenth century, at least half the population of Madagascar was of Malayo-Indonesian origin, having arrived there from the east around the tenth century. The dominant physical features of slaves on St Helena for a century or more, would have been of the Indian Ocean.

Some of them were from India, St Helena writing to ask the Company stations there, usually for specific types of workers. In 1669, they wrote to Masulipatam, asking for four *Gentues* [a corruption of a Portuguese word for Gentile, or heathen, and used for Hindus, as distinct to Mohammedans] and their wives, procured from Bengal to be sent to reside on the island *as our servants.* They were considered *more usefull and ingenious than those people who came from Guinea.* No force was to be used, and accomodation on board ship was to be provided.

A later request to the Company in Bengal received the answer, *We have tryed to obtayne eight men and women slaves for St Hellena, but cannot this yeare procure them; the natives seldome selling themselves or children, except in a famine, which (God be thanked) hath not this yeare happened to the countrey.* As late as 1716, St Helena wrote to the Company saying they needed 200-300 more *blacks,* from Madagascar, as they were better than those from the Gold Coast; or they could be *the slaves that are sometimes in great plenty in Bengal.*

Generally though, Indians were brought in for specific craft skills, or as household servants. The Company sought barbers expert at blood letting, building artisans, and unsuccessfully, indigo growers. *Lascars,* Indian sailors, were a small, and specifically identified, community on the island, certainly until the 1820s. I have spent some time on these specifics, partly because I had been struck by physical similarities to Indians I know, and partly to demonstrate the very mixed origins of imported labour, slave or otherwise.

In the latter half of the eighteenth century, the island had more direct contact with west Africa, but fewer and fewer slaves were brought in. In 1789 the last slave arrived on the island, although the import was not legally forbidden until 1792, and slavery would not finally end until 1832.

Records of actual numbers of slaves are fragmentary. In 1689 there were 92 male slaves on the island. In 1714, there was a *white* population of 405, and another 125 soldiers, with over 350 male slaves, with 81 women and 247 children. Between 1769 and 1800 the *whites* numbered between 350 and 400, the *blacks* between 700 and 1200. By 1812 the total slave population was around 1200.

In 1747, Teale quotes a visitor describing the island as comprising some 150 families, all of English extraction, and about 300 soldiers. *There are also 300 slaves, brought from Guinea, Madagascar, and Bengal.* The island girls were friendly*, extremely easy, and good natured,* they joined in with the officers, *while the slaves, or black girls, are still more obliging with regard to the sailors. It is indeed a very odd scene sometimes to see the wanton behaviour of these last.* He reported the slaves to be prolific breeders, *in which the sailors who come hither have a good hand.*

In 1673 the Company had insisted that *all negroes both men and women* on the island that embraced the Christian faith and were baptized *shall within seven years be free planters and enjoy the privilege of free planters both of cattle and land.* But fifty years later, only eighteen people were listed as 'free blacks'. The number had risen to 331 in 1803, and 448 in 1812.

Freed slaves therefore became a part of island society, very slowly for a long time, but more rapidly as the nineteenth century started. Maps of the time show a number of land holdings, especially in the west, probably granted to freed slaves, including women. But as numbers increased dramatically, freed slaves became difficult to absorb. There are references to women turning to prostitution, for there was little other choice, and as many as a thousand ships a year called at the island.

In 1810, there was an extraordinary indication, or rather indictment, of economic and social policies at the time. There were in excess of 400 freed slaves on the island, yet Gosse writes : *Governor Beatson's desire to improve the cultivation of the island was at first held up by the shortage of labour, but in May, 1810, there arrived from Canton the first consignment of Chinese labourers.*

The Chinese came in on five year 'engagements', and numbers rose to more than 600! There is no doubt they did remarkable work. Some of the finest masonry is Chinese. They brought running water for the first time to Longwood, you can see parts of the channel today, and their farming skills were extraordinary by island standards. They appear to have kept, or been kept, much to themselves, and most of them had been sent off the island by the 1820s. But some clearly stayed on, and physical characteristics are displayed by a small percentage of today's population.

So contributions to the population of the island continued to be drawn from a number of sources, and the admixture continued. There is an interesting Council record of 1824, *The Vestry having recommended a Tax on Free Blacks the Governor points out that they cannot recognize any distinction of Colour in legislation, and that in the case of hundreds of individuals it would not be an easy matter to determine whether they ought to be classed as Whites or Blacks.* In 1832, the Company finally abolished slavery on the island, and purchased the freedom of the final 614 slaves.

Then in 1839, the island was pitched into the battle, economic, moral, and politically self-righteous, of the western world's attempts to restrict illegal slave trading, and eventually its suppression. The West African Squadron moved its base to the island, a Vice-Admiralty Court was set up, and the Liberated African Depot was established in 1840. Over the next thirty years, at least 25,000 liberated slaves passed through the island, and when the Depot closed in 1874, fifteen hundred west Africans had chosen to stay on.

Melliss, who was born on the island, in his book of 1875, says of the *natives* of St Helena, ie the population there when the Liberated African Depot was established : their *general colour is a very light brown or copper, sometimes deepening into nearly black, and in other cases becoming almost white.* Their ancestors were *chiefly from Europe and Asia, and there is now some difficulty in tracing the prevailing element in their composition, or in saying which predominated, whether it is Portuguese, Dutch, English, Malay, East Indian or Chinese.*

He also wrote of the inhabitants from the Liberated African Depot who stayed on the island : *With the "natives"* [St Helenians] *they do not blend, but live apart in little colonies or settlements; not half a dozen instances of intermarriage have occurred during thirty years ....* But that was a hundred and twenty five years ago, when the Depot had only just closed.

There was one further development. Between 1900 and 1903 the island was host to some six thousand Boer prisoners-of-war. Although in two main camps, they were allowed considerable freedom of movement, and many were incorporated into the, particularly the skilled, work force. With cessation of hostilities, the majority returned to South Africa, but a few stayed on and married St Helena women. That was the last historical addition to the island's gene pool. So yes, the population has an exceedingly mixed history.

Islanders then as a whole are a blend of all sorts, and the character as you'd expect is just as varied. Saints are friendly people, with great senses of, sometimes hard to follow, humour. They are interesting people, and interested to whatever extent they want to be. They're very helpful, and they don't generally interfere. They can be talkative much of the time, but you only find out what they're prepared to tell you. Some questions are better not asked, but it can take a long time to work out what those questions might be. It's sometimes difficult to understand that with a population so small, there are as many complexities as you'd find anywhere.

You might think that such a cosmopolitan background would result in some pretty way-out food, but not really. Tasty, yes, but not exotic, although pokes (tuna stomachs) stuffed with potatoes and onions are pretty distinctive. As the editor of *What's cooking in St Helena* says: *Like life in general in St Helena, the food is wholesome and uncomplicated without too many frills or fripperies.*

The East India Company was in part to blame. From the earliest days, the staple food was salt beef and rice, subsidised. And for the slaves it was yams. All the good stuff, all the fresh fruit, veg, and meat, was sold to the ships, at inflated prices, the histories would have us believe. Rather leave it to rot in the fields than sell it at a price the islanders could afford, that's what we're told. But not now, though corned beef was subsidized until the 1990s, and St Helena corned beef hash is dynamite.

There's probably a three-way toss up for the national dish, corned beef hash being a definite front runner. Then there's the food of the gods, perhaps why they chose classical names for the Peaks, fishcakes. Eat them any time, anywhere, snack, filler, main course, side dish, you name it, delicious. And with a dish of tomato paste, sometimes called *bread 'n dance*, which combines chilis with tomatoes and more chilis, food doesn't come much tastier.

The third contender, and main staple, is 'plo', probably from the India connection, *pilau*. You can also have white plo, which is the same as ordinary plo but without curry powder. And curry powder is another staple, backs up the green chilis to put a bit of 'bite' into dishes. 'Chutney' is a good example; tuna chutney, which is really a curried tuna variant, but it's very distinctive, a marvellous meal. Brinjal is the local word for aubergine, that's standard in India too, thought to be from the Portuguese. Bacon is a staple, and goes into a lot of dishes.

And the vegetables? Well a lot depends on the season, what happens to be available. For vegetables, and that includes potatoes, the greatest staple of them all, can suddenly disappear, lack of water, too much rain, 'worms', forgot to plant, forgot to spray, whatever. And then there can be sort of gluts, cabbage coming out of your ears for a fornight, and then not a green in sight for a month. Carrots are so staple, they could be exported. If the island ran out of carrots, they'd probably evacuate the population.

Pumpkin is a tremendous vegetable, comes in a variety of kinds, and goes in a variety of great dishes. Cream of pumpkin soup is a wow, pumpkin fritters are a devastation, you can't stop eating them. And pumpkin *Do down* (stew), which is like cabbage *Do down*, but with the veg changed over, is a feast all in one pan.

What is so good of course, is the range of fresh fish, and seafood in general, octopus, shark, lobster. But tuna, cavalli, soldier, bullseye, old wives, jack, wahoo, mackerel by the dozen, the fish are wonderful. And they smoke tuna.

Local honey is delicious, and there are some good home-made jams and jellies. And there's an extraordinary cake, made of dates or mixed fruit, or both, called *boiled pudding* which looks like an old fashioned medicine ball. It's about the same weight, and it certainly reaches places other cakes haven't even heard about. There are some oddities which I never saw, beetroot top omelette, mock caviar (which is brinjal), poke mince, or citric fluff. But all told, St Helena cooking, or more particularly St Helena cooks, do you proud.

Fruit and veg are produced by individuals, and much goes through a Growers' Association with a shop in the market. But something of the old system still exists, in that it takes a while to learn where certain things are available at certain times, "Oh there's brinjals at So and So's," or grenadillas, or capsicums. You might be out walking and someone will ask if you want to buy some tomatoes, or guavas, or Cape gooseberries. I was once offered half a conger eel as I walked back to town. And if you like bananas, it's best to find out who has access to Sandy Bay varieties, undoubtedly the tastiest around.

Fishermen now mainly work for the Fisheries Corporation, which has a new handling plant in Rupert's Valley, built to EU specifications. But most fish is sold to Argos, next door, with its even bigger handling plant. Argos then exports the fish. For meat (mainly excellent beef) there's an island butcher, private and family, though a lot of meat is imported frozen from the Cape. Pork is largely handled by Solomon's, but raising a pig or two is a cottage industry (the slaughtering and butchering being carefully controlled). An interesting occurrence is someone calling at the door to see if you want some pork. Once he's got enough interest, the pig is killed, and he delivers however much of whichever bits you wanted.

I haven't said anything about occupations mainly because it's a microcosm of anywhere else. At the beginning of the chapter, The Castle rush-hour was in motion, and the Government is the largest employer, education, administration, Agriculture and Natural Resources (ANRD), Public Works Department (PWD), health sector. Privatisation over the last few years may have changed the outfit, but it hasn't changed the paymaster.

Most people still set about building their own houses, calling on those with specialist skills as and when required. There's little building in stone now, it's virtually all in concrete blocks. But you can still get most things repaired that in the outside world require the object to be thrown away, or cost an arm and a couple of legs.

Talking of a couple, reminds me to mention the local variety of English. I had been sent a bowl of eggs, and when I saw the old lady who had sent them, to thank her, she said she thought I might "take a couple of eggs." A *couple* is a number greater than two and usually less than a dozen. A *nice couple* would be in excess of ten. The expression is a little imprecise, so it is used with material objects, a couple of brinjals, a nice couple of mackerel. It isn't used for example in distance, which is more important, and therefore requires specific numbers, like two miles. Christ, a couple of miles could be half way to Ascension.

It's an odd language till you get your ear in. Come to think about it, it's a pretty odd language even if you have got your ear in. Nicknames are a way of finding out about the language, and local lore, behaviour, humour, all kinds of things. Almost every male has a nickname, some have two, but the second may have come from his or her father, as a sort of surname, like Pudgy (rotund) Dover (originally to some physical resemblance to a 'Dover', popular make of, stove). Not as many woman have them.

Nicknames fall into certain categories, like physical attributes or peculiarities, behavioural quirks, personal habits, prowess. Some may be rude, some most certainly are, but they are used quite openly. Particular foods you like, or liked as a child, stay with you for ever. Sometimes they are related to specific events, some of which have been forgotten, or were never known to many people. Most people are quite content about their nickname, of whatever origin, but a few are touchy, so it's well to be careful.

Try to work your way through some of these : Muscle, Moonshine, Christ, Conger kidneys, Pickaxe, Sweetheart, Iron Dick, Cheese, Chicken (skinny legs), Bow (legs), Dumb boy, Boer, Porky, Sperm, Skipper, Baked beans, Flea, Boot, Spade, Breadbelly, Huggy bear, Hitler, Gas, Lampshade, Chili, Crasher.

Some of them require a little more background, as for example Charlie Burndown. Charlie Peters was the ancestral figure in this. He was burning off dry growth round the house and lost control a bit, and it took his house too. Chief was an illigitimate son of Chief Dinizulu Suzy Darkdale was born the night the *Darkdale,* the ship supplying fuel oil to the island, was spectacularly torpedoed just off shore, on October 21st, 1941.

I asked someone about Moses : "I don't know, he looked so wild he must have come out the bulrushes." And one of the gentlest of all was earned by a little lad on the first day of school. His mother had taken great care, sending him all freshly scrubbed, in smart new shorts, crisply ironed white shirt. So when they saw him his mates called him Eggshell. You can never be sure with St Helenians, exactly what to make out of what appears to be on the surface, or when they're "bending you up."

# CHAPTER 5

## JAMESTOWN
## ONE STREET WIDE: 500 YEARS LONG

*When the ships come hither, every man maketh his lodging under a tree, setting a tent about it, and the trees are there so thick, that it presently seemeth a little town or an army in the field. Every man provideth for himself, flesh, fish, fruit, and wood; for there is enough for them all: and every one washeth linen.*

Captain Thomas Cavendish, 1588

Anchored in the Road, waiting to go ashore, two particular features of Jamestown strike you. The main one is that James Valley, cut through hundreds of feet of lavas, is narrow and steep-sided. So the town is a thin strip, filling the floor of the valley as it climbs up it. The second feature is Jacob's Ladder, a stark stairway of concrete steps rising straight up the side of the valley. The top of the Ladder is a useful place to take in Jamestown and its place in its valley in the barren north of the island, to set it into an island perspective.

Every visitor has to climb the seven hundred steps of Jacob's Ladder. For many, perhaps most, this implies climb *up*. But you can also climb *down*, which is both physically less challenging, and aesthetically more pleasing. From here it's like seeing it from a hot air balloon, or a cable car, except the Ladder doesn't swing in the wind. Coming down at night, the town, strung like Christmas decorations below you, is wonderful. So, for a start get a ride up Ladder Hill, get out at the top of the Ladder, and take in Jamestown from above.

Some form of barracks has been up here from early days. Ladder Hill got its name from a makeshift rope ladder enabling troops, or settlers in the militia, to get down the valley side faster in times of emergency. Jacob's Ladder is much later, it was constructed in

1829, to haul manure out of town.

The idea to clean up the town dated from a year earlier, when the new Governor, Brigadier-General Charles Dallas, arrived after long service in India. Eight days at post, and he proposed that a mule-cart should work every day, from daybreak till eight in the evening, removing *Soil, Rubbish etc proper for Agricultural purposes from the Houses, Stables, or Yards of such Persons as may be willing to submit to a trifling charge per week each for the use of the said cart.*

At the time, such materials, if at all cleared away, were dumped into the sea off the front, just outside The Castle, Dallas's office. A charming practise. His solution, of carting all such agriculture-friendly waste, *except the cleansing of privies*, to the top of Ladder Hill was a realistic introduction to urban rehabilitation and recycling. It would clean up Jamestown, and provide manure for up country farmers at sixpence a cart load. Best not to ask what continued to happen to the cleansing of privies .....

The system functioned well enough. Then Dallas had another idea. In 1829, using private funding, he arranged the construction of his 'Inclined Plane', for the transport of the mule-cart's burden. It was an extraordinary piece of engineering. It took a year to level the rock face, and then install a double tramway, divided by steps running a length of 900 feet up the valley side.

A capstan and winching device allowed mules at the top to run one load up the tramway, and one load down, up to four tons, and a journey time of twenty minutes. Rails rested on sleepers and rollers, and there were three miles of half inch chain round a two feet diameter capstan. Simple as that! Manure got rid of, heavy loads for up country handled, farm produce for town and the ships brought down. Dallas was full of bright ideas.

He subsequently issued a proclamation that all manure etc would be handled by the Inclined Plane. Monopoly it may have been, but it worked. And in 1831, he even persuaded London to buy it. Then in 1836, his successor, the first Governor appointed by the Crown after transfer of the island from the East India Company, rescinded the proclamation and allowed all manure etc to be pitched in the sea again. Such to-ings and fro-ings of progress are the history of the island's administration.

In 1871, the Inclined Plane was restored by the army, but only as a stairway, seven hundred steps and two thin handrails. And for years, before cars were so common, it was the fastest way into and out of town. It is far less commonly used today According to guidebooks you can go up it in a few minutes, and in the 1960s there was an annual competition to see who could run up it fastest. The record then was 6 minutes and 20 seconds!

I can just about trot *down* it in that. Youngsters had, very rarely still have, an even faster way of coming down. They rest their feet on one rail, shoulders on the other, and using their feet and hands as brakes, slide down. Zip! One minute you were in the dust of Half Tree Hollow, the next you're nicking across the square to go swimming. Dallas would have been proud of them.

The flagstaff is a mast taken from an iron ship in 1879, and the flag is hoisted in the morning and lowered at dusk by the Police, when a visiting ship is in the Road. The existence of a flagstaff here is much older. Up to the start of the nineteenth century, miscreants, civil or military, were flogged at the flagstaff, possibly even hung from the flagstaff. A little earlier the practice had stopped of displaying, festooned above the town and anchorage, as a warning to others, the heads of those sentenced to death, slaves or mutineers.

Look down Jacob's Ladder for a start, it's like a narrow ribbon plunging away, rippling slightly, its guard rails looking no more than bits of string, and thank God you didn't climb up it. Six hundred feet below you, the Wharf, The Castle, the Square, all of Jamestown laid out, warm and friendly, like a brightly coloured model. The other side of the valley is Munden's Hill, and beyond are barren ridges as far as Sugarloaf. There is an awful lot of brown, in a variety of shades perhaps, but a lot of brown, arid rocks and cliffs. Full of its town, James Valley looks decidedly welcoming.

Da Nova was incredibly lucky when he chanced upon the island. The Portuguese had only rounded the Cape of Good Hope six years earlier, heading into the Indian Ocean, and his was only the third or fourth fleet, if you could call it that, that had gone to India after Vasco da Gama's historic landfall in Calicut in 1498.

So the island became a lifesaver for the Portuguese, neatly dividing up the several month homeward voyage. They quickly introduced goats and pigs, fruit trees and vegetables, to provide fresh food for their ships' crews. St Helena was an oasis, without which they might well have joined the Portuguese equivalent of Davy Jones. The valley below you was then called Chapel Valley, after da Nova's wooden chapel.

Ten or twelve years after its discovery, the link with India produced the island's first resident, one Fernando Lopez. Those early years in India had been somewhat chequered for the Portuguese. In one of the numerous disputes with local rulers, Lopez made the mistake of joining one of them against his own team, and his side lost. As a friendly gesture by his local host, Lopez was handed back to the Portuguese, with a plea that his life be spared. Of course, no problem, said Admiral Alfonso de Albuquerque, and had him mutilated instead, removing his right hand, left thumb, ears, and nose.

When Albuquerque died, Lopez stowed away in a ship sailing for Portugal, hoping to return to his wife and family. On the long voyage, he had plenty of time to think about the kind of reception he was likely to receive, looking as dreadful as he did. So, he jumped ship. He hid in the woods, and the crew couldn't find him. Understanding his feelings perhaps, and anxious to get on, they left him some food, and a fire. Lopez hollowed out a shelter in some volcanic ash, and settled down in Chapel Valley as St Helena's first resident.

Over the years Lopez lived his solitary life, hiding when ships anchored, but eventually, possibly feeling his age, he sought passage on a ship to Portugal. He had an audience with the King and Queen, and they arranged for him to go to Rome, where his penance was heard by the Pope himself. Lopez then asked to be returned to his island, taking more livestock and plants with him. He cultivated gourds and pomegranates, planted palm trees, and raised ducks, hens, pigs and goats, trading them with ships' crews. He died supposedly in 1546, and Chapel Valley was empty again.

Over the next century or so, British, Dutch, possibly a few French, joined the Portuguese in using the island. They could offload their sick and dying, for here was wonderful water, shelter, fresh meat, fresh fruit and veg They could repair damaged vessels, they could leave messages carved into rocks, leave letters for ships going the other way to take on. St Helena was a sort of glorious maritime free house.

Of course there was strife from time to time, and the sinking of the Dutch ship *Witte Leeuw* (White Lion) in 1613, must have been one of the most spectacular disagreements. In its eagerness to capture a Portuguese East Indiaman, the Dutch vessel fired into its own magazine. It was witnessed from the shore by English sailors. Very colourful, they said, ducking bits of flying debris. What's left of the *Witte Leeuw* lies close to where the RMS is anchored. She was located in the 1970s. Most of her cargo of Chinese porcelain is in Amsterdam, but they say the jewels the captain was carrying were never found. Royal Air Force divers more recently brought up one of her elegant bronze cannons, of which the Museum is justifiably proud.

The Dutch actually laid claim to the island in 1633, but didn't leave permanent settlers. It was left to the English East India Company in 1659, with a commission from Richard Cromwell, Lord Protector, to land the first band of intrepid settlers under Captain John Dutton, and a few hiccups apart, they never looked back. James Valley it became, and Jamestown, after James Duke of York, later James II. And over the centuries they came, into the bay and through the collection of dwellings: more settlers, slaves, sailors, soldiers, travellers, lascars, Chinese, the French, the West African Squadron, a few whalers, Boer prisoners-of-war.

The Bay looks so gentle from here, spot of action on the wharf, fishing boat or two, a visiting yacht. You can doze in the sun just watching. But in January and February most years, the bay is livened, sometimes considerably, by the rollers. Waves the size of Hawaiian surfers' dreams, originating somewhere in the north Atlantic, appear literally out of the blue, and crash into the shore.

I saw them in 1966. Out of nowhere they reared up and

came in, breaking with a noise like tearing metal, and a Crump! you could hear miles away, and feel it shake the front. They swept the length of the wharf, clearing anything in their way. Over a few days they dug into the sea wall and dragged most of its centre into the bay.

Then in '96, I was back and so were the rollers. So, in the space of a week, were three cruise liners, including the *Canberra,* and the seas were so rough not a single passenger was allowed ashore. These were bad enough, but in 1846 they wrecked the wharf, and destroyed thirteen of the twenty or so ships anchored in the Road. One was pitched across the seafront. So it's not always quite so pleasantly peaceful.

Right from the start, this valley was a focal point. With its permanent supply of good water, and its safe anchorage, it was the obvious place from which to start the settlement of the island. It was easy to fortify, and of course, it was the point of contact with the outside world. But it was really only in the later eighteenth century that it became a place for many to live full time.

Planters lived up country and came into town when ships were about, or on business or military duty. The Castle was the Governor's official residence, it was the hub of the Company's rule over the island, but the Governor had his main residence, Plantation House, up country. Jamestown got hot in the summer, and although the breezes from the Peaks cooled the valley, it was humid and dusty, and must have been pretty smelly.

It was the place to set up stores and shops for the settlers' needs, and for people on the increasing numbers of ships. It was the place to set up ale-houses, wine-shops, spirit and arrack shops, depending on what the Company wanted people to drink at the time, and to a lesser extent, what they liked. It would also have housed the brothels, for servicing the crews of ships, after months at sea. And of course the soldiers, once the garrison was manned by the Company's professional troops, needed their R and R. It was very much a 'working' town, rather than residential.

It was the business centre, so it had timber yards, coal yards, yards for the repair of boats and ships. It had stables for horses, for oxen and for cows. For a long time it had the island's only church. The Court was there, and the Council met weekly in it. But above all it became a port. All provisions for the island from the outside world, all provisions for ships from the island farms, passed through Jamestown, carted in and out by ox or bullock carts, until Governor Dallas that is.

In the first half of the nineteenth century, a thousand vessels or more a year anchored in James Bay, ten or fifteen a day in the season. That's an awful lot of seamen looking for shore leave. Jamestown earned a notoriety as the roadhouse, or alternatively the whorehouse, of the South Atlantic. At its peak, Jamestown would have been a wild town, a bomb burst of rowdy colour in the vast emptiness of weeks on the ocean. Governor Beatson, fresh from the relative order of India, wrote:

*Upon my arrival in 1808, I was forcibly struck with the disorderly conduct of the soldiers. Scenes of the grossest intemperance were daily exhibited at the spirit houses. Crowds of soldiers and sailors were in constant attendance, rioting and boxing in the public streets. The roads leading to country were often strewed with drunken men, laying insensible, both white and black.*

It may be quiet today, but Jamestown has a long and unbroken history, wild and subdued, orderly and mutinous, religious and ribald. It keeps its secrets well, and small though it is, there is an awful lot there for the finding.

Today's population is around a thousand. More than that live behind you, across the broad and rather desolate sweep of Half Tree Hollow, between the fort of High Knoll and the line of the barrack wall. And about the same number live four miles away in Longwood. So in 2003 that leaves barely another thousand living elsewhere, spread through the interior of the island.

The island has been settled and so closely travelled for so long, that every rock, tree, bit of road and track, every feature has a name. The longer you stay, the more you learn, or the more you're prone to forget. You come across a lot, even on a brief introductory visit, but the names are not there to bog you down, they're there to help, you the traveller, or you the local, for they are not only points of geography, they are points of history, points of society. Some will know them, some won't. Using them usually helps, if you're trying to find the way.

But they can hinder, if they're no longer in fashion. Try for example asking for Fiddler's Green, or Black Bridge, in Jamestown. They're both in, or perhaps just out of, the upper town. Fiddler's Green, an early red light district, lots of drinking, lots of fighting, music, and of course the whores, was more a 'concept' than a specifically named entity. It was near Chubb's Spring, and everyone knows where that is, it's where the town water supply comes in. Not far away a famous, or infamous, duel was fought at Black Bridge in 1809. People pass it every day, but the duel is as long forgotten as the name.

Take Side Path on the valley side opposite where you're sitting. Just as you get out of the houses, there's Sentry Box, nothing but rock and rubble. A bit further, more rock and rubble is Ten Pound Rice, and nobody knows why. Someone dropped a bag of rice? That's what they paid the Chinese for rebuilding the road up to there? Further on there's Condwall, or corner of the wall, of the road down to The Briars, and Fibre Gate, well it sounds like that, but it's Five-barred gate, except it only has four. Then Button Up Corner, where you did up your coat after the humid warmth of town, before the cooler breezes of the higher ground hit you, and Two Gun Saddle. You've almost left the valley by then.

There are six ways out of Jamestown, and you have a magnificent view of them all from here. You can even see the traces of earlier attempts to civilise the accessibility of the rest of the island. You're sitting on Jacob's Ladder, and you're virtually on Ladder Hill road, so that's two at the same time. Side Path is opposite, and above the wharf there's the old road round the cliffs to Rupert's Valley and further fortifications, that's four. Higher up the valley there's Barnes Road, an old military road going up onto Francis Plain.

That's five, and then the sixth, perhaps the least welcome, is back out to sea. In all his years on the island, Napoleon only ever used two of them, each of them only once. Side Path, when he rode out to look at a house soon after he'd landed in 1815, and the sea, when his remains were carried in state back to France in 1840. Yes, it's a good place, the top of the Ladder, to sit and watch the town and think.

In the afternoon, you can watch the morning rush hour in reverse. The school buses sort out the young, and at four Government cars sort out most of the rest as they speed homewards. Five o'clock and it's the shops' staff, and soon after peace settles over the early shadowed town.

Jamestown's a lovely place to walk around and discover at your leisure. St James' Church, the library and the Public Gardens, the Market, the Run, half a dozen other churches, what's left of the Friendly and Benefit Societies' buildings, the shops and the handicrafts, the Post Office, and one or other of the current or former hostelries.

Memorial plaques, particularly in St James', provide glimpses of people in the island story. The town had several cemeteries over the years, but they have been moved out, the school yard used to be one, and behind a wall at China Lane was the old Chinese cemetery. In the later eighteenth century the islanders had been piqued at the speed their cemeteries were filled by people off-loaded from ships, to die in peace, or be buried in solid ground. Saul Solomon, the founding father of Solomon's, the island's oldest company, was on a ship bound for South Africa, when they thought he was dying. So they off loaded him at the wharf, but he sat up and set up the printing press, and then the company.

I like Jamestown. With or without people, it's very friendly, people help with questions, and whether or not they know the answers doesn't really matter. On my first morning back in '98 I went to the Post Office, post some cards back on the RMS before she sailed, and to Eva Benjamin's shop for a loaf of bread, and the Market for some fish and veg. About a hundred and fifty yards all told, there and back, and I had conversations with more people than I *know* in London, and I've lived there for forty years.

Looking down, the town is attractive, the coloured houses, the trees, the toytown layout. It is subdued rather than sleepy, but you can bring it to life yourself when it's quiet. It is so easy to see the ships in the Road, to picture East Indiamen at anchor, the *Endeavour* or the *Beagle* coming in under sail. And with a bit of a prod, you can watch the *Witte Leeuw* blow itself apart.

It needs a little, but not that much, more imagination to see the redcoats, the country planters on horseback, ladies in their ox carts. Flags flying on The Castle, on the wharf, and from the assorted batteries livening up the cliffs and bleak sides of the valley. Parades, performances, the handing over of power, or prisoners-of-war, or Napleon's remains. You can picture them in this solid, gentle, little town.

What is much more difficult to see, maybe impossible, is the reality of Jamestown in the past. Perhaps the collection of ramshackle cottages and huts and tents in those very early days. But the thriving port? The ocean whorehouse? Do you want to remember what it really was once like? Indeed what it was probably like for most of its life?

Official reports of the 1840s offer an insight : *Throughout the town heaps of filth and rubbish with pools of fetid and stagnant water ..... decayed fish bones, stable manure, ordure, rotten bedding, and gunny bags, as the constant contributors of foul gases ..... The banks of the Run are loaded, for nearly the whole length of the town, with filth of every sort ..... The combination of evils now mentioned, creates a wretchedness physical and moral among the poor which baffles description. The dwellings are not houses; in each case the occupant resorts for his evening hours and diversions to the wine shops, and he is driven there by the dirt of his home which he only enters to forget himself in sleep.* Dallas's vision and the Ladder hadn't lasted very long ...

Almost a century later, the Colonial Office Blue Book of 1932 commented on the great shortage of houses. It spoke of the shocking slum property of Jamestown, and overcrowding, reflected in high rates of infant mortality. Yet by the 1950s St Helena was winning Commonwealth prizes for the health of its children. Amazing changes.

Can that really be the same town as today, or indeed as I remember it in the 1960s? Perhaps these are parts of the past best brushed under the carpet, for it's certainly hard to picture them. Yes, I think it's best to enjoy what remains, just fill your own bits onto the dusty bones of Jamestown's history in whatever way you want. Think on it as you go softly down the Ladder, as the lights of town are going on.

# CHAPTER 6

## NAPOLEON : AN ACCIDENTAL WELCOME

*This is therefore to warn all the inhabitants or other persons on the island from aiding or abetting hereafter in any way whatever, the escape of the said General Napoleon Bonaparte or that of any of the French persons who have arrived here with him, and to interdict most pointedly the holding of any communication or correspondence with him or them, excepting only such as may be regularly authorized.*

St Helena Government Proclamation, October 17th, 1815

A lot of historic places can bring colour to the pages you have read about them. A building, a ruin on a hillside, a fading piece of tapestry, can add so much. On St Helena, the exile of Napoleon, not far off two centuries ago, can almost come to life. So many elements of the story are still there, seemingly undisturbed, that without noticing you find yourself falling into it.

You walk down Main Street looking at the buildings where Countesses Bertrand and Montholon shopped. You stand where Sir Hudson Lowe and Napoleon shouted abuse backwards and forwards, you look out of the same windows, at the same views. You sit in the shade, where Napoleon sat to look at the Heart-shaped Waterfall, and walk through the trees where General Gourgaud thought lusty thoughts of island maidens. You walk where the troops guarding him lived, where they drilled, you stand in their sentry positions, and wave from one of their distant signal positions to another.

You can picture the *Northumberland*, riding at anchor in the Road, and stand where the settlers and slaves stood to watch him disembark. You can stand too, where they stood and watched his funeral cortege, where twenty years later the islanders watched his mortal remains shipped off in pomp, home to France. It's not only Napoleon that you feel, it's the day to day atmosphere of the island

and the people that surrounded him.

On that day in 1964, when I knew I was going to St Helena, I can't honestly remember if I knew that Napoleon had been banished and died there. I definitely knew his mortal remains were in Paris, so perhaps I was a bit hazy.

I'd been fascinated by the Napoleonic Wars for 'O' level, so much so, that I'd asked for a copy of Arthur Bryant's *Years of Victory, 1802 - 1812* for my birthday. Napoleon had been the Enemy with a capital 'E', Nelson was the hero at sea, and Wellington, *The* hero on land. I'd got immersed in The Peninsular War, loved it, the battles had an exotic ring about them, Vittoria, Badajoz, Salamanca, Cuidad Rodrigo. Wellington had won them all! He was *victor ludorum* with a vengeance, and Napoleon was on the run. I knew Waterloo was important, but basically England had won in the Peninsula, Wellington was top gun. It had all been over by the end of 1812. Bryant's book was finished, *and* there was Tschaikovsky's overture.

So when I was on St Helena first, Napoleon didn't mean a great deal. I was too busy being overwhelmed by the physical diversity and beauty of the island. Napoleon was just another chapter in the island's long story. But Gilbert Martineau, and his wonderful sense of ironic humour? He was Consul for France at the time, living in Longwood House. Now *he* was a real life character, but sadly he had died just before I returned.

So in the '90s, although I knew more about Napoleon, he was still just another piece of the island story. I had after all returned to walk and rediscover the island's natural beauty. But visits to the Tomb and the Pavilion, to Longwood House and the house of the Bertrands, they changed all that. They were emotive. There was an aura of Napoleon, man and legend, an aura of time not so much past, as suspended. In the gentle sunshine, or the swirling mists, they were real parts of the island's natural beauty, integral parts of its diverse fabric.

Napoleon's time on the island is of course documented more fully than any other part of its story. The translation of Martineau's *Napoleon's St Helena* is eminently readable, Dame Mabel Brookes' book is as delightful as The Briars. And there are so many others, of varying literary and historical standards and persuasions. Considering all the characters, being able to put them physically into place or places, brings a realism to the events and the period.

But Napoleon was another of the birds of passage. He just left a more indelible stamp. Of course, after his death and with time, he became a legend again, even bigger than at the height of his power, a sacred figure. How many million lives had been lost didn't matter. He was the man who implemented the revolution, developed the French education and legal systems, laid the communication systems of Europe, and yes, won great battles, made the rulers of Europe dance, took France to heights it would never see again.

So what you have on the island could be artificial, what the world wants to remember, a deified mask of the man. But it isn't. What remains on the island is the story of a great man become a lonely man, stuck on a lonely island. It isn't a cosmetic re-enactment of a scene, it is the atmosphere of those few years, the places, the people, the everyday events of the man himself. And you can walk them, walk through the pages of the endless diaries and endless rehashes, true or false, of his time there. You don't just step back in time for a moment, for a quick glimpse of the past. No, on St Helena you can live in it.

During the Napoleonic Wars the island had barely been on the periphery of the conflicts. Its inhabitants had continued to service the fleets of the East India Company. In the early years, they had seen the British navy, coming to guide the fleets back through waters threatened by the French. But it was always months after the events, that the islanders learned of Britain's defeats, and with time, of its victories. It impinged barely at all on their lives. They were concerned, but they were no more or no less comfortable, than they had been in collective memory.

Until, that is, September 15th, 1815, when out of the north appeared a ship bringing the news that the war in Europe was over. Napoleon had been defeated once and for all by the Duke of Wellington.

Now was a time to celebrate. Royal salutes were fired, a

festival was organized for the garrison, extra rations of wine were issued. All prisoners were released, with the exception, and for no clear reason why, of one miscreant awaiting trial for burglary. It was a marvellous few days. The war that had almost completely ignored them, was over. So they celebrated with vigour, there were few enough occasions for such good times, especially with an extra wine ration. And when the festivities ended, the island went back to the start of another summer.

But only until October 11th when another ship, the *Icarus*, appeared. This time it was a very different kettle of fish. It confirmed the news of the end of the war, the victory of Waterloo, the surrender of Napoleon and his abdication. Cheers all round, but we knew all that. Not only had Napoleon surrendered, but he had been sent into exile. More cheers, serve him right.

Oh, we almost forgot, they said, Napoleon's been exiled to St Helena. In fact he's due any day now, and there's an interim Governor coming in place of yours, and a Regiment of foot, so your garrison's disbanded, and there's artillery, and restrictions to movements, curfews, and a naval blockade, and .....

That really set the cat among the pigeons, in fact several cats among very few pigeons. St Helena was to become the home in exile, the gaol, of the most feared man in Europe, indeed the world. The twenty years when Napoleon pulled the strings of all the crowned heads in Europe, as far as St Helena was concerned, could well have been on another planet. Now at any minute, the erstwhile puppeteer would arrive in the Road, with a supporting cast half the size of the island's population to pull his strings.

What was known of Napoleon Bonaparte, the person, was no more than he was an ogre, who ate small children. You can imagine the uproar the news the *Icarus* brought started. In a community where gossip was a way of life, where the merest hint of a rumour rapidly magnified into biblical cataclysmic certainty, the news exploded like a direct hit on the powder store. Every corner of the island was awash with wave after tidal wave of rumour and counter rumour, so many rumours in fact, that the locals didn't have to make up any themselves, for a while.

Four days later, the elderly *Northumberland* dropped anchor in James Bay. On board were Admiral Cockburn, Napoleon and his French entourage, women and children, half a regiment of foot and its band, the equivalent of a small town. Some of the fleet had already arrived, and in the next few days, the rest of it, ten, a dozen, ships in all, escorts and store ships and troop carriers, *Icarus, Zephyr, Redpole, Ferret, Havannah, Bucephalus* and *Ceylon*, perhaps even the *Peruvian* and the *Zenobia*, too many to keep track. If the island had had only four days to prepare for Napoleon, he had had seventy days at sea to prepare for St Helena. What wasn't clear was who was going to be the more astonished.

Commanding the fleet, and personally responsible for Napoleon, was Rear Admiral Sir George Cockburn, Knight Commander of the Bath. The British Government had informed the Court of Directors of the EIC that their island would have to pass temporarily into the surer hands of a Regiment of the line, and a Governor who was *a General Officer in His Majesty's Service.* Until this man, already known but not publically identified, arrived, Admiral Cockburn would act as Governor.

Cockburn was a distinguished sailor, he'd served under Nelson at Cape St Vincent and was an Admiral at 43. He had been quickly, but carefully, selected for the job. Rear Admiral Cockburn was not a man to be meddled with. Almost exactly a year earlier, Cockburn had captured Washington, in the American War.

He had taken the Capitol first, and set it on fire, making sure that it, and its contents, which included the archives and the embryonic Library of Congress, were well ablaze, and then marched off to the President's house. The handsome stone building, already called by some 'The White House', was deserted. But a table had been set for an American celebratory feast. So the unexpected, and certainly uninvited, British ate and drank, toured the house, admired the furniture and fittings, oohing and aahing. Then Cockburn set The White House on fire too. He was quite satisfied, twenty hours work and Washington captured. So, yes, it was generally believed, that Cockburn was a man well able to look after Bonaparte.

The day after the *Northumberland* anchored, Cockburn went

ashore, and escorted by Governor Wilks, who he was in effect deposing, went looking for a house for Napoleon. At six that evening, Cockburn returned and informed Napoleon that he had found one, but it would require some alterations, taking perhaps three months. Until this accomodation was ready, Cockburn explained that he had rented suitable rooms in town.

It was dusk on the 17th, when the French party left the ship, to be taken ashore. The island population had already been warned by numerous proclamations that they were to have nothing to do with Napoleon or the French. Even so, they waited round the wharf, round The Castle, in the Square and Main Street, for a sight of the man.

The French party, under escort, crossed the moat on the drawbridge (the archway wasn't there then), and entered Jamestown from the side of The Castle. By this time it was dark, but what seemed like half the population had stayed in town to see the island's new resident. In the guttering light of torches, soldiers had to hold back the crowds to make way for the party.

Staring in silence, they watched the French party walk along the side of the square, past the courthouse, to Porteous' House, on the corner of the public gardens, opposite St James' Church. Henry Porteous was 'Superintendent of the Company's lands', but he also ran this modest guest house. Indeed it was very modest, but he was already dreaming of a more lucrative future, when he could boast that Napoleon and his French court had stayed under his roof. He lived on that shaky story for some time, but his House had a shakier future for it burned down (possibly *was* burned down) in 1865.

But to return to 1815. The next morning, the 18th, Napoleon and General Bertrand, Cockburn and an aide de camp, rode out of town, through the grim heat of Side Path. Napoleon noted the barrenness of the narrow valley, and the fortress of High Knoll dominating its western wall. Troops clattered past, he could hear bugle calls from a meadow above a waterfall, and he noted a farm house and a few cottages on the fold of the valley side below him.

Three miles, and several sentry posts, later, the party rode onto Longwood Plateau. Troops were already encamped on Deadwood Plain, and there was a major sentry post at Longwood Gate. The atmosphere was distinctly military, the kind of thing that Napoleon had enjoyed throughout his life, but now it rang more of the rattle of gaoler's keys and the clang of iron doors. The plateau was featureless, but beyond it, on the north-eastern corner of the island, was a solid, square black hill called The Barn.

Napoleon was in poor humour when, about a mile from the Gate, through the scrappy fields, scrubby trees and coloured clays of the plateau, the party reached a little farmhouse. Cockburn announced that this was Longwood House. The Lieutenant-Governor, Colonel Skelton, and his wife, were waiting and they welcomed the party warmly and ushered them indoors.

It was a good lunch. The Skeltons spoke French and were excellent hosts. Napoleon relaxed, warming to them both. Bertrand may have been taking note of the house that was to be their home in a few months, but Napoleon seemed to have paid little attention to his surroundings. The Skeltons only lived there from October to February, the warmer, drier season, spending the rest of the year in Jamestown, in the first house in Main Street, next to the church, opposite Porteous' House. But they left the impression on Napoleon that the house and Longwood were habitable.

Napoleon and Cockburn took their leave, and rode back in silence towards town. At the top of the barren descent down Side Path, Napoleon announced that the ride and the heat were tiring him. He wished to stop at the farm on the shoulder, just below them, for some refreshment.

So out of nowhere, the Emperor and his riding companions arrived at The Briars, the home of William Balcombe, his wife and three of their children. Balcombe was in bed with one of his not infrequent attacks of gout, but Admiral Cockburn was staying there, so was able to present the astonished Mrs Balcombe, and her family, to their unexpected visitor.

Chairs were brought out, and Napleon sat on the lawn. It was very pleasant, there were sounds of the farm, sheep and chickens and ducks. There were cooling breezes, and shade in a little grape arbour, there was a fish pond, and the smell of oranges, lemons and pomegranates. English flowers were mixed with hedges of plumbago and hibiscus, and cascades of fiery bougainvillea. On the side of the lawn, about fifty yards from the main house, on a small knoll, was a little wooden pavilion.

William Balcombe limped out to be introduced, and to take charge as master of the house. He was friendly, and as lively as his gout permitted. Napoleon was relaxed, he liked this rather bluff man, he liked children and the warmth of the family atmosphere. Mrs Balcombe reminded him vaguely of Josephine, and the younger girl, Betsy, spoke some French.

With no more ado, Napoleon announced that, with Mr Balcombe's permission, he would like to stay there, pointing to the Pavilion. The town was hot and noisy, he had no space in that dismal hostelry, he couldn't concentrate, he couldn't work, couldn't dictate. The house at Longwood would take months. He needed peace and quiet, and here it was. The Emperor bowed.

Balcombe was effusive, of course he must stay. But he mustn't stay in the Pavilion, Napoleon must have their house, Napoleon must have their servants too, he and the family would move into town. No, said Napoleon, you are too kind, the Pavilion is excellent, so be it. And so it was.

Napoleon continued sitting on the lawn, talking to Balcombe and Cockburn, General Bertrand could organise the French side of things. The Pavilion had one modest main room, a bedroom, some tiny side offices and two attics. Cockburn would arrange for a marquee on the lawn, to provide kitchens. Napoleon was delighted. His private secretary, Las Cases, and his young son, Emmanuel, could be sent up. They would sleep in the attic, and he could dictate his battles in peace. Two of his valets, Marchand and Ali, would come up and could sleep on the verandah.

It was all sorted out, in Napoleon's customary way. He decided what he wanted, and Bertrand and the others did it. Cockburn was bemused, but he was a pragmatic man, recognizing that Napoleon's security would be no greater a problem than in town. Francis Plain virtually overlooked The Briars, and half the 53rd

Regiment was camped there. The bulk of the French party could stay in town, visiting their Emperor as and when he demanded. Cockburn knew that if Bonaparte was secure, then it was probably in the best interests of all for him to be as contented as possible. So it was settled, just like that. And would Napoleon please join the Balcombe family for dinner?

There is a peace about The Briars on its little step on the valley side. It has a charm, onto which the stark high ground does not intrude. It is close to town, yet high enough to catch, and be cooled by, breezes coming down from Diana's Peak. It was a magic garden, a rustic retreat, it's fresh air scented with fruit trees and flowers. Surrounded by the higher cliffs and evidence of the military, it was strangely oblivious to it all. It was a haven, where the real island was immaterial.

Napoleon had been landed on this isolated rock, he had already been introduced to its different world, the barren cliffs, the crowded, humid, smelly town. And then, quite by chance, he found a totally different world at The Briars. He liked the life he saw around him. William Balcombe was a respected figure on the island, as was his company, Balcombe, Fowler and Coles. In the HEIC Register he appears as *William Balcomb, superintendent of public sales.* He had bought The Briars early on, and its hundred acres of land, much of which was not developed, stretched as far as the waterfall.

Balcombe had been in the navy (his father, a ship's captain, had been lost at sea), and had fought in the Battle of the Nile. Napoleon had a ready rapport with seamen, as had been witnessed on the *Northumberland*, and the two men were not short on subjects to discuss. Mrs Balcombe was a good housekeeper, mother and wife, and clearly made Napoleon feel if not exactly at home, at least most welcome.

The three children were Jane, aged about 18, Betsy about 15, and Alexander, who had been born on the island in 1811. Jane was already a young lady, and she and her mother were pleased at the arrival of so many eligible young officers with the 53rd. Betsy was on the edge of puberty, an attractive mix of tomboy and young woman. She was unaffected by Napoleon's position of former greatness.

Because she spoke some French she was a natural point of contact for him, and was young enough not to be embarrassed using the language. An improbable 'uncle - hoyden niece' relationship developed.

Napoleon quickly set up a routine. He sat outside and worked in the shade of the arbor. He dictated each morning and afternoon to Las Cases, or to Gourgaud or Montholon if Las Cases was writing up his notes. The marquee appeared on the lawn, and his cooks, Pierron and Le Page, came up and prepared his meals. He ate on occasions with the Balcombes, and often spent evenings in the house with the family, playing cards, or talking, or listening to the girls singing.

Napoleon had gone through the traumas of Waterloo, and abandonment by his government and many of his closest political supporters, friends and relations. He had abdicated his throne, and surrendered to the British. He had survived those shocks. He had wanted to leave France, leave Europe, leave politics and power, and go to America. The Allies were agreed on all of these, except America, and they delivered their answer, the ultimate shock. He was going to St Helena, with a much reduced private staff, for the rest of his days. From the eve of Waterloo, when he knew he would *dine tomorrow in Brussels*, to learning of banishment to an ocean rock, had been barely forty days.

Napoleon was no stranger to political ups and downs, or military defeats, but those forty days had delivered a succession of massive body blows. Seventy days at sea had at least begun to let it all sink in. But Porteous' House, and his first exposure to Longwood House and its bleak plateau, had disturbed him. Then The Briars and its setting, and the life and warmth of the Balcombe family, quickly reversed any depression, and all accounts indicate that he enjoyed his time there.

There was a different side of the coin in Jamestown. The French party was not a happy one. They found the climate oppressive. The women, used to Europe's finest Courts, tired quickly of the 'country village'. The men were frustrated, to-ing and fro-ing between Napoleon's whims, and town. Bertrand and Montholon visited Longwood regularly, which provided a break, and they had their wives with them. Gourgaud missed feminine company, and was jealous that Las Cases had the Emperor's ear and his company all the time.

One of the great joys of The Briars for Napoleon must have been the absence of the claustrophobic, all enveloping, company of his compatriots. He had had it for three months on board the two ships, and he would have it again, with a vengeance once they got to Longwood.

He was also free from the British troops. Of course, he was reminded daily, as squads clanked up and down Side Path, carting the materials to convert Longwood House from a small summer farm house into a small residence for an erstwhile Imperial party. And above his head, was the camp on Francis Plain, and the fortress bulk of High Knoll.

But there were no sentries, no guards. He wasn't stared at as he walked in the gardens, his compatriots could come and go at will. The Orderly Officer, Captain Poppleton of the 53rd, was supposed to keep him in his sight when he went outside the house. But Napoleon liked Poppleton, and his somewhat schoolboyish sense of duty and respect, and even started teasing him. There was no atmosphere of gaol and gaoler.

Napoleon played hide and seek, and blind man's buff, with the children, and enjoyed teasing Betsy. He growled at younger children, including Alexander, pretending to be the eater of small children that rumour had of him, and then gave them sweets. His childish pranks with Betsy, outraged Las Cases and Gourgaud, but for quite different reasons, Las Cases seeing a threat to the position of Emperor, Gourgaud seeing competition to his own idolization of him.

Today at The Briars, there are satellite dishes and aerials, antennae and the other high tech communications equipment of Cable and Wireless. But there are gardens, bananas and brightly flowered hedges, cottages and frangipani and funny hanging monkey toes, firs and aloes, myriad trees of different shapes and sizes and provenances. There is a tiny pond, chickens scratching at whatever, and mynas bossing anything that moves. It is rural, trees shade a patch of 'pasture' and a couple of bleating sheep.

The Pavilion, hardly large enough to warrant such a description, is L-shaped. It has a verandah on two sides, with cast iron poles holding up a pitched grey roof. It fits unobtrusively into the greenery of the setting. Originally, it had been a place where important Company visitors could spend a few days while their ships were re-provisioning. There are brass plates on either side of the entrance, one informing of Wellesley's sojourn there in 1805, recovering from his near-drowning in the Road. The other tells of Napoleon's longer stay. Things are delicately balanced at The Briars.

Inside is a sort of entrance-cum-waiting room, a little bedroom with a view of the Heart-shaped Waterfall, a small sitting room, and a larger reception room more or less at the rear. It is modestly furnished, in pieces representative of the time, some from India including a huge Burmese chest with brass inlay. There are fireplaces, though they would hardly have been necessary. There are a couple of busts, and a wonderful collection of contemporary prints, sketches, cartoons and maps.

Behind the Cable and Wireless buildings, up the valley a little, the vegetation is profuse, bananas and mangoes, and vast banks of night-flowering Cereus climbing high into the trees. The foundations of Balcombe's original house may be here, or perhaps the bits of wall are from other times. There are fertile fields for a little way up the valley, and the hills, if steep and rocky and barren in places, are accessible and normal, nothing threatening here in any way. The contrast with Longwood House could not be more extreme.

In 1815, of course there were regulations and counter regulations, the islanders were inundated in proclamations of this and that and the other, more accurately, don't do this, don't do that, don't do the other. There was a curfew, *the parole for the night,* though it was much more lax in town than in the country, as the French would discover. Shipping, even the Company's own, was tightly controlled, and there were naval vessels patrolling the island's approaches at all times.

Fortifications were being strengthened, even new ones installed. Ascension Island was garrisoned for the first time by

Royal Marines, and there was already talk, which would materialise somewhat later, of putting a company of soldiers on Tristan da Cunha. None of this impinged on Napoleon at all. His staff might have been aware of such matters, but he wasn't.

The period at The Briars was the equivalent of the 'phoney war' of World War II. Napoleon lived his life, dictating, refighting battles, discussing former strategies with his generals. When his meals were ready, they were preceded by Marchand announcing "His Majesty's dinner is served." Napoleon had started to put on a little weight, he had colour in his cheeks, he was less moody. It was the phoney exile. The weather was pleasing, the gardens and orchards blooming, the breezes soothing, and the 'freedom' tangible. The Briars clearly had a magic.

Then in the first week of December, Cockburn informed Napoleon that Longwood House was ready. Napoleon played for time. But very soon there were no more workmen, no more clatter, no more smells of paint. And to be honest, there was no more of Cockburn's patience. Napoleon was furious at having to leave The Briars. Cockburn was impassive, either Napoleon moved or he would bring guards to move him. Take it or be taken. Napoleon took it.

On that Saturday evening, Napoleon dined with the Balcombes, and the Skeltons and Las Cases were included. It was an evening of mixed emotions, the family had grown close to the man, and he to them. Playing blind man's bluff with the children, Napoleon cheated, as he always did. The adults talked of India and China and Australia, and Napoleon talked of European affairs, and teased Balcombe about his fondness for port. It was informal, enjoyable. Napoleon took his leave and returned to the pavilion.

But it was also rather sad. Perhaps that was the real end of an era. Not Waterloo, or the *Bellerophon* or Torbay, but the departure from The Briars. There is no doubt at the time that Napoleon knew, and in hindsight we all know, that the island would not be the same again for him. The phoney exile was over. On December 10th, 1815, accompanied by Cockburn and their assorted staffs, Napoleon rode away from The Briars to Longwood. Here was the start of the real exile.

Napoleon never rode back down Side Path into town, neither on that day when he'd left Porteous' House to look at the Skeltons' house, nor later. With his move to Longwood, a new life, and yes, after the fairytale atmosphere of The Briars, an increasingly ugly life, started. The next time Napoleon went down Side Path, was after his exhumation, in the set of coffins he had lain in for twenty five years, in the Devil's Punch Bowl.

# CHAPTER 7

## FORTIFICATIONS, AND THE BUTTERMILK SPECTRE

*Nature, indeed has been so wonderfully profuse in giving strength to this place, and has left so little for art to perform, that out of twenty-eight miles of coast, the fortified lines of defence, collectively, do not exceed eight hundred and fifty yards.*

Governor Lieutenant-Colonel Alexander Beatson, 1810

Several valleys round the island are accessible to ships wanting to land men for water. But it was just one or two on the leeward coast that offered a safe anchorage, and a stream providing water year round. The obvious choices were Chapel, later James, and Rupert's Valleys. They were slightly broader, with boulder and sand beaches, allowing relatively easy access, and space to camp and work once ashore. In fact, only James Valley has year round water.

To the west, Lemon Valley has excellent water, a good anchorage and a safe landfall, but it was perhaps uninvitingly narrow. That didn't bother the Dutch on New Year's Eve, 1672. Their first assault, was repulsed from Lemon Valley.

The Dutch second assault was successful, forcibly demonstrating to the Company that the island could be stormed from a dozen or so valleys, including several on the windward side. All of them would have to be defended in time, but the most pressing need for the new settlers was to make the northern coast, centred on Chapel Valley and its rudimentary settlement, as defensible as possible. The cliffs of the north-east, towards Sugarloaf, are rugged rather than vertical, so early on, a track was made to connect them.

You can see all this from the top of Jacob's Ladder. And the walk along the track is a rough but simple way to see something of the defences, and also to start the process of assimilation for more testing journeys. Most excursions on the island require a fair bit of vertical movement. With the exception of the Ladder, and you can always get a lift to the top of that, the trail of the fortifications keeps vertical endeavours to a minimum.

Jamestown itself was massively defended. Ladder Hill Fort stretched along the clifftop, batteries were dotted down the edge of the cliff face, then right across the bay. The eastern headland, from sea level to the top of Munden's Hill, bristled with gun positions. On the top, the smallest of them, Sampson's, faced inland, overlooking upper Jamestown and Side Path, more protection against mutineers than invaders.

Ladder Hill and Munden's, were fortified from the time the castle was built until the troops departed at the end of World War II. Ladder Hill Fort has been to all intents and purposes, a town in its own right for most of its history. And encompassing as it does, the entire period of English rule, it must be one of the historic building complexes in the Commonwealth with the most extraordinary potential for development. I find it impossible now, to visit it without seeing it as a restored historic 'recreation' centre, a massive attraction for islanders and visitors.

But where to start? It stretches along the cliff tops, across the hillside below Half Tree Hollow. It controls all approaches to Jamestown, and most of the leeward side of the island. On the corner, above James Valley, is the Flagstaff, and Signal House, perched on the edge of not one, but two cliffs. It could have been called the Eyrie, its walls on two sides drop 600 feet, one straight down, the other bouncing you irregularly before you attain the glacis.

A grand arch, its most recent reconstruction dated 1873, lets you enter Ladder Hill Fort. Step through it from the tarmac of the present day, into what? The nineteenth century? Eighteenth? Difficult to be sure. Difficult to be sure too, where you are. Is it Mediterranean? Is it Caribbean? Is it African? Warm sun, brilliant blue skies, gentle breezes, canaries and mynas, tropical and temperate flowers. The shore is invisible, you just look out over hundreds of square miles of Atlantic ocean, cloudscapes and sunsets. Doesn't that sound attractive for a hotel room or a restaurant? But it isn't that yet .....

The fort fills one end, the long barrack block along one side. The military prison, the Guardhouse, officers' quarters, batteries, guns, magazines, are spread round the others, and the parade ground fills the centre. The gymnasium building has some of the finest stonework anywhere on the island, the irregularly cut blocks fitting with a beautiful precision. But at some stage a quartermaster, or government administrator, decided to have them pointed with totally unnecessary mortar. Some of the grey basalt blocks have even been painted - that's right, grey!

The barracks are a simple, colonnaded building, of a single high storey, with latest dated stones of 1824 and 1827. A verandah runs the length of the colonnade. Doors, every four windows, open onto the verandah, and there is an outer, low stone wall between the columns. Opposite each door, a semi-circle is cut into this low outer wall, and a circular base installed. Below is the open, now dry, drain. What a delightful idea, I thought, plant pots brightening up the colonnade.

Plant pots, my elbow, said my guide, they were for buckets. The latrines were on the far side of the parade square, far too far to walk in the middle of the night. So buckets, their locations precisely engineered along the full length of the verandah, for night time essentials. A policy of 'last man up empties the lot' would have guaranteed a pretty crisp reveille.

Inside, the barracks are on two levels, stairs to upper half-open quarters. There is parquet flooring throughout, all the woodwork is teak, some iron girders, individual blocks connected by rounded archways through the heavy stone walls. Hammocks were hung cross-ways, and there are still wall racks for rifles. For decades the barracks were Government stores, mainly for essential foodstuffs which the Government had subsidised for generations. But in 1996 subsidies were removed and all trade in foodstuffs went to the private sector. So that has left the barracks, like the rest of the bulk of Ladder Hill Fort, temptingly empty.

Another arch takes you out of the parade ground area into a little 'village' of cobbled lanes and colour-washed stone cottages, that were presumably married quarters. They are all lived in, unchanged a couple of centuries later. They are low, with barred windows. There are horseshoes over doors, cats sleeping in the sun, window boxes. And they step down gently to the final wall on the cliff top.

Switching centuries again, beyond and onto rubble are two WW II six-inch naval guns. Beneath them the lavas are a warren of tunnels and magazines, more in need of attention than the older stonework.

Whether or not Ladder Hill Fort is turned into a major tourist complex is for the future. In the past it saw its troops marching out for centuries, on excercises and church parades, in 1795 to join an attack on Cape Town, in 1806 to join an ill-fated expedition to Buenos Aires. They paraded to guard Napoleon, to counter, or sometimes participate in, mutinies, and to guard the Boer prisoners. They watched the *Graf Spee* sail past, and had the sense not to fire. A salvo or two in reply would have made an awful mess of Jamestown.

One evening in '95, when I'd been on the island a week or so, there was a blackout in Jamestown. It wasn't all that late, but I'd gone to bed early after a day's walking. I still wasn't particularly fit. It was a day or so off the full moon, and the night was clear. What a chance to see Jamestown at night, I thought, like it used to be without street lights. So I went out onto the broad step at my front door. I was in a dressing gown, unlikely to offend anyone on a night as dark as this. It was lovely, the town in the moonlight, at the bottom of the valley, under a canopy of brilliant stars.

Out of nowhere, a teenage girl appeared, and stopped to say that the power cut would last all night. Her uncle worked for the electricity, she said, and they usually called him out, but she knew he wouldn't get up this late. QED. She lived just around the corner, she continued, but in the dark the dogs frightened her. So I offered to get dressed and walk round with her. That would be all right, she said, and I went inside. I heard a car pull up, and an exchange between a man, presumably the driver, and the girl. There was a cheery good-night, and the car drove off.

I went downstairs. "That was the police," said the girl, "they stopped to see if I was OK. So I said the man was taking me home." So the man walked with her, down the little lane off Napoleon Street. Her house was just round the corner, where the lane joins the path to Rupert's Valley, and a dog or two did indeed bother to complain. The moonlight accentuated the shadows, but her house was as clear as on a dull day. She opened the front door, thanked me and went in. The dogs complained again as I walked the couple of hundred yards back.

It says a lot for St Helena, when a young girl is frightened of the dog next door, but is in no way concerned by a perfect stranger (wearing a dressing gown rather than a gabardine), and neither were the police. The lights came back on just before midnight, so somebody must have woken her uncle up.

The house of the trusting young lady was on Munden's Way, an impressive title to the track round to Rupert's Valley. The old, solid, stone warehouse, tucked almost into the hillside, is now the Scout Hall. I should have known something was happening as I set off this Sunday morning. Napoleon Street had exhibited a scattering of freshly scrubbed Scouts, Guides and Brownies.

From the direction of the Hall, on one or two evenings a week, came the sounds of the ritual torture of bugles, by young lads. It's not just Scouts that do it. Cadet Forces do it, Boys Brigades do it, I suspect even Sally Army trainees do it. But what defeats me, is how successive generations of trainee buglers produce the same abominable noise, the same painful rendition, note for ruptured note, that they did in my village fifty years ago. It's the indiscriminate scything through the scales that is so disconcerting, and that final choked discord. It's a sort of musical equivalent of the teacher's fingernail screeching down the blackboard, except trainees don't feel the pain and repeat it, endlessly.

This morning, someone was still trying, as though somehow, in a sort of Munden's Way to Damascus scenario, an island Herb Alpert would rise from the ashes. And that ghastly metaphor is perfectly in keeping with the sound quality. I hurried along the path behind the Consulate Hotel. This track, once so strategically important, indeed photos show you could drive an Austin Seven round it in the twenties, has fallen considerably from grace.

Behind the houses of Main Street are a jumble of low, ruined outbuildings, like sloughed skins of the town's narrow street of houses.

Fitted in between the path and the Public Gardens, behind The Castle, another walkway is being restored. This was Sisters' Walk, built by Governor Patton in about 1805, for his two daughters. Built with flower beds, shrubs and trees, it was a few feet higher than Main Street, but it caught the breeze, avoided the worst of the smells, and offered a little shade for the ladies of his house. Now, nearly two centuries later, they are tackling the barren dustscape it became, on their way to restoring some of its charm.

The bell of St James' sounds repetitively over Lower Jamestown. Then behind me a big drum thumps, and Lo! miracles are still to be found, for the bugles start up, pretty well in tune. Invisible from here, the band and its music channel their way down Napoleon Street.

Outside the Canister, the assembled guides and brownies and their banners would have been lined up, ready to join in. The bright and musical sounds continue down Main Street, and the marching ranks eventually appear across the Public Gardens. There is no one out to watch. Main Street is a sadly empty stage for this monthly fixture in the Church calendar. It is a delightful vignette of past youth - nostalgia on parade.

The big drum now overpowers the church bell, and few will be able to sleep off much more of their Saturday night. The parade disappears behind the trees and the library, and silence indicates its safe arrival. It puts a spring in your step, physically and mentally, a parade like that. Nostalgic it might be, but it can't quite drag you back to the army bands on parade, and great functions in the Square with forests of masts in the bay. But it reminds me of the importance of Banks Lines, which is where I'm heading.

On the morning of June 1st, 1706, two ships flying Dutch colours were seen approaching the island. Britain was at peace with the Dutch at the time. The alarm gun was duly fired, and they passed close to Banks, acknowledging the signal from shore. Then, as they came into the Road, the ships opened fire on a Company ship, the *Queen*. Running down the Dutch flags and hoisting French colours, they boarded her, and cutting her cables, and those of a second Company ship, the *Dover,* fired on the shore batteries, and sailed off with their prizes.

It had been a swift and skilled operation, but the shore batteries had had plenty of time to return their fire, had they not been out of shot, powder and the sponges used in charging the guns. Perhaps they'd been on church parade. Whatever, in the South Atlantic Cup it was very much France 2, England nil. And this was the event that installed the procedures of all ships identifying themselves at Banks.

As the track turns away from town, you stand propped by the wall against the breeze, looking over the bay, across the boat-life in the Road. The lighters lie quietly tethered, with those fishing boats that had not departed long before the early morning bugle call. Occasionally esoteric vessels arrive at St Helena, a Chinese junk, or a Brazilian tall-ship, even a copy of Captain Cook's *Endeavour*. But on any good day in season, half a dozen yachts, masts rocking in the swell, are evocative enough.

The seaward end of Munden's Hill was even more strongly fortified than Ladder Hill. From the shore up to the hilltop, the lavas have been cut and sliced, tunnelled into and built onto. Roadways and haulways zig-zag through a maze of walls, concrete and stone, depending on the age. There are bits of cobbled yard, complex masonry, iron girders, concrete trackways, a VR crest above an entrance to covered passages, quarters, batteries, and magazines. There are vaults for men, for machines, for shells and weapons, vertical chimneys for hoists.

Spalled masonry and rusted cannon lie on the shore, and the installations are veneered with rubble, graffiti, beercans and broken glass. There is rusted barbed wire, there are abandoned searchlight batteries, sliding metal screens, and steel lifts for shells. How many generations of gunners, St Helena Militia, St Helena Artillery, Royal Artillery, Royal Marines, Royal Navy? How often were they ever fired in anger? Most of them, probably not since 1673.

It's all so desolate, so sad, all these carefully constructed defenses. One minute nostalgia of the proud Scout band and Church parade, the next, the products of three centuries of killing machines gone to rack and ruin, forgotten, rubbished. And the roadway itself? Much of its retaining wall has fallen away. For long the most important thoroughfare for the island's fortifications, it has fallen on hard times.

A large gap in its retaining wall has been filled by poles resting on two stone-filled barrels, whitewashed as is their right. The fortifications are of the past, dead. The graffiti are of the present, alive and well, uplifting after the desolation of Lower Munden's: *Faron Crowie love Sexy Peggy Moyce his best girl in the world*, reads one barrel. *Faron Boogie Secret Admirer and dreamer of Darling Peggy Moyce want her like crazy*, reads the other.That's uplifting for the rest of the relic roadway, where a patch or two has followed its retaining wall into the sea. There's a notice in Rupert's, a bit late if you missed the one on the wharf:

*Warning. The St Helena Highway Authority hereby warns members of the public that Munden's Point Road from Ruperts Valley all the way to Jamestown is in a very danerous* [sic] *state. Any persons using the road do so at their own risk - Government will not accept liability in the event of an accident arising. You are strongly advised not to proceed further.*
Danerous it might be, but you wouldn't want to miss a great historic walk, or graffiti like that. (Unfortunately in 2003 Munden's Way had been closed to the public).

In its heyday, Rupert's Valley was protected by a massive wall from side to side, bristling with cannon. Today, it is a strange mix of ancient and modern, collapsing fortifications contrasting with the cluster of pristine fuel storage tanks for the Power Stration. Up the valley are a few houses, and some oleanders offering a touch of colour to its monochrome drabness. The rock walls of its containing hills stretch, drab and unwaveringly austere, to the skyline. I shall return to Rupert's, for this is where they built the Liberated African Depot in 1840.

On the other side of the bay are the remnants of the path, half buried in samphire, between the fuel storage dump and the fish handling plant. Originally the path was wide enough for a gun-carriage, with a retaining wall two or three feet high all the way to Banks. Now, not only has most of the retaining wall gone, but the path itself, so carefully engineered, has largely slipped away.

Nothing grows. It's dusty. It's hot, heavily hot, from the sun directly overhead, and its reflections from the rocks. The sea, a hundred feet below, looks delicious, washing the rocks with lines of foam, laughing at you sweating. It's worth watching the sea, when you've stopped, not when you're walking, there's not enough path for that. You might see a manta ray, or you might walk along more or less in step with a turtle. Very occasionally, in season, there may be whales, huge T-shaped tails waiting to dive. You might see the odd dolphin, but far better for that is to go out in a boat to see them. The fishermen will tell you the best times, and you can watch a couple of hundred of them (pantropical spotted dolphins) swimming, jumping, somersaulting, all round you - truly spectacular.

Banks' Valley, barren and grim, runs down from Flagstaff Hill and the end of Deadwood Plain, in their cooler, breezier world. The northernmost part of the island, Sugarloaf Hill, stands sentinel above it, a fine observation point for shipping, friend or foe. And yes, you can land at Banks, and you could stagger up to the interior of the island, but miles from anywhere. So why was so much trouble taken at Banks, for the fortifications here, and the cluster of batteries on the other side, are the jewel in the island's military engineering crown?

Banks' importance lies in its position on the northern point of the island, and the approaches to James Valley. Ships coming from the east and south, had the full backing of the winds up to The Barn. They then had to turn across Flagstaff Bay, and to make the anchorage in James Bay they had to come in close to the cliffs at Sugarloaf, to hold the lee of the island. Come in too wide, and the Trades carried you out to sea again.

If the ships weren't yours, you'd had early warning from the lookout on Sugarloaf, and as they rounded the point, they came immediately into range of the batteries on the east side of Banks. If they decided to turn about to question your authority, they came into the field of fire of the great Half Moon battery and the cannon across Banks Line itself.

And we mustn't forget the fiasco of June, 1706. It was really that that guaranteed the importance of Banks. All ships after that had to heave to off Banks, and send in a small boat with identification, to seek permission to anchor in the Road. Anyone ignoring the regulation was fired on.

It looks very peaceful today, the sea wall and its platform, and the wall of the path round to the forward batteries. It all looks rather small from the path, before you drop down towards the bay. In the '60s, the wall across the mouth of the narrow bay was intact, its platform of imported limestone slabs, and patterned cobbles scattered with most of its ten 32 pounders. The stream, when it flowed, came onto the beach through a magnificent arch.

But times change, nature and man have both played their roles. The sea wall has been breached, with more than half of it, and half the platform, claimed by the sparkling Atlantic. Soon the rubble fill behind the seawall under the platform will be breached, ironically leaving the arch for the stream the only part left standing. The cannon have all been removed, not by the sea this time, but by man, collected by boat and lighter and taken round to Jamestown, to replace others long removed from there.

A few hundred yards up the valley, is a lime kiln. It is in need of restoration, but much of its intricate brick and stone structure is revealed. With no limestone or shelly beaches on the island, lime was at a premium, having to be shipped in from England. Then in 1797, shelly sands were discovered in Banks Valley, and this lime kiln was built. The calcareous sands weren't on the beach, so they haven't all been quarried away, they were up the valley, almost where it reaches the clifftop above Flagstaff Bay. What's left of them is still there today, seven or eight hundred feet above sea level.

Tens or hundreds of thousands of years ago, those sands were beaches, when the ocean was warm enough for the tiny shelled creatures that make them up. During the Ice Ages, with the northerly shift of Antarctic ice, the South East Trades would have been stronger. In fact they must have been ferociously strong to blow the sands up the cliffs from the beaches in Flagstaff Bay, to drop them as sand dunes on the lee slopes above Banks. That's why a lime kiln, built two hundred years ago, stands solid in the spoil heap rubble and prickly pears, at the back of Banks' Line.

What you've really come here for is on the headland on the other side of the bay, the exceedingly handsome Half Moon Battery. It's the first of a spectacular complex of five batteries, at a variety of levels in the cliffs, each seemingly more inaccessible than the next. Beyond Half Moon, a roadway takes you to Middle Point, Repulse Point, Buttermilk Point, and Lower Crown. All are flagged in imported stone slabs, their approaches in impeccable stonework. The last two are in three tiers with passages and stairways cut through the lavas. There are magazines hollowed out too, and sitting on ledges are what is left of guard houses and quarters for the gunners.

Hundreds of feet above is the distinctive Sugarloaf, a landmark for incoming ships and an excellent vantage point. It was a lookout post and signal point connecting Flagstaff Hill and Ladder Hill, which between them had contact with the rest of the island. From the top, you can see into the barracks of Ladder Hill, and the whole of the north-west coast beyond. But it's funny, you can't see Banks, so you had to signal the forward battery at Buttermilk, and they relayed the message.

The batteries were started in the late seventeenth century, and most display signs of Chinese masonry work, so they were improved upon when Napoleon was on the island. So you have a hundred and twenty five years or so of extraordinary engineering and masonry skills. But I leave it to you, fair reader, to imagine the effort of manhandling the blocks of cut stone, and several tons of cannon ten feet long, up and down the hillside, round corners, down steps, into and out of boats, in places with hairsbreadth precision.

The fortification are a pleasure to wander round, to touch and to absorb, to try to envisage something of the men who built them and the men who manned them for so long. It's warm and the breezes are soft, there is the steady scrape of the sea. It's beautiful sitting in the sun admiring the workmanship and the setting.

And here may be one of the most reclusive spirits of the island, the wraith of Buttermilk Point. Captain Oliver's book of 1881, *On board a Union steamer*, recounts the original story of Richard Keating. No one I spoke to on the island knew of this particular ghost, and it is an odd one, in that it's such a complicated tale. You may believe it or not, but when you've scrambled all round, and all over, the batteries and the buildings, you know exactly where it all happened. It's easy to understand what this setting might do to one's imagination.

Keating was a sergeant in 1835, when Banks was manned by an officer and 35 men. There was a day guard on Half Moon, and a night guard on Buttermilk. One bright, moonlit night, Keating was in charge, sitting in the guardroom. Men were on the battery, and sentries were at post. Between nine and ten o'clock, a sentry shouted that Keating was wanted by the officer in his quarters, up above the battery.

So up went Sgt Keating, and reported to the officer, who was reading. The officer was puzzled, what on Earth did he want? No, he hadn't called him, he had been reading in peace, and perhaps the Sergeant would be kind enough to leave him that way. Or words to that effect.

Puzzled, and annoyed, Keating went down again, eager to sort out whoever had played the trick on him. But all the men on duty swore they had heard the officer call, "Sergeant of the guard!," three times. They had all seen the officer leaning over the low wall above, outside his quarters. Keating still thought someone was having him on, but he shivered, remembering the old adage, "He who sees the wraith first, is wanted in the other world." But nothing happened.

A week later, it was midnight, and Keating was outside with the guard. The officer's servant, Pat, came up, greatly disturbed. Pat had been asleep, when he woke to see his wife coming towards him with blood dripping from her mouth. She came to his bed, and told him to get up and follow her. He followed her to the door, but she vanished. Pat, having recounted the events, refused to go back to bed.

Pat's wife stayed in Jamestown, so next morning as the orderly was leaving for town, Keating asked him to check on her to be on the safe side, Pat had had a disturbed night. That afternoon the orderly returned with bad news. Pat's wife had died the night before at about midnight, from a broken blood vessel.

About a month after the funeral, four of the men of the battery went fishing in a boat in Flagstaff Bay, round the point of Sugarloaf towards The Barn. A sudden squall capsized and sank the boat, and two men were drowned. The two men were Pat, and the first man to have seen the officer calling for the Sergeant, on that moonlit night several weeks earlier.

So endeth the tale of the spectre of Buttermilk Point, an odd, but perhaps appropriate, ending for a visit to the intricacies of the island's finest military installation.

# CHAPTER 8

## GHOSTS : A PHANTASMAGORIA

*Many of the islanders believe to this day that the ghost of the murdered slave is seen to make the circuit of the wild spot wherein he carried on his nightly orgies; a superstition easily accounted for from the circumstances of the summits of the mountains being generally encircled by light mists, which wreath themselves into all kinds of fantastical shapes; thus to the eye of superstition giving to 'an airy nothing a local habitation and a name.' In St Helena every cavern has its spirit, and every rock its legend.*

Mrs. Abell, (late Miss Eliza Balcombe) Recollections, 1843

When I went back in 1995, I stayed for several weeks in town, at the classiest address I've ever had: Bishop's Rooms, Napoleon Street, Saint Helena. Well, I thought it was pretty good.

The house was on the open part of Main Street, across from the Post Office, at the very start of Napoleon Street. It was Georgian, a sort of grand three up three down. It extended back from the road towards the valley side, through a threadbare, narrow garden with two lemon trees, and cobblestones from some distant former life. It was called Bishop's Rooms, as it had been used from time to time in the past by the Bishop and his staff. In Napoleon's time, it had been the residence of the American Consul, (and by 2000 it was the town offices of Cable and Wireless).

A lovely broad wooden staircase rose round a central 'well', and at the top of the stairs, the landing, of polished wooden planks of unknown age, connected the bedrooms at the front with the bathroom, off a narrow balcony at the back. It was a very open house, doors and windows letting in light and breezes, and I would discover in time, occasional wafts of rain upstairs, and a particularly audacious pair of mynas into the kitchen.

On that first evening, Barbara and Basil took me home for dinner. When I returned to the house, feeling very glad to be back, my head was in a whirl from trying to absorb some of what had happened over the last thirty years. So many changes, large and small, but I had plenty of time to take them in.

The street lights in Main Street stayed on all night. In the '60s they went off at 10, and walking home later than that you might get pinned in the beam, often rather feeble beam, of a policeman's torch. He was only making sure he would be fully *au fait* with the morning's gossip, who had been where and when and why and with whom. But with today's outside illumination so bright, I could turn off the lights upstairs and wander about in peace, should I so wish.

And that's when I heard the gentle sound of heavy breathing. At first, I thought it was coming from the little room on the left, that had long before been an office. But it was silent, and when I walked to the balcony, the sound wasn't there either. There was just the breeze, brushing the sides of the valley and stirring the leaves of the peepul trees. It must be my imagination, I thought. But no, crossing the landing again, the heavy breathing was still there. It seemed to be in the stair well.

I was rather pleased. St Helena has many ghosts, in some of the old houses, and a few in town. And now I had come back, and I had my very own. But thinking about it, I decided it was rather sad, because my ghost must be the only one on the island that was asleep.

The island's stories of ghosts are of all kinds and forms, in all kinds of places. There are eighteenth and nineteenth, and very definitely twentieth, century ghosts White ladies are quite common, in town, up country, even one running along the now non-existent ramparts of Sandy Bay Beach. Up country, there are babies crying, and slave women wailing. In many cases they are in locations where there was once a house, though so long ago that even the ruin has disappeared.

There are stories of blazing houses seen from afar, but nothing when you get close. But you mustn't take stones from certain ruins, because if you did, then your own house would appear to be on fire.

Up country, horses and carriages are almost run of the mill, in the dark nights and mists. Sometimes you see them, sometimes you hear them, but not always do you do both. Sometimes one of a pair of travellers will see, and the other will hear, or one might not see or hear anything at all. In the 1890s, the Governor's wife was up late with a sick child, when she heard horses' hooves, carriage wheels and voices under the front windows of Plantation House. She heard them go past the house and straight through a locked gate into the woods. The sick child woke asking who was there.

There are a number of very specific ghosts. In the far south-west, there are a woman's footprints on Castle Rock Plain, and fishermen scuffing them out on the way down to fish, find they are back when they start for home. There is a sow and her piglets in a wind blasted pasture filled with boulders, known as The Churchyard. And William Burchell, writing in his journal of a visit to Longwood in 1807, went to a *fertile gut* below Longwood wall, where locals said there was the ghost of a large white boar.

You can look from where Burchell never saw the white boar, across to the brooding bulk of The Barn, where there is, or was, the ghost of a white goat. I wonder if the boar actually became the goat, as a tale rather than a genuine piece of ectoplasmic transformation? They don't appear to have overlapped historically. And unlike the early rare reference to the boar, the later goat had a longish run. In the nineteenth century, an eccentric known as London Ben used to go onto The Barn and stay for days at a time. It was when the white goat called him, he said. And it's gone into the language. "White goat calling you?" they ask, when they believe you've gone potty.

There are redcoats in the trees below Alarm House, ten or eleven of them, the returning spirits of the soldiers hanged for their part in the mutiny of 1787. They were buried with stakes through their abdomens, it is said. They reappear at midnight on Christmas Day, but that was the anniversary of the ending of the 1811 mutiny. Dates may be hazy, but details are pretty exact: men in scarlet coats, three-cornered hats, dragging their rusty old cannon through sulphurous vapours. Military anniversaries aren't uncommon. At Cox's Battery over by Turk's Cap, there's a red hand, which appears once a year, on the anniversary of a soldier's suicide.

It's strange that there are so few ghosts related to the sea. I heard of only two. One is of a fishing boat rowed out of a cave near Egg Island, by six boatmen without heads. Very odd. And the second is of a ghostly schooner near Egg Island, which sails between the shore and the boats out fishing. Fishermen, who know every rock of the shore, and often fish all through the night, must be very unreceptive, or perhaps they just have their feet firmly on the ground.

Particularly interesting is the complete absence of ghosts of Napoleon, and very little of the French household. While Napoleon was at Longwood House, it was Mme Montholon who was disturbed by ghostly rumblings in the loft. You have to remember that the attics were inhabited by several members of staff, and late night visits from whores were not uncommon. The only suggestion of a ghost left behind after the French had departed was of Count Montholon. Perhaps there was a family predilection.

There are still tales of Napoleon's buried treasure, secret manuscripts hidden in bottles, and even hordes of diamonds on The Barn. Shades of London Ben Calling. But there are no ghosts of Napoleon, and let's face it, the Tomb and the House are both pretty spooky in the driving mists. I have an explanation, but that's definitely another story.

No, the closest Napoleon seems to get to ghost stories was when he was staying at The Briars. William Balcombe brought in a tale of a ghost near the Heart-shaped Waterfall. The Emperor certainly teased Betsy about it, more so when it was discovered that the strange noises were from a pair of runaway slaves hiding there. Mrs Abell's recollection, quoted above, which is supposedly about a manifestation near Lot, sets me to thinking that she might have got a couple of her memory wires crossed over the years.

General interest in ghosts and unnatural occurrences is waning on the island today. Certainly it is with the younger generation. Videos and TV probably show far more frightening, real or unreal, manifestations. But then waning too, is young peoples' interest in walking from place to place, especially at night. You use the car if you want to go somewhere, or if there is no car, then you stay at home watching a video. And electric light is now provided all over the island. So there is far less opportunity to frighten yourself.

In the '60s it was very different, especially up country. Ghostly and related talk was standard. People kept garlic, tied it to doorposts, wore it, ate it, popped it in their boots, to ward off the evil-eye, known as gilly-gilly. Children, country and town alike, could be threatened with the Gunnybag Man, an unspecified character rather like a bogey man, the Old Nick of my childhood.

At that time, half the male population carried gunnybags. Whether you were a flax worker or on relief, a fisherman or a farmer, you carried a gunnybag, to hold whatever it was you needed to put into a gunnybag. So children were wary if elders invoked some shadowy figure, roaming the dark lanes of town or the mists of country paths, all too ready to pop them into his bag.

There was Jack o' Lantern too, in those far off days, and he was more terrifying, probably because he was much less easily envisaged. Some kind of light appeared in the distance, and you were well advised not to go in that direction. There are still stories, but not quite so easy to find. But it doesn't need too much to kindle or re-kindle an interest in ghosts, as is only to be expected in such isolation.

On the ship in '95, I travelled with two German amateur entomologists, coming to the island for a week's holiday over Christmas. If mine was a love for the island born of close proximity, then their's was a gentle obsession born of distance. Their interests were in lace-wing flies and moths, certain species of which are unique on St Helena's central ridges. With the support of the Agricultural Department, they had gone onto the Peaks to collect at night, using special yellow-green lamps.

At the time I didn't know these details, but I was able to guess them the following morning. As I walked to the market, someone told me that ghosts had been seen on the Peaks the night before, yellow-green ghosts.

Later that morning, a leading island figure, came up to me in the street and introduced himself, he explained that he had been away at school when I had been there first. And Nick Thorpe and

I talked a while, and he eyed up the figure he had heard about, the solid 'rock man', the 'scientist', who had been all over the island looking at stones. At one point I'd laughed, saying I'd just heard about the transformation of last night's entomological expedition into psychedelic apparitions.

Nick nodded, "Yes, but you really saw a ghost, didn't you? John Bailey told the story."

John Bailey had certainly tried putting the fear of God into me, in the flickering candles of a half ruined house I'd lived in for a time. "Well, John told me the story about the ghost in Distant Cottage, but I never saw it."

"No, not that one. When you were camping on the ridge between Sugarloaf and Flagstaff" This was on the edge of the high cliffs at the head of Banks' Valley.

"But I never camped that side. I only went along those cliffs a couple of times, and never at night."

"You must have done. John told the story. John said that there was a ghost over the cliff top, down one of the fishing ropes. You'd been camping there one night, and you'd felt its presence and had had to leave. John said it must have been a real ghost, if a scientist who studied the rocks could be made to pack up his tent, and leave because of it."

"But I never camped ...." I stopped, there was no point. John's marvellous way with words had provided initial veracity, and it was then carved in stone because it had been told on St Helena Radio. You couldn't argue with that.

Jamestown has its ghosts, entrenched in memory long before John Bailey needed to keep the spooky pot boiling. There is a white lady on The Castle ramparts, but nobody has seen her for a while. There is Free Molly, another white lady, up Main Street. She comes out some nights round Seales's Corner, from down by The Run. Some say she was a freed slave, and a soldier had fallen for her charms. More likely a soldier had acquired her charms by promising he would take her with him when he left the island. Well when he left, he didn't take her, he didn't even tell her he was going. He just sailed away. And Free Molly still runs through the dark street looking for her would be suitor.

In the town's tiny gaol, a lovely little building next to the church, there used to be Lowry's cell. In the days when boys were boys and not delinquents, the police held an ultimate threat. Any talking back, any larking about, any attitude, and they'd be locked for a while in Lowry's cell. It saved an awful lot of time and paperwork. Who they might have found in Lowry's cell, I don't know, but Lowry was certainly in the gaol before he was hanged.

Up on the side of Rupert's Valley, just below Napoleon's Tomb, is a shoulder of pasture where a house called Fox's Folly used to stand. A pleasant enough walk, down from the police post at Alarm Forest. The story I'd been told was that the owner of Fox's Folly had a burly, and surly, negro slave called Lowry, and a young slave girl. One day the girl disappeared. A few days later, the owner was out riding, when his dog started barking and scratching at the ground. A hand was sticking out of a mound of earth, where the girl's body had been hastily buried.

The farmer assumed Lowry to be the perpetrator of the crime, because he was a violent man. He was afraid of Lowry and wanted him out of the way, so he wrote a letter to the Chief of Police, saying "Arrest this man, he's a murderer. I will explain later." He knew Lowry couldn't read, and sent him to town to deliver the note, and thereby get himself arrested. They hanged him, and his ghost returns to his cell to terrify naughty children. That was the story I'd been told.

But the St Helena Herald of February 17th, 1853, carries the genuine, detailed account, *Trial of Lowry for the murder of Elizabeth Ann Booms.* So whether or not you see the ghost, at least on this occasion you know exactly what he had supposedly done. The young girl worked for Ebeneezer Hastings, who lived near Fox's Folly, which was then an inhabited dwelling. It was Ebeneezer's dog which found the body, but there was no note saying "Please lock him up." Otherwise everything else was there in the paper.

Lowry, *a negro,* was found guilty, on evidence that would have had the police arrested today. He was sentenced and hanged.

The newspaper report went on to contrast the good behaviour of the public attending the hanging, with the conduct of similar crowds in England, where *oaths, lies, obscene jokes, picking of pockets, and all other improprieties are the order of the day .... But here the most perfect stillness and order reigned, whilst very few females were present; and those who were were mostly of a class not much respected.* The account does however point out that the hanging was arranged very early, so the 'audience' would be as small as possible.

Perhaps that linkage of factual past to a subsequent tale is a necessary aside. Lowry was a well known ghost, as are some of the others. But I found an obscure reference to the 'Shamrock ghost' in an old *Wirebird*, an island magazine which went out of circulation in the late '60s. But it offered nothing more than the name.

At about the same point of Main Street where it is said Free Molly appears, there had been an ale-house called the 'Rose and Shamrock'. After the Second World War, this had become a shop with the same name, and now it was half a shop. Next door was the island's main disco, Barry Dillon's bar. So I asked Barry what he knew about it.

"Oh yes," says Barry, "I remember that, as a boy. My father [Sergeant Dillon of the island police force, a legendary figure, equally respected by the general population, and feared by the children of his day] helped the Bishop and the priest to exorcise it."

That would have been in the 1950s, but I'd never heard it mentioned in the '60s. So I asked Barry who it was. "No idea, but I'll ask my mum about it, she'll remember."

If she did, it slipped his memory to tell, and mine to ask. But about a month later, I was up country with some people and mentioned the Shamrock ghost, and Sgt Dillon's involvement in the exorcism.

"Best example we ever had of a human ghost," said one. "Couple who lived in the house weren't getting on. She used to see her boy friend on the side. Whenever he came, he'd make some funny noise or other, so the husband would think it was a ghost, and keep his head down. They bothered him a lot, the ghostly noises, so he asked the Bishop to get rid of them."

Plantation House has, or had, its share of ghosts, not just phantom carriages. Joshua Slocum stopped off in 1898, on his voyage round the world. He wrote that the Governor specifically chose the 'West room' for him, because it was haunted. But Slocum slept very soundly. Yet at about that time, there were a number of cases that may have been poltergeists. These are not otherwise referred to in the island ghostlore, but you'd expect a different, if not necessarily better, class of manifestation at the Governor's residence.

The rooms in Plantation have special names, and in 1960, a woman and a child were staying in the 'General's Room', when a ghost proceeded to open and close the drawers of the chest of drawers. This even woke the woman's brother, who was sleeping in the 'Baron's Room'. He saw the ghost, and so did the child, but both were unperturbed. The eiderdown was taken off the bed, the reading lamp was taken from the bedside table, and somewhat erratically moved up and down along the floor. So perhaps the poltergeists lived on, in a manner of speaking.

The woman stayed on the island, and on a later occasion was in the passage upstairs, going for dinner past the 'General's Room' towards the room named 'Chaos'. The curtains on the doors were held back by a man in a black silk coat with velvet revers, his cravat was loose and hanging, and he had a deformed thumb. He watched the woman, with a *saturnine case of countenance, with very dark and markedly winged eyebrows.* She opened another door, turned on the light, and the man disappeared. In spite of that detailed description of dress and looks, no identity of the man was offered.

The uplands are the setting of some of the best known houses on the island, Wood Cot and Oakbank, Luffkins Towers, Woodlands and Rose Bower. They are not particularly large houses, but they have great, often simple, character, partly intrinsic, partly from the histories attached to them. Their gardens contribute to the richness of the up country landscape, with their plants from all corners of the planet. Some of course have ghosts associated with them.

The original house at Oakbank was seized from one of the ringleaders of the 1684 mutiny. In Napoleon's day it was the town Adjutant's main house. Later that century it was the official residence of the Bishop of St Helena. One Bishop died there, when his pony and trap overturned. And a man *looking like a Bishop* supposedly passes through one of the bedrooms. Or the Bishop-like man may be a figure like a nun in a cowl, with her hands tucked into her sleeves. She, or he, has been known to walk through one of the interior walls, and some years ago, renovation work revealed an unknown door buried behind plaster in the place in the wall through which she, or he, walks.

Perhaps the oddest apparition of all from this part of the island, is a very twentieth century one, but nothing to do with any of these fine houses. It was recorded in another issue of the *Wirebird*. A man was going in his car from Francis Plain to Hutts Gate, when the engine suddenly died on him. It was daylight, but mists closed in and obscured all but a yard or two from the car. He was puzzled at his engine stopping, and was trying to remember when he last filled up with petrol.

Suddenly, two pairs of booted feet and the lower few inches of trouser legs appeared on one side of the car, walking, at window level. He watched the pairs of feet turn and walk across the bonnet of the car, and out into the mists on the other side. Some time after they had gone, the car engine just re-started. The island's mists have a lot to hide.

It was known that I was interested in ghost stories and one evening a senior lady, having regaled me with the most excellent of dinners, told me of a ghostly occurrence. This had occurred five or six years before at Rose Bower, a late eighteenth century house across from Oak Bank. It's a lovely house, its rambling gardens so peaceful the only sounds are of ripe fruit falling. Rose Bower at the time of Napoleon belonged to the man who managed the Emperor's funeral, but those few years ago it was the residence of John Bailey, the island dentist and racconteur, his wife Evie, and their two young sons. This was the good lady's story.

Evie was putting the boys to bed one evening, when she noticed a distinct smell of honeysuckle in the room. She asked the boys if they had brought some back, or had been playing with the flowers, and they assured her they hadn't. Strange she thought, tucked them in and went to the lounge, where John was reading. "When you say goodnight to the boys, see if you notice an odd smell in their room," said Evie, and off went John.

When he returned, he said there had been a scent of honeysuckle, "Did the boys bring some in?" Evie explained there was no honeysuckle physically there. In the morning, John, always interested in island history, went to the Archives to try to look up a bit of history of the house that they had somehow missed.

When he returned that evening, he indeed had a tale to tell. At some stage in the nineteenth century, the house had been owned by a woman who lived alone, and was very fond of horse riding. One day she had gone out on her favourite horse, but it had returned to the house on its own. Just before night fell, the servants found the woman dead, her skull fractured by the rock onto which she had fallen.

More amazing, was that John had also found an old plan of the property at that time, and the boys' room had then been the stables. And to cap it all, the woman's favourite perfume was honeysuckle. It's amazing what you can find in the Archives. My hostess sat back to watch as that all sank in. Duly and deeply impressed, I had another cup of coffee.

A month or so later, I was at Rose Bower, having another excellent dinner, this time provided by Evie. Sadly, John had died about a year earlier. But Evie had been weaned on a nice couple of ghostly tales by John, and I asked if she would tell me more about the horse riding lady and her honeysuckle perfume.

Evie looked puzzled at what I was rambling on about, and I explained about the after dinner story. Then she remembered. Some years before, she had indeed noticed a strange scent one evening when she was putting the boys to bed. And yes, John had noticed it too. It was two or three evenings later before they realised it was the new mosquito coil they were burning for the boys.

I know the feeling. Back at Bishop's Rooms it was several

nights before I found my ghost and his heavy breathing. It was the motor of the elderly fridge in the kitchen downstairs. John Bailey would have enjoyed my ghost, and he'd have exacted a terrible price from me for it. I might even have had to agree that I'd been chased from my camp by a ghost up on the cliffs above Sugarloaf.

Plate 1

Top: Jamestown from the Road

Btm: Jamestown from the Ladder

Plate 2
Ladder Hill Road and earlier generations

Plate 3

Top left: The Seaside, The Castle, and Jacob's Ladder

Top right: Archway to The Castle

Btm: Jacob's Ladder (down)

PLATE 4
TOP: CHURCH PARADE LEAVING NAPOLEON STREET
BTM: THE RUN

Plate 5
Top: Waterwitch Memorial and Public Gardens
Btm: Sugarloaf Hill with Banks' Bay and batteries

PLATE 6

TOP LEFT: THE PAVILION AT THE BRIARS

TOP RIGHT: WINDOW OF NAPOLEON'S *CABINET DE TRAVAIL*

BTM: LONGWOOD HOUSE

PLATE 7

TOP: MARSHALL BERTRAND'S HOUSE AT LONGWOOD

BTM: NAPOLEON'S TOMB

PLATE 8
TOP: THE NORTH-EAST FROM THE PEAKS
BTM: DEADWOOD PLAIN AND FLAGSTAFF HILL

PLATE 9
TOP: THE BARN AND TURK'S CAP VALLEY
BTM: EASTERN CLIFFS FROM THE BARN

PLATE 10

TOP LEFT: TURK'S CAP VALLEY : ALGAL AND MINERAL STRIPES

TOP RIGHT: TURK'S CAP VALLEY : ALGAL COLOURS

BTM: TURK'S CAP

Plate 11

Top left: Eighteenth century cannon at Portugee battery

Top right: Prosperous Bay Beach and King & Queen Rocks

Btm: Headwaters of Fisher's Valley

PLATE 12
TOP: FISHER'S VALLEY FROM PROSPEROUS BAY BEACH
BTM: PROSPEROUS BAY PLAIN TOWARDS STONE TOPS
(WITH BABY'S TOES AFTER A WET 'WINTER')

PLATE 13

TOP: PROSPEROUS BAY PLAIN AND SIGNAL STATION

BTM: PROSPEROUS BAY SIGNAL STATION AND THE BARN

Plate 14
Top: Bencoolen and coloured 'marls'
Btm: Stone Tops Ridge and Levelwood

Plate 15
Seaward end of Sharks Valley (Basil for scale)

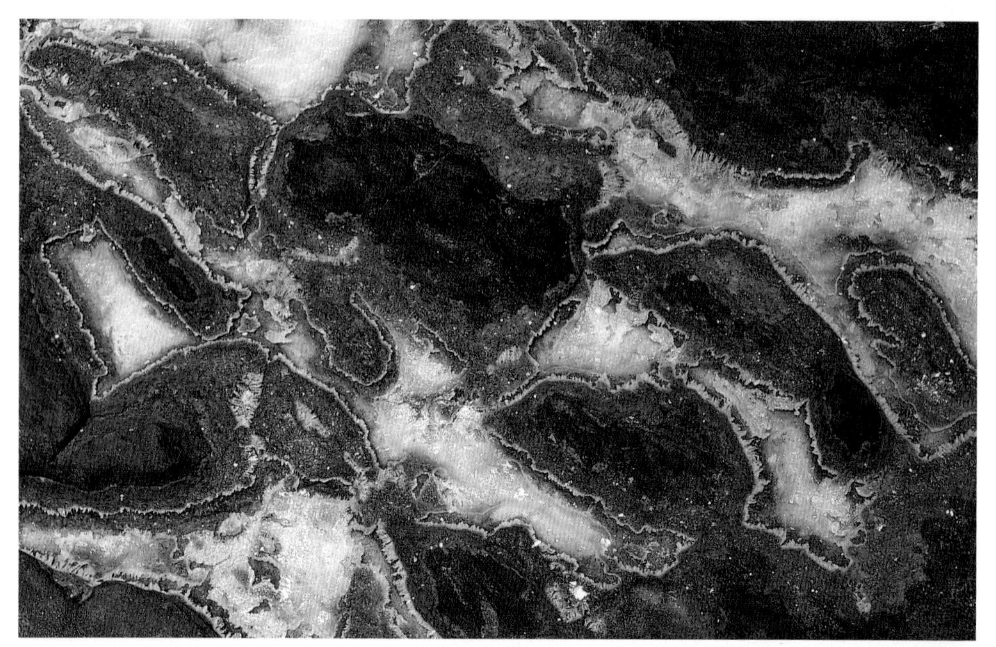

PLATE 16

TOP: SALT CRYSTALS FROM SPRAY AT GILL POINT

BTM: SHARKS VALLEY BAY AND GREAT STONE TOP FROM GILL POINT

# CHAPTER 9

## THE LIBERATED AFRICAN DEPOT

*I went on board one of these ships as she cast anchor off Rupert's Valley in 1861, and the whole deck, as I picked my way from end to end, in order to avoid treading upon them, was thickly strewn with the dead, dying, and starved bodies of what seemed to me to be a species of ape which I had never seen before. One's sensations of horror were certainly lessened by the impossibility of realising that the miserable, helpless objects being picked up from the deck and handed over the ship's side, one by one, living, dying and dead alike, were really human beings. Their arms and legs were worn down to the size of walking sticks.*

John Charles Melliss, 1875

Opposite the church, at the end of the Courthouse, sprinkled by the flame petals of a *gulmohar* tree, is the Library. It is a building as welcoming as it is short on space, but not short on books or popularity. The side windows relax onto the Public Gardens, a gentle brush of slightly dusty green, of flower beds and lawns, a fish pond with lilies and a fountain.

There are cannon and anchors, from the past, and seats in the shade for the present. Ann's Cafe is through to the back. And at the rear on the other corner, is an old colonial style, one storey house, once called Garden Hall, when it was the museum. Outside, an oval plaque set in the grass informs that: 'Captain Joshua Slocum the first man to circumnavigate the world alone lectured in this building in 1898.'

Viewed from beneath the heavy canopy of branches at the entrance to the gardens, lying between the little fountain and the erstwhile Garden Hall, is a simple white marble obelisk, topped with an urn. The inscriptions on the four sides are a tribute to seafaring people, and a harsh reminder of man's inhumanity. This is the Waterwitch memorial, which, in this gentle setting, is for me one of the most moving places on the island.

*This Column was erected by the Commander, officers, and crew of Her Majesty's Brig Waterwitch to the memory of their shipmates who died while serving on the coast of Africa 1839 - 1843. The greater number died while absent in captured slave vessels: their remains were either left in different parts of Africa, or given to the sea; Their graves alike indistinguished; this island is selected for the record, because three lie here; and because the deceased as well as their surviving comrades, ever met the warmest welcome from its inhabitants.*

On three other sides are listed the ship's dead, from only the first four years of its fifteen of service. Gunners and mates, ordinary seamen, marines and boys, who died far from home, their own or even their adopted one.

*Thomas Bush, A.B. Died at this island 16th July 1841, Aged 29 years From the effect of exposure on shore, after a gallant attempt to rescue a watering party on the coast of Africa by swimming through the surf with a line.*

*Samuel Knight, Marine. Drowned in an attempt to board a slave vessel 10th February 1842, Aged 24 years.*

*James Eddington, Boy. Died at sea, 24th December 1839, Aged 18 years.*

*James Collins, Boy. Died at sea, 12th February 1842, Aged 17 years.*

The *Waterwitch* was just one of tens of British ships that worked for over a quarter of a century trying to reduce the numbers of illegal slave ships plying from the Guinea Coast. I find it amazing that Melliss, naturalist, scientist, historian, great observer, and an islander, had to describe that harrowing visit to a vessel over twenty years after the *Waterwitch* had started its work. The vessel Melliss described was of about a hundred tons. On it, a thousand souls, alive and dead, were packed into an atmosphere of foetid heat, filth and indescribable deprivation. The cargoes from such vessels were unloaded in Rupert's.

Rupert's Valley is broad by island standards, its flat floor running half a mile inland. In the '60s, I knew little of the enormity of its story, yet it was for me the *only* depressing place on the island. Its dust and dried out stream bed, its scenery of barren rock walls and slumped piles of broken hillsides, were made all the more desolate by ragged traces of ruins.

Virtually nobody lived there, and half the handful of cottages were empty. Very little of anything grew there. In 1938, Gosse had written: *There is only one person in the island suffering from leprosy. To be thoroughly isolated, he lives all alone in Rupert's Bay, a God-forsaken hot, stony valley next to James Valley.*

In the sixties, the sea fortifications were solid, and behind them was a yellow brick chimney, its surrounding ruins so low they may have been no more than rubble on the valley floor. In the dust I found broken cast iron tripots, originally for rendering whale blubber, and the fragments of china and bottles of regiments long, long departed. Up the valley, were the ruins of three or four buildings that had been part of the slave village, and, I was told, unmarked in all this desolation, were burial grounds.

That then, was the atmosphere I remembered. But time and some reading and talking, had teased out pieces of an extraordinary story of freedom, of the rescue of slaves in their tens of thousands. It is a powerfully depressing story, much more significant for the island and her people than Napoleon's incarceration.

It's a bit of an odd name, Rupert's. Why should it be named after Prince Rupert of Bohemia, cousin of Charles II and James II? In the Civil War, Prince Rupert, at the age of 30, was the Royalist General of the Horse, and later Commander-in-Chief. But in 1650, he had to flee the country, and became instead commander of the Royalist fleet. A man of many parts, this Rupert. Chased by the Commonwealth navy through the Mediterranean, he escaped south in 1652/53, and cruised off the Cape Verdes and the coast of Guinea, before heading back northwards. But I could find no record to suggest that he called on St Helena.

After the restoration of the monarchy, Rupert went from strength to strength, and by 1673 had become First Lord of the Admiralty. So he was an important naval figure, when the British returned to St Helena after their brief dismissal by the Dutch. He certainly didn't visit the island after the colony was re-established, so it seems most likely that the Bay and Valley and Hill were named in his honour, in the hope of future patronage.

Rupert's Bay, as you see it from the path from town, is impressive. Rimmed with stark lava cliffs, turquoise water washes against the remnants of a black sand beach beneath the massive stone wall of Rupert's Line. Rupert's was protected by batteries and this great wall, 15-20 feet wide, which at one time had as many as 32 cannon to protect the landing, an easier one than that in James' Valley.

Through the stone archway, built to allow the stream, fed by periodic flash floods, to reach the sea without tearing the wall down, the first submarine cable was brought ashore in November 1899. The Eastern Telegraph Company connected the island with Capetown in the first stage of a direct England - South Africa cable. It went up the valley, over the ridge and down to The Briars, where Cable and Wireless are today. Although not needed today the cable's still there.

That great wall today is already being eaten away by the sea and by development. Here now, is the bulk fuel storage depot, and a long girder frame carries a pipe out for the tanker that calls every other month. Between the fuel tanks and the gantry is that immaculate yellow brick chimney. It is all that remains of, and a memorial to, a desalination plant installed in 1901 for the camp on Deadwood Plain, for half the island's contingent of Boer prisoners-of-war, and never used.

Now the front line buildings are the modern fish handling and processing plants of the St Helena Fisheries Corporation and Argos, and an accumulation of outbuildings acquired by them from earlier fisheries ventures. The Fisheries HQ is in a long, restored, stone building, more obvious because of its shiny corrugated roof, than its single storey walls and their distinctive pointing. This was originally the hospital for The Liberated African Depot.

Today there are patches of colour in the dusty monochrome of the valley, a bright lawn near the pipeline, flashes of red and pink and white hibiscus by the Fisheries' buildings. Stretching up the flat floor of the bleak valley is a double line of oleanders, bougainvilleas, palms, acacias and bananas, planted fairly recently to bring a little more hope to the valley. This reassuring brightness takes up more space than the handful of cottages, reaching up the valley.

In the early 1860s this stretch of valley was designated Hay Town, an urban renewal project of the Governor, Sir E. H. Drummond Hay, a 'new town' for the overcrowded and termite devastated Jamestown. Stones dated 1862 and 1866 above two cottage doors are all the evidence that remains. A model prison was imported from England, to relieve congestion in the one in town, but a prisoner burnt it down in 1867. One of the ruined shells may have been its replacement.

A few modern cottages have been added, and a new Church was built and consecrated (St Michael's) in 1996. A little further up valley is the Power Station, functional and hard pressed. So today there is a real start for a Rupert's Valley revival, into a sort of island Silicon Valley. Indeed there are some who would like to see all ship handling transferred to Rupert's, and the main heavy access road inland avoiding the town, going up the side onto Deadwood.

In reality a road snakes out of the valley, over Munden's Hill to join Side Path. And beyond the Power Station, the valley divides. Up at that end, the valley is hotter, the rocky sides have closed in and reflect more heat. There are prickly pear, and the floor is thick mud and rubble. There's a new veterinary quarantine station, though I never saw it in use. The valley feels airless and still. A family of partridges scuttering up the barren side, is a rare display of life.

From 1840 to 1874, ten years after the fleet had been disbanded, this valley was the home for thousands of former slaves rescued from illegal slavers. It was also, particularly in the higher reaches close to the divide, the burial ground for some of the many thousands who were dead on arrival, or died soon after. Rupert's Valley is a testimonial to the island's involvement in the slave trade and its eventual suppression. It is oddly ironic, because slavery had been instrumental in St Helena's development.

In London, in 1807, the Bill for the Abolition of the Slave Trade was given Royal Assent, and the dealing, trading, purchase or transfer of slaves from any part of Africa was prohibited. Ships under British colours disobeying the law were subject to forfeit to the Crown, and a fine of £100 per slave. Such sweeping legislation had little effect on the island. The import of slaves had been forbidden since 1792, but there was no change in island practices. All that happened was that the price, when resident slaves changed hands, increased.

Then one day in 1818, Sir George Bingham, Commander of the troops guarding Napoleon, and presiding magistrate, saw a young slave girl in the street, who had been severely beaten. He was incensed, immediately ordered the perpetrator to be brought to Court, and tried and fined him on the spot. Bingham was appalled that the statuatory fine was only £2, so he dressed him down severely to make up for it. The perpetrator was so annoyed at this treatment, that he complained to Council! This brought the affair to the attention of the Governor, Sir Hudson Lowe.

Lowe had been concerned about slavery on the island for some time. Now he had good reason to implement the changes he felt were required. He proposed to the slave owners, that in the first instance all children born of slave women should be free. The slave owners concurred, and the act came into force on Christmas Day 1818. So they were born free, but until the age of 18 they were considered as 'apprentices', and were encouraged to go to Church and receive an education.

It wasn't until January 1828 that the government declared that all slaves would be liberated in five years. And on July 14th, 1832, the remaining six hundred or so individuals classified as slaves, were freed by order of the East India Company, with compensation payments to the owners of about £45 a head.

Freedom for the remaining slaves coincided with two other events which were to change dramatically the future of St Helena. The first, was the transfer of the island from the East India Company to the rule of His Majesty's Government, to take effect on April 22nd 1834. The garrison would be dispersed, and the Civil Establishment broken up. Things had not been too bad after the death of Napoleon, but this was a major incentive to the economic decline that was starting. Charles Darwin wrote during his visit in 1836:

*The lower orders, or the emancipated slaves, are, I believe, extremely poor; they complain of the want of work. From the reduction in the number of public servants, owing to the island having been given up by the East India Company, and the consequent emigration of the richer people, the poverty will probably increase. The chief food of the working class is rice with a little salt meat; as neither of these articles are the products of the island, but must be purchased with money, the low wages tell heavily on the poor people.*

The second event, was the establishment on the island of a Vice Admiralty Court, for the trial of vessels engaged in the slave trade off the west coast of Africa. Ships of the Royal Navy had been patrolling West African waters since at least 1825. They had been using the spartan facilities of Ascension as a rendezvous, but in 1839 the West African Squadron was delighted when St Helena became its base. In 1840, the Liberated African Depot was established in Rupert's.

Whatever Governments in Europe might decide about slavery, the realities of the real world were very different, and it's worth a quick look at that world as St Helena started a new chapter of its story. In America, slaves costing perhaps $30 in Guinea were sold for up to $700 in 1820, and a staggering $2,500 in 1845. In 1820 there were an estimated 3,000 'Yankee' ships in the trade, and skippers were said to be able to make a million dollars a voyage. 1850 marked a peak in demand for cotton, and slave labour was deemed essential.

In the early part of the nineteenth century, before the abolition of the trade, an estimated 80,000 slaves a year were taken in West Africa and shipped across the so called Middle Passage. By 1835 numbers may have been as high as 135,000. In the period 1825 - 1865, more than a million West African slaves were successfully *landed* in America. But during the same period, only 130,000 were released alive from the 1,287 vessels captured by naval patrols trying to enforce the prohibition of slave trading. Brazil, in the 1830s imported 35,000 slaves annually; and slavery only ended there in 1888, when the final 700,000 were freed.

This was the picture in the 'real' world into which St Helena was thrust in 1840. With the opening of the Court on the island, there were some twenty naval vessels of the West African Squadron using the island while on duty. Although the navy caught only a small percentage of the shipping involved, in the first year of operations 1,824 liberated Africans were landed in Rupert's. Of those, 467 died in the same year, 136 were placed out as servants, and 1221 were under the charge of the Collector of Customs. The new Depot in Rupert's was quickly overwhelmed by the scale of the operation.

The liberated slaves urgently needed food, medicines, proper barracks, clothing from Britain. There was no water in Rupert's most of the time, nobody lived there after all, so it was sent round by boat daily from town. A surgeon was on duty, but you didn't need a surgeon to distinguish the dead from those still alive. A hulk was moored in the bay for use as a Reception Depot, principally for male slaves. Lemon Valley, to the west of Jamestown, was used for the reception mainly of women and children, and another hulk was moored there. Lemon Valley had been used as a quarantine station for seriously ill sailors from passing ships, or soldiers of the garrison, so the worst of the sick males were sent there as well.

This situation could not go on for long. In 1841, a quarter of the island's population of 5656, were liberated Africans. There were no proper facilities. To receive them was one thing, but once returned to passably good health, there was no work. What to do with these mounting numbers of people? They clearly had to be shipped out again.

There was an initial shipment of 650 to the Cape Colony (at least get them back to Africa, was one line of reasoning), but the Cape couldn't absorb them, and although another 681 went in 1842, the Cape refused to receive further shipments. That year more than 400 went as paid labourers to British Guiana. Gradually a system was worked out to cope with an average of another 400 souls from every captured ship landed on the island.

And that was not all that arrived. One of the ships captured and confiscated in 1840, and tradition has it that it was a Brazilian vessel, was duly condemned and broken up, and its timbers landed in Jamestown. Those timbers were infested with termites (white ant), but it wasn't until the 1860s that the devastating effects of white ant became obvious, and Jamestown was described as looking as though it had been hit by an earthquake.

The vessels used by slavers were many and varied, but almost all were armed, some quite strongly. Ships of the Navy could fire warning shots, but could not fire into them because of the fragile nature of their suspected cargoes. The slavers on the other hand could, and indeed did, fire at will, and many sailors were lost through such hostile action.

It was a foul business, but there are few specific accounts of the horrors of the slave ships. Captains were totally unscrupulous, they were after all conveying cargoes of serious value. They hung onto their cargo as long as they could run, but if in any doubt they dumped the slaves overboard. After 1845, it was the Brazilian vessels that came into prominence, but America was still a major participant, and there are records of the construction of a paddle steamer custom-designed for the trade.

The Vice Admiralty Court was in operation from 1840 to either 1868 or 1872, when the last ship was brought to the island. After 1851 however, the number of ships brought in was rarely into double figures for any one year, in 1863 for example only three vessels were taken and condemned, and 1026 *rescued negroes* were passed through the Depot awaiting, once fully recovered, transhipment to the West Indies. In the years of the Court's operation, 425 vessels were tried. Only nine of the ships charged, were declared as not liable to be condemned.

The Royal Navy vessels would cruise off the West African coast looking for suspicious vessels, chase them, and if sucessful board them, with varying degrees of violence, put on a prize-crew, and bring them to St Helena. Or they might find the illegal slavers in mid-ocean, give chase, and repeat the above procedures. Once back at St Helena, they off-loaded the slave cargo, participated in the trial of the captured vessel, and then sailed back to station.

The most famous of the British ships was the *Waterwitch*. She had been built in 1832 in Cowes, and was reputed to be one of the fastest ships of the day. She was taken into Royal Navy service in 1834, and appears to have joined the West African Squadron five years later. She brought the first ship captured into St Helena for trial at the new Court in 1840.

The *Waterwitch* headed the list for most captures by British vessels, with 43 between 1840 and 1853. In 1842, she took 18 out of the year's total of 31. The *Styx* in two years captured 26, the *Cygnet* 18, and the *Brisk* in 1840 and '41 captured 13. Finding some of these statistics in the Archives is more disagreeably thought provoking than the gentle marble monument in the Public Gardens.

Rupert's Valley, that desolate sliver between its barren walls of rocks was the home of the Liberated African Depot. It is difficult to get exact figures of the numbers of slaves set free on the island. Records are fragmentary, and statistics were not kept of the very large numbers of slaves who were dead on board on arrival. Figures from the Court records show that certainly 21,500, and probably more than 25,000, slaves were landed and surviving at the times of the trials of the ships that brought them.

To those, many thousands of slaves dead on arrival must be added, and of those alive, many thousands died on St Helena before they could start new lives in whatever form. How many were buried in Rupert's or Lemon Valleys? Numbers will never be known, but the scale of the work related to the Liberated African Depot, made a massive impression on the little island.

In 1874 the Liberated African Depot closed, and Rupert's was emptied of its living transient inhabitants. All that was left were the buildings that would soon be shells, and later only ruins, except the 'hospital'. It's work was done, but the legacy of those years still remains. The Liberated African Depot left liberated slaves, pure West Coast Africans, constituting a quarter of the population. White ant was on the island to stay, and the town was already devastated.

The Navy had gone, the Court had gone, and with them a

significant part of the island's economy had gone. Over that same period as many as fifteen hundred islanders, without work without money, had departed, as had substantial numbers of better off landowners and their families. The island was poorer than it had ever been, poorer than it would ever be again. Events around the third quarter of the nineteenth century had many different origins, and it is sad that the economic and social bleakness of this period should tend to hide the most extraordinary humane role played by the island.

# CHAPTER 10

## THE NORTH EAST :
## SKELETONS IN THE VOLCANO'S CUPBOARD

*Rendered as extraordinary by its Geological singularities, as it is by those political events, which caused it to become the "prison house" of that man who thought the world too circumscribed for his ambitious views, St Helena, perhaps, contains within its ironclad cliffs, a gem of information which, in the hands of the scientific geologist, may assist in throwing some additional light upon the structure of the globe.*

R.F. Seale, 1834

In spite of the island's small size, different districts are quite distinct. Physically, differences are of course topographic, modified by an extraordinary range of microclimates. That's fairly simple. If it's higher, it's probably windier, cooler, wetter and therefore greener. If it's closer to the coast, it's probably warmer, more barren. These variations are one of the great joys. Wake up in the morning, and decide what kind of morning, or afternoon, or day, you want to have, wild and alone in Sandy Bay, windswept on one of the high plateaus, warm and humid with snippets of history in one of the wooded bits.

If you're indecisive, it may even be a problem. What kind of wooded bit? Just how cool and windy? High cliffs and huge views, or rural fields and cows? And what if it's raining? Well, you phone up people in different parts of the island, until you find a dry patch. Mind, by the time you get there, it may all have changed, thick mists there now, or widdling down, and the town sweltering in sunshine. But I'm getting off the point.

People are different too, from area to area. It may be hard for us to recognize that, but to islanders it's easy enough. There are differences in the language. I find it hard enough to follow the accent if it's broad anyway, so I couldn't spot much on that front. But Jamestown people, those from Longwood, Levelwood, Sandy

Bay, Blue Hill, they're all something else. Keep your eyes open, because they do say they even dress differently. Keep your ears open, as much from what is said as how it's said. Then you might start picking bits and pieces up, but it takes quite a while. I'm still watching and waiting.

The area I've called the north-east stretches from Deadwood Plain and Flagstaff, round to the broader, less easily defined, Longwood Plateau. You could see the edge of it from Banks'. You could see the start of it from the top of the Ladder. It has more 'woods' in place names and less trees on the ground than anywhere else. And Longwood has the third biggest concentration of population after Jamestown and Half Tree Hollow.

When Seale wrote the piece above in his *Geognosy* of 1834, he was referring to the whole island. And please note that even when making a scientific point, Napoleon had to be brought in. So, in the north-east, where Napoleon lived for most of his time on the island, it's worth bringing in some scientific points. They won't throw much light on the structure of the globe, but they throw enormous light on the violence of the island's volcanoes - something the scenery of the north-east hides so successfully.

Please don't get me wrong, I've as much time as the next for Napoleon, probably a lot more. But there is much more to this island than even that special bird of passage. No, if someone's banging on about Lowe cutting Napoleon's budget, or the toughness of his mutton, or how big the perimeter fence of Longwood was or wasn't, ask them if they know, or indeed have ever even thought about, why The Barn lords it so emphatically over the desolation of Turks Cap Valley?

Or for that matter do they ask themselves why the thick black lavas, or brightly coloured ochrous stripes, of the east are almost flat lying? Don't volcanoes slope down to the sea? Don't their lava flows elsewhere on the island slope down to the sea? Yes they do, but not here. Just beyond Napoleon's nineteenth century doorstep, a story, ten million years old, of unspeakable violence lies hidden. Almost accidentally it is this obscured geology which gives the area its physical character.

Forget for a moment any conflict of interest between Napoleonic and volcanic histories, because here's a good example of St Helena's bizarre geography. In many cases it takes you ages scrambling to get to a particular piece of scenery, yet in others you can see the most extraordinary scenery with almost no physical effort.

One of the most outstanding viewpoints, and one of the simplest to get to, is Flagstaff Hill at the end of Deadwood Plain. There are views over more than half the island. All you have to do is sit there and turn your head. You don't even have to get out of the car to see most of it! But add on a ten minute stroll you have all this, and much more besides.

Deadwood Plain is long and slim. The few houses at the Longwood end have a few trees for shelter, but the line on the Rupert's side tries vainly to shelter on the break in slope between plain and steep valley. The grass is thin, and what little there is, after a spell of hot weather, is bleached almost white. In winter Deadwood is grim, what little you can see of it through driving rain and mist.

I don't do Deadwood on wet days. And I prefer to walk up from Rupert's. You can go up on the Boer Road, far grander in name than in what's left of the prisoner-of-wars' impressive handiwork. I prefer the Pipe Path, which doesn't actually exist any more, although the hill it went up does. It was named after the pipeline from the desalination plant that was never really used. You just follow your nose, picking your way through prickly pear and rocks till you breast the slope. Then it's a clear ramble along Pipe Ridge till you reach the top end of the plain.

But on a fine day Deadwood is a different world. The air is crystal clear. It's warm, balmy almost, and it's probably the best place to see the island's only endemic bird, the wirebird (*Aegialitis sanctae-helenae*).

It's a sweetheart, the wirebird, like a little ringed plover, with legs like the wire grass after which it supposedly derives its name. They do fly, but prefer to run between the tussocks, the little grey-brown body leaning slightly forward as its thin legs scissor away. They nest on the ground too, so are prey to the feet of clumsy cattle, and of course to the taking ways of rats and the increasing numbers of feral cats.

A recent population survey showed wirebird numbers down on a decade ago, but at about 400 they are still healthy. Apparently more of a problem than predators, is the changing pattern of pasture management. This does mean that you come across them in some of the apparently most barren areas, below Lot's Wife for example. But on the Plain, keep your eyes open, or have an islander to help, as they can seem even more reclusive than they really are.

Parent birds are very protective of their nest, but give an indication of its existence with their diversionary tactics. They make themselves much more conspicuous, having flown, or more likely run, a little way from the nest. They then head erratically further away, sometimes lowering their body and fanning their wings and tail feathers in some strangely submissive way. But where that might fool humans, I can't see it working with rats and cats, or clumsy cattle.

The Plain's a good place too, for some of the other birds. It keeps you entertained with brilliant red cardinals, the Malagasy Fody or weaver (*Foudia madagascariensis*), sometimes in flocks of fifty or more, and the dullish yellow Cape canaries (*Serinus flaviventris*). With traditional St Helena simplicity, these are known locally as Red birds and Yellow birds. Cheeping sprays of averdevats (*Estrelda astrid*) from South Africa, so small they are just pink and grey spots, go past ringing like tiny bells.

It was to Deadwood Plain, as well as to Francis Plain, in October 1815, that the British army came to set up camp. The first garrison for Napoleon consisted of the 2nd Battalion of the 53rd (Shropshire) Regiment of Foot. They were replaced by the 66th (Berkshire) Regiment in July 1817. Starting in 1819, and I'm not clear how, officers and men of the 20th (East Devonshire) Regiment appeared on the island, serving alongside the 66th, possibly from India, or possibly en route there.

It is hard to picture the camp, the wooden barracks, the more solid quarters for the officers, and the mud. Even more difficult, is to try to picture the balls that were held there. The island girls arrived in bullock carts, carrying their dresses, then traipsed through the mud before changing for the Ball. Because of the all night curfew, balls continued until day break, and as the islanders went home to rest, the garrison resumed duty guarding the great man.

There were regular horse races on the Plain. During the exile Betsy Balcombe disobeyed her father and participated once, on a horse lent to her by Napoleon. Balcombe was furious, Betsy was gated, and Napoleon thought it a great joke. But when, in September 1818, his coachman, one of the Archambaud brothers, rode down the course so drunk he had to be horsewhipped off it by the stewards, Napoleon was not amused. He had been watching this through his telescope and gave Archambaud another rollocking when he got home.

From 1900 to 1903, Deadwood was even more overpopulated. It was one of the two camps for Boer prisoners-of-war. There was tented accomodation for 3000 men, though wealthier prisoners were allowed to build wooden huts. Mainly Transvaalers were here, and the Orange Free Staters were at Broad Bottom on the other side of the island. More truculent prisoners were locked up in High Knoll, and on the slopes below the fortress, in Kent Cottage, General Cronje and his wife stayed.

Erich Mayer's recently published study of paintings and drawings made at the time is a wonderful and emotive addition to the sketchy material otherwise available. I learned of a second general, General Ben Viljoen, who stayed at Myrtle Grove, then moved to Rose Cottage above Mount Pleasant.

In the late 1960s, the site of the Boer camp was taken over by a forest of aerials for the Diplomatic Wireless Station. But that was short lived, and in the '70s the Plain returned to its more traditional emptiness. Then, just before the new millenium, three wind generators rose, to help the island's growing needs for electricity. There they stand today, motionless in the South East Trades.

It seems such a natural development doesn't it, wind power? It's such an attractive alternative to oil, so long as you can keep its structures discreetly placed, or in this case so long as you can keep the structures working. What went wrong is about as straight forward a question as 'how long is a piece of string?' But come what may, they'll have to get it sorted out one day.

Deadwood was treeless long before Napoleon, and Flagstaff Hill at its end was a lookout post from the earliest days. It has a commanding view of the approaches to the island from the north, east, and south-east, so it had a flagstaff, to signal shipping movements. But in the winter months the top of the hill is prone to disappearing in the mists. So your views of anything, and anyone's views of you, were hidden for hours, perhaps even days, at a time. The main lookout moved to Prosperous Bay Signal Station, and Flagstaff's working role was dropped, leaving only remnants of the stone wall of a hut as a reminder

Even if you only have a few hours on the island, Flagstaff Hill is pretty well obligatory. But if you haven't got a head for heights, stay below the topknot of junipers on the Deadwood side, the views are just as vast.

Looking towards the centre of the island, the northern cliffs to Sugarloaf are on your right. Inland, those lavas have been altered to multicoloured eroded wastes stretching across to Rupert's. Behind them is High Knoll and the houses of Half Tree Hollow, and the west beyond. In front is the full spread of Deadwood Plain, and the striped ochre palette of Longwood. There are little cottages along the edges, and most of the housing is on Longwood Plateau. A distinctive cluster of trees surrounds Longwood House.

To your left is the sheer cliff edge of The Barn, and a great hollow where a huge part of the landscape has been removed by erosion, and a black promontory ending in Turk's Cap. Beyond is the sheer eastern wall of the island, to the ragged outlines of King and Queen Rocks. Long slopes back away from the cliff tops, rising gently to the Alpine greenery of The Peaks, nearly five miles away.

So obvious from here is one of the north-east's most striking features. After the ignominy of the loss of the Great Wood, the land so cleared gave rise to the island's broadest scale agriculture. Wheat has been grown here, and there was so much space there were free range ostriches at one stage.

Nowhere are the contrasts between savage wildness and agricultural domesticity marked as indelibly. The agricultural calm is huge, Longwood and Deadwood Plains, Sheep Pound Gut, Mulberry Gut, Bilberry Field Gut, bucolic in name and all under control. Miles of fields, a whole region of grazing cattle, crops and peace, it's a way of life, an entire landscape, not just a couple of patches of vegetables, and a peach tree or two. Yet it's only a matter of a few steps from that into the totally different world of staggering cliffs and wild shorelines.

Where else on the planet can you sit in such peace, the only interference from inquisitive butterlies, and see scenery from half the world's climatic zones merely by turning your head? But climb the last few feet through the trees, and just over the top, take a deep breath, and sit down again. Here, you've been moved from one world onto the edge of another, and you can actually fall off it if you're not careful.

There are some big drops on the island, but at twelve hundred feet to the first bounce, and a thousand more to the splash in the sea, this is one of the most spectacular. It's certainly the easiest to reach, you can stroll up to it. There are no signs of vegetation of any kind, no signs of life except an occasional seabird. It's majestic this side of Flagstaff, this is big cliff country, between the big sky and the big ocean. The view back onto the island was beautiful, this is awesome.

St Helena is built up of two large volcanoes, the older in the north-east, and the much larger in the south-west. Eruptions at both were mainly from fissures, like those you see on TV when Kilauea erupts in Hawaii. Pressure inside the volcano, from its magma chamber two or three miles down, fractures the structure above it in a long 'crack' which opens into a fissure as magma is forced upwards to be erupted at the surface.

Most of the eruptions on oceanic island volcanoes are relatively quiet, because the viscosity of the magma allows gases to escape easily. So none of the violence of Montserrat, or Pinatubo, but gentle explosive activity and very fluid lavas. When the eruptions are over the lava solidifies in the fissure, and you are left with a dyke, a near vertical wall a few feet wide and perhaps several miles long.

These volcanoes were built up not as typical pyramids like Mount Fuji or Vesuvius, but as shield volcanoes, broad domed structures reflecting their gentle eruptions and fluidity of the lavas. Here, at Flagstaff, you are standing close to the centre of what is left of the island's first volcano. It stretches from Rupert's Valley, through Sugarloaf, Flagstaff, The Barn and then south to King and Queen Rocks and beyond towards Gill Point. I'm not ready yet for the skeleton, we need to look at the aged volcano itself first. Don't be put off by its academic importance, for what is revealed here is outstanding.

The lavas and ashes dip away west, north and east, you can see them. And you can see one of the island's most striking features, indeed one of the most striking anywhere in the world, the enormous central swarm of dykes which fed the flows that built up the volcano. Below Flagstaff and The Barn, down into Flagstaff Bay, and particularly just south onto Knotty Ridge, and all the way to the coast at Turks Cap Bay, hundreds and hundreds, even thousands, of dykes. In a Volcano Olympics this dyke swarm would have won St Helena the gold medal.

So far we've seen the wildness of the scenery relatively effortlessly, but taking a closer look and getting into it physically is a different ball-game. That shoreline below Flagstaff, for example, is almost inaccessible these days, except to a very few fishermen.

The Barn is attached to Flagstaff, indeed to the rest of the island, by the narrowest of cols. That's worth the effort of a closer look. It's a remarkable structure, The Barn, a great block of dark lava flows, a mile long, 2000 feet high, sheer-sided all round. It's an island in its own right, isolated and emotive. It's separated from the rest of the island by harsh, arid yellow-brown valleys, clawed into the entrails of the ancient volcano.

You have to drop nearly a thousand feet onto the col, and then climb up to the roof of The Barn. The col is razor thin, a drop of a few hundred feet on one side, or a slide of much the same height, through the rubble, on the other. But the path, though barely as wide as your boot, is just below the edge, on the gentler, more scenic side. It's a typically St Helenian path.

The surface you are trying to move on is a mixture of rock fragments, broken and breaking from the rocks themselves. There is no soil, just a harsh brown surface with no hand holds, and very little in the way of footholds either. St Helenians aren't bothered by surfaces like this, they call them *gritty*, which translates simply as "if you put your foot wrong you'll go whatsit over elbow."

Much of the rough walking is like this in the wilder parts, but at very few places on the island is it actually like this on what is called the path. Try it out carefully a couple of times, you get used to it, you learn to treat it with the respect (as opposed to the initial abject terror) it deserves. But when a St Helenian *tells* you such and such a path is 'a little gritty', you may be better advised going to the library.

But once across things rapidly improve, and the climb onto the top of The Barn is fine, any inconvenience quickly forgotten. On top, you can relax, the rest of the island is literally not so much at your feet, as in the far distance, of no direct concern. The Barn is like that, it brings out a sense not so much of isolation as of independence, which is probably why London Ben took to going there. It's unusual to be on top of a 2000 feet high cliff which looks *inland*. It's certainly very different.

It's another marvellous place to sit in the silence, and watch the splendour of the eastern seaboard, protecting the splendours of the island. You are as far away as you can get from the Peaks, and the rugged spine they form is no more than an irregularity on a distant horizon. The full sweep of the eastern cliffs, near vertical walls a thousand feet and more high, is majestic. But you can't get a real idea of scale because you're looking down on them. They're like a beautiful model, every detail so perfect, yet so far away.

From The Barn to the end of Prosperous Bay Plain the lava flows, some of them several hundred feet thick, are almost flat lying. Surrounded by such a vista, now you can ask the question that is the real puzzle. Surely volcanoes pour their lava flows down their sloping sides to enter the sea in explosive violence? So why, in this part of the island, are the lavas like so many frozen layers, filling a broad saucer-shaped depression cut into the spoil-heap monochrome splendour of the volcano's oldest rocks? Well, leave looking at the scenery and walk into it.

It's easy enough from Longwood to walk to Turk's Cap Ridge. Just ask at the Meteorological Station, and follow the track, to the end of the black ridge. Like the Turk's Cap at its broken end, the ridge is two or three hundred feet high, jutting out across the lower rocks like a landing stage. A scramble down to the right finds one of the few remaining collections of the endemic Old Father Live Forever (*Pelargonium cotyledonis).* It gets its name from the fact that most of the time it looks like a piece of dead wood, fitting in well with the rocks and rubble. But give it some rain, even after a few years without, and leaves burst forth, and sprays of small, pure white flowers.

The bay below Turk's Cap was considered a possible landing place, so from about 1700 there have been two batteries on the ridge, Cox's and Gregory's, one with its annual red hand. And there's another much bigger battery, a thousand feet below on the shore of Turk's Cap Bay. What is left of a fishermens' path drops down the face of the ridge, skirts the base of its cliff, and then zig-zags down to the valley bottom and along to the sea. It's called Portuguee Battery on the map, or Dutch Battery in some of the records, but there are no logical reasons for either name.

Records from August 1734 explain that *Turk's Cap valley - fortification commenced by inhabitants,* and on July 24th 1735, *The Battery for eight guns; Guard House and Powder Room, are near finished at Turk's Cap valley.* Positioned about twenty feet above the shore, its guns covered the wave cut platform where boats could land in moderate seas. It is, or it was, a gem, constructed with an elegant curved wall two to three feet thick, for its gun platform. It, or the beach, still hold six cannon, all grotesquely rusted, and bits of a picquet house remain.

It is an amazing setting, one of the most spectacular of all the island's batteries. Overhead on one side, are the sculpted walls of Turk's Cap and its Ridge. On the other side, almost three times as high, the towering mass of The Barn. It is at batteries like this, and there are plenty of others, that you feel great respect for the men who built them, and for the gunners who manned them. There is no shade, no fresh water. It is a two thousand feet climb out of the spoil-heap sun-trap, and a six mile walk into Jamestown for a touch of R and R.

There was no machinery to haul the heavy paraphernalia of a cannon battery, and often no animals. It was all manpower, and if you felt rough because of the hardships, so did your officers, so they were twice as hard on you. You could swim if you were careful, to help scrape some of the dust and grime off you. You could fish, to help out the salt beef and rice. It was the wrong Age for enjoying the scenery, the peace and ever changing sky, or to write sonnets to sweethearts in Jamestown, or the village back home. Manning these batteries was pretty well a no-win situation. And I doubt if they looked at the rocks, but now we must, if you want to find the monstrous skeleton.

Going across to The Barn you saw the dykes, and going down to Turk's Cap Bay, you saw them too, and here you see the broken and altered rocks they are cutting. Some of these fragmental rocks originated under water, some were erupted violently into the air, but they all formed the earliest bit of the island to break the surface of the Atlantic twelve or so million years ago.

Very melodramatic, but that's how it was, just where you're standing. Curtains of molten lavas fountaining, ashes and smoke and steam rising thousands of feet, a multi-million year old beacon in an empty ocean. Dramatic it was, and dramatic it is now.

After that early violence, eruptions calmed down and over a long period produced the ashes and flows of The Barn and the broad flanks out to Flagstaff and to King and Queen Rocks. The north-eastern volcano would have been six or seven miles in diameter, well over 3000 feet high, with its centre around Knotty Ridge. Then something catastrophic happened, at about the end of its active life.

Possibly magma was intruded into the upper levels of the structure lifting up a part of the central area and destabilising it. Certainly something destabilised it, for in an event of enormous magnitude, a huge part of the volcano collapsed catastrophically on a vast slip plane from Deadwood to the sea, from Turk's Cap Ridge to Fishers Valley and beyond to Prosperous Bay Plain.

That entire flank, almost a quarter of the huge volcano, several thousand feet thick and perhaps three miles by three miles, plunged away into the ocean in one gigantic event. Much of it sank below the surface, cascading down the sides of the submarine mountain, but the slipped mass was so big it formed a wall, a barrier, across what today is Turk's Cap Bay. It left behind an enormous depression in the side of the volcano, and formed a wall of jumbled lavas over a thousand feet high blocking it from the ocean. It formed in effect a huge saucer-shaped emptiness.

The south-western volcano was already growing, from fissures in the area of Sandy Bay. But this catastrophic event possibly caused voluminous outpourings of lava from fissures in the upper reaches of Fishers Valley. These poured into the hollow filling it as if it were a pond, from the bottom up, one flat-lying flow after another. There was no way out for the lavas until they filled the depression, up to an elevation of about 1200 feet, and only then could they flow out round, even over, the great 'wall' and into the sea.

Several million years of erosion have removed the collapsed flank which blocked the depression, and have cut the cliffs back into the near horizontal lava pile. They have left the Turk's Cap flows, the cliffs down to Holdfast Tom and the great black stepped flows at the lower end of Fishers Valley. You can see them from where you were sitting on The Barn, massive cliffs in part, sculpted remnants in part. They rest on the smooth, gently curved slip surface from Prosperous Bay Plain all the way to Turk's Cap. And this is the volcanic island's most important skeleton in its cupboard; here it is revealed if you know what you're looking for.

The views of these eastern cliffs, from The Barn or from the Signal Station, are truly majestic, presenting a scene of permanence, of stability, indeed a scene of great tranquility. But now you know better; that calm hides an event of truly monumental violence.

Standing on Flagstaff or The Barn, or on the wave cut platform of Turk's Cap Bay, you know about it so you can see it, you can walk into it and through it, you can touch it. Enjoy it, for very few others know the skeleton is there. Or isn't there, if you think about it.

# CHAPTER 11

## FOOTFALLS OF NAPOLEON

*I obtained lodgings within a stone's throw of Napoleon's tomb: After the volumes of eloquence which have poured forth on this subject, it is dangerous even to mention the tomb. A modern traveller, in twelve lines, burdens the poor island with the following titles, - it is a grave, tomb, pyramid, cemetery, sepulchre, catacomb, sarcophagus, minaret, and mausoleum!*

Charles Darwin, *Voyage of the Beagle*, 1845

Darwin spent five days on the island in July, 1836. He stayed in lodgings at Hutts Gate. From what he wrote, I don't think he had a great deal of time for Napoleon. And although living so close to the tomb, and the body was still there in 1836 if you're particular about that sort of thing, he didn't visit it, though several of the *Beagle* crew signed the visitors' book.

Joshua Slocum was similarly indifferent, writing: *St Helena has been an island of tragedies - tragedies that have been lost sight of in wailing over the Corsican.* That's a pretty Gallic statement for a start, but he didn't expand.

For two months Napoleon had been coccooned by the Balcombe family and The Briars, oblivious of the harsh realities of everyday life that were settling onto the fair isle. Most of his staff however, had lived in town and ridden about the island. They knew what the real world was like, the real world that awaited Napoleon on December 10th. The higher plateau of the windswept north-east of the island, and the strictures of Longwood House, were very different to the pavilion and the grape arbor tucked onto the sheltered side of James Valley.

Cockburn and his party left The Briars and rode slowly away. At the sentry post at Longwood Gate they were saluted by the guard. They looked north, along the windswept pasture of Deadwood Plain and the muddy camp of the 53rd. They looked east, along the desolate sweep of the Longwood plateau, and its ochrous clays. And that's where they rode, along a lane roughly cleared through what were left of the gumwoods and scrub, scrappy grazing areas and some rough fields.

The plateau extended for a mile or so at an elevation of about 1700 feet, and before it started to drop away was the house Napoleon had visited in October. As they went inside, even with all its repairs and extensions, it looked to Napoleon little bigger and certainly no better, but General Bertrand assured him that all was well. This was to be home for Napoleon, and most of the French contingent, for the unforseeable future.

Longwood House had very much the character of what it was, a building that had been cobbled together. It was a single storey building, boasting six principal rooms, and a gaggle of outbuildings, offices and sheds, round a little muddy courtyard. The main part of the house was T-shaped, the main entrance at the base of the stem, into the newly added billiard room. Next was the drawing room, with a handsome black stone chimney piece.

The cross part of the 'T' had a dark dining room in the centre. To the left was a large room and two smaller ones, which Napoleon gave to the Montholons. To the right were his own diminutive quarters, more like a series of interconnected boxes than a suite. His study, or work room, had a separate door and tiny porch into what would become a garden. Then came his bedroom with his camp cot. Through that was a tiny bathroom with his great copper bath. Initially water was heated on a fire outside the window and passed in in buckets.

Beyond the dining room it was very congested, with an ante-room where servants on duty at night could sleep on the floor, a tiny kitchen with a smoking stove, a silver room, pantry, linen-closet and the kitchen stores. Gourgaud had a bedroom and a separate small office. The attics provided a series of cell-like rooms. Las Cases and his son had one, so their stay at The Briars had been good practise. Servants had the others, Marchand being immediately above his master.

There were more little offices, and some added tented accomodation, providing space of sorts for the Orderly Officer of the 53rd, and Dr Barry O'Meara, Napoleon's personal doctor. There was a room for a group of English sailors who worked as servants, but without access to the principal rooms of the house. There were stables, a coach house, assorted sheds for gardeners. In all, fifty-three people inhabited the little complex that was Longwood House.

It would take a while for the French party to settle in, and for the building to settle down. It would be unbelievably restricted for Napoleon, impossibly cramped for the others. For a man who had been at home in palaces throughout Europe, and who had done not at all badly with accomodation on Elba, he could hardly have conceived of such an opposite end to the spectrum. But to be fair, at the beginning everyone seems to have tried to make the best of a pretty poor show.

When the fleet arrived carrying Napoleon, the population of the island was 3587. The security forces, their administrators and camp followers, for this one man, added more than another third to the population. The strain on the island's food resources, placed by this overnight jump in population, was enormous.

The last three Governors had endeavoured to improve agricultural production, though their experiments hadn't necessarily endeared them to the inhabitants. But there was no way the farms could cope with this influx, and their rather different demands. The staple diet of the island population and the troops was salt beef, and bread or rice. The troops topped up with whatever alcohol was available, and the slaves existed largely on yams. None of that put much demand on the island's production, but for the more genteel palates of the French party, and the senior British staff, there was not enough to go round.

Things sound as though they had slipped back to February 1770, when the redoubtable William Hickey visited the island on his way to the East. Although he tells of dances every evening, *an amusement the damsels of St Helena are very fond of,* he added somewhat petulantly: *I certainly never left a place in which I had resided a fortnight with so little regret as I did St Helena. The comforts it affords are few indeed; scarce any fruit, bad bread, and no fresh butter. Yet the charges made for every article of life were enormously high.*

Quality fresh produce was traditionally intended for the Company's ships from India. Now there were major conflicting demands on it. Blame for shortages, and the prices which rocketed as the availability plummeted, was largely levelled on Napoleon and the French. One attempt to alleviate the situation, though coincidental in terms of Napoleon's arrival, was the Company's purchase of the island's first sloop for its own use in improving the flow of foodstuffs, the first *St Helena.* This was to run regularly to west Africa, particularly in search of fresh meat.

While Napoleon had been at The Briars, Bertrand and Montholon had looked for accomodation close to Longwood, where they could secure some degree of privacy for themselves and their families. Montholon was unlucky. Bertrand was successful, and found a cottage at Hutts Gate, on the edge of the Devil's Punch Bowl. Napoleon was piqued, accusing him pretty well of desertion, and over the next year he could be positively bitchy to his Grand Marshall because of it.

Climatically, the first six months were pleasant enough, for it had been summer throughout. By the end of March, the French might even have been mildly pleased to note a cooling in the temperature, a freshening of the breezes, an increasing frequency of mists sweeping across the plateau. Soon they would experience their first winter, which would be wet and windy, and generally somewhat enervating.

Longwood House was dark. It was damp and cold, and mould grew as easily on clothes and boots, as it did on walls and curtains. Fireplaces were essential. The house was home to large numbers of rats, which were, in fairness, a veritable plague over the whole island. Such was the closeness of their confinement in the house, that on occasions the French had evening 'games' catching rats. Water was a problem. Originally it came in casks, until a couple of years later, a stone water course was built, largely by the Chinese, to bring good water from Hutts Gate.

The deterioration in the weather at Longwood more or less coincided, in April 1816, with the arrival of Sir Hudson Lowe and his staff, replacing the interim Cockburn. From the start, Napoleon took against Lowe. It wasn't just that it was difficult to please Napoleon in the situation in which he had been placed. But Lowe had been hand picked for his job.

Napoleon was a Corsican, and Lowe had been the founder commander of a regiment of Corsican deserters who had fought against the French. Although Lowe had seen considerable action over the years, he was more an accomplished administrator than a field commander. Balmain, the Russian Commissioner, summed up the mismatch in his famous description *the man who only knew how to command, and the man who only knew how to obey.* In four months Napoleon had five volatile meetings with Lowe, after which he refused to see the Governor again.

The next five years were difficult for the island. Only with time has their fascination steadily increased, again much more for the world than the island. At the time there was certainly much more frustration than fascination. For the principal players, they were destructive years, embittering, claustrophobic years, petty, and belittling. We, with nearly two centuries of hindsight, have so much to look back on, we can enjoy them. There were so many characters involved, directly, indirectly, willingly or hesitantly, and so many wrote so much. We can savour it all.

All of these characters are woven into the fabric, the legend, of Longwood, that was Napoleon on St Helena. The British had their prisoner, their responsibility to the Allies. The French protected their master, but they interacted at all levels with the British and with the island population. All the accounts of this time on the island make entertaining reading. But it is patchworked reading, for everyone writing had particular axes to grind, and the nature of those axes colours the history.

Who in the end are we to believe? Does it really matter? Contemporaneous accounts vary, even between members of the French household. With degrees of variance too, are those of Lowe and his staff, and fragmentary accounts of assorted visitors to the island, and to Longwood. Even more voluminous are later accounts, based in varying degrees on selected elements of earlier material, where each of the new writers had yet another agenda to support.

The legend of Napoleon that grew up, as France returned to greatness, grew when their Emperor was dead and buried far away. But on St Helena his legend grew in the years when he lived and died there. It is that legend, much more of the man than the idol, that lives on here, and that is what you can become a part of so easily.

The road from town to Longwood turns at the head of the Devil's Punchbowl, at the church of St Matthew's and the obscurely named Hutts Gate. What used to be Hutts Gate Store is still there, it has a sign but is no longer a store. On the opposite side of the road is St Matthew's Vicarage, a low building trying to crouch even lower to get away from the winds blasting in from the eastern cliffs. Whether or not bits of the original outer walls still exist, this was where the Bertrands first stayed, before their own, rather more elegant, house was built for them close to Napoleon.

The road leads on to Longwood Gate, which was a fortified sentry post in 1815. From there, a broad Avenue with small bungalows, some suggestive of pre-fabs, now runs down to a sort of village green. On the right, just before the green, is 12, Longwood Avenue, the house of Maurice and Maisie Thomas, where I camped in 1966. Interesting, Darwin had been a stone's throw, damn good arms in those days, from Napoleon's tomb, and I had been a stone's throw from his former residence.

Maurice was working with the construction of the new Diplomatic Wireless Station, and Maisie was a primary school teacher. Their shop now stands in the front garden, where I'd pitched my tent. Maisie overfed me, and they introduced me to something of Longwood, past and present. Electricity had just made it there, so I could work on my maps in the house. It was a delicately balanced luxury, for the power supply was low, and when Maisie turned on the kettle to make tea the light nearly went out.

A little way beyond number 12, on the corner of the sort of village green, is Longwood House. Its red ochre buildings, in the setting of gardens, flowers and fine trees, looks as though that is how the French left it in 1821, but much has changed, much has happened, since. The lovely setting in the trees for a start, for in spite of Napoleon's periodic interest, and the work of the Chinese gardeners, even by 1821 the rudimentary garden was more concept than reality.

The buildings had to be totally restored, because following the departure of the French, the house reverted to its bucolic origins. When Napoleon died in exile in 1821, most of the world felt he had got no more than his just desserts. It is all too easy to see Napoleon, the great leader, in hindsight, but at the time he was hated, feared and vilified. Many would have rather the Prussians had taken him after Waterloo, and executed him, as they had wanted to.

So after the funeral, the contents of the house were removed, and it was ransacked. Long before the French had packed, Hudson Lowe had selected the pieces of furniture he wanted shipped back to Britain. What the French didn't take, the senior British did. What was left went to the soldiers, sailors and islanders. When they had finished, it was left to the rats. Oh, and occasional visitors peeled off bits of any wallpaper that remained.

By the time the French returned in 1840, to collect the mortal remains of their Emperor, the house was in a sorry state. There was a windmill in what had been the garden, and it powered a threshing machine in the billiard room, next to the room in which Napoleon died. It wasn't even a farm house, it was a farm building. It waited in desolation until 1858, when Queen Victoria made over the house, and the tomb, to the French, and Napoleon III sent out a team of specialists to restore his uncle's former residence.

Today the buildings, protected in their delightful setting, are welcoming, even in winter with the mists streaming in from the Atlantic. By an empty sentry box, is the gate into the gardens. The house is low, but larger than I had remembered, pale blue one end, red ochred the other, tall white chimneys and roofs in varying shades of grey. It has the air of the seat of a successful farmer rather than a country squire. The buildings behind are slightly higher, and their solid red ochre gives an air of greater permanence than the delicate, almost fragile, main entrance.

It is across the lawn, in that part of the building more suggestive of the prow of a ship than a farm. Under a portico, hollow sounding wooden steps take you to the narrow door, and straight into the billiard room, or waiting room. Napoleon used the billiard table to spread his maps on, but it was a good table, from, says its little nameplate, *J.Thurston, Manufacturer by Appointment to her Majesty Queen Charlotte, Consort of George III, Catherine Street, Strand, London.*

The room is cool, subdued light from shuttered windows, pictures on the walls, a chaise-longue, chest of drawers and display cases. But it is more than a peaceful museum room. It has a life, it isn't dead, it has a character, I wouldn't say aura. Perhaps you create that yourself, because it was Napoleon's house. Perhaps too, it is because there are so few places on the island like this, which are so devoid of the island's immediate physical presence.

You feel an empathy for the house, it's not just a shell filled with museum bric-à-brac. You can look closer. The chess table is there, where he played Mme Montholon, and frequently cheated to try to beat more skilled opponents, Mrs Skelton perhaps. The shutters do have spy-holes cut in them for Napoleon to look up the plateau towards Longwood Gate to see who was coming, so he could decide whether to be available or not. There are the orders he usually wore, the *Legion d'Honneur*, and the *Couronne de Fer d'Italie.* His famous globes stand either side of the door into the *salon.*

If the billiard room looked lived in, the drawing room is cooler, and something jars. This is the room where Napoleon died. Sofas and paintings, the fireplace with a long mirror, side tables, an ill-looking *General Bonaparte franchissant les Alpes*, and later engravings. What disturbs the whole room, pervades it somehow, is his death mask.

More reassuring is the small dining room, with a table that at best would seat Napoleon and ten others. In the drawing room the wallpaper was subdued, but here it is floral gilt on red, more like a pub trying to put on airs.

There is virtually no natural light from the small window, and its table with candles would be like a forerunner of dinner on the Orient Express.

There is a lovely account in the diary of Sir George Bingham, Commander-in-Chief of the garrison, of a dinner here on January 8th 1816, soon after Napoleon had taken up residence:

*Dined with Napoleon; it was a most superb dinner. The dessert Service was Sèvres china, with gold knives, forks and spoons. The coffee cups were the most beautiful I ever saw. On each cup was an Egyptian view, and on the saucer a portrait of the Bey .... The people who live with him scarcely spoke out of a whisper and Buonaparte was so much engaged in eating that he hardly said a word to any of us. He had so filled the room with wax candles that it was as hot as an oven.*

Outside the dining room is the Library, now with books for sale and reprints of assorted academic papers. Initially the Montholons lived here, but very soon they moved to rooms on one side of the courtyard. There were scurrilous comments at the time, that Napoleon could peak from his quarters into Mme Montholon's bedroom. His neck would have had to have a very strange physiology to manage that. Like much else to do with his relations with Mme Montholon, I see more malice than fact.

On the right of the dining room are the three diminutive rooms, referred to grandeloquently as his suite by some, where Napoleon spent most of his time. The *Cabinet de travail* has a campaign cot which could also serve as a desk, and on the side is his writing desk. His long coat hangs there, with the famous hat. From his desk he looked into what would become a little garden, and beyond to Deadwood Plain. There is a bronze of a small, dejected old man in a dressing gown seated, apparently dozing, in a chair with a map on his knee. The house and setting are like that, changing your mood almost every time you move your head.

The stem of the house blocks any view of The Barn. So working at his desk, his views were not onto that, but the sights and sounds of the army camp. Some writers say he found The Barn depressing. It is dark and solid, and so often in winter its top is shrouded in mists, so yes, it can be seen as brooding. But it is some way away. Infinitely more dominating, overwhelming, was High Knoll from the Pavilion, at The Briars, but nobody refers to that. I think The Barn became a useful feature on which to hang the writer's own feelings of guilt.

Next door, in his bedroom, is an elegant 'camp' bed, curtained in green and white, and some small pieces of furniture. The walls are not papered, but draped in fine white material. Through the door is his bathroom, a dark room with a single window. There is the deep metal bath, a huge wardrobe, wash stands with a mirror by the window, and a small table where he shaved. And that is the entirety of the living quarters of the erstwhile Emperor of France.

Behind are several rooms and corridors, now full of exhibits, some fascinating, some almost irrelevant, many of them emotive. Of course it has become a museum, of pieces related in some way or other, sometimes very distantly, to Napoleon, his life and residence here. But it is separate from the house he lived in. So you return slowly through the rooms, more feeling than seeing. In time, and you may not be sure how long, you walk out, down the steps onto the lawn, with banks of agapanthus, so many trees, and the broad view beyond.

The garden is another story. You know it wasn't like this when he was here, but you'd like to think that the rudiments were. The fish pond, the slightly sunken paths, the grape arbor, and the summer house shaped like his famous hat. They are mostly re-built rather than restored. They should hint at formality, but there is an overriding spontaneity from the great mixture of colours and varieties of the plants. The gardens are a pleasure. You can walk and admire the plants, you can lift your head and reflect on the rest of the island, or you can sit and think.

Longwood House is an experience, moving in a contemplative, not a tear-jerking, way. I had the luxury of being able to go several times, when there were no other people there. It helps you put Napoleon into perspective, and it helps you put the island into perspective too. The accounts of 1815-1821 are fascinating enough, but Longwood brings them to life so easily. The cast of players, major and minor, even the walk on parts, the stage directions, the prompter's cues, are real, no longer just pages and paragraphs or one liners. Visits in swirling mists and driving rain, or brilliant sunshine, show very different sides of the coin.

In the house and gardens, you can see where Napoleon had that final show down with Lowe in August 1816. You can hear him ranting at Bertrand, insisting he break up some of the Imperial silver because Lowe had reduced the allowances. You walk where he started to garden, where he shot at animals with the temerity to graze on his land. You can feel the oppressive heat of the candles in the dining room, the damp chill of the drawing room, or his little bedroom. You can just about hear the servants bribing the sentries with bottles of wine, to let in the whores from town for their night's entertainment.

Yes, Napoleon died here, but he lived here too, as did so many others. They are all here, the great and the good, the ordinary and the not so good. There are no ghosts of the Emperor on St Helena, but his presence and that of his entourage and the British, Governor and troops, officers and servants, wives and whores, they're all here, maybe larger than in life, even if they're only in your mind. It's not just the mists that blow across Longwood plateau.

Tradition has it, that one day when Napoleon was visiting the Bertrands in their cottage, he scrambled down the side of the Punch Bowl and found a spring, in a wrinkle of the valley side. Two legends survived that chance encounter. One is that one of his Chinese gardeners brought him water every day from the spring. And the second is that Napoleon told his colleagues that when he died he wanted to be buried near his spring, in Geranium Valley.

On May 9th, 1821, they were able to do just that. The funeral procession, with all its pomp and grim finality, went up the plateau, through Longwood Gate, round one side of the Devil's Punch Bowl. It turned at Hutts Gate, passing above the ground already prepared for the coffin, and stopped on the road where the little lane led down to the Tomb.

There are many more trees today along the road and into the Punch Bowl, most of the hillsides were bare then. The grassy path drops gently down the side of the valley, below the road, little white posts with chains suggesting that the path is going somewhere. Firs grow sporadically above the path, and clumps of flax have been put in as a sort of raggle-taggle hedge, their blades rustling.

The backdrop of the entire north-east is wide open. It is sunny, there are white clouds, and fairy terns play below in the valley. You can't see the barren rim of the island from here, or even the threadbare bottom of the valley, just these green headwaters, pastures and trees. So much more beautiful than in 1821. No mists, no rain and mud, no damp cold wind today, no dirges, just sunshine and the hum of insects.

The trees close in, shading the path covered in moss. At the bottom is a clearing in all this vegetation, dominated by the great black trunks of half a dozen Norfolk Island pines. In its naturally landscaped hollow, it is like a cavern in the hillside of tall trees. Small stepped terraces scalloped on one side add to a feeling of a natural theatre. And not quite in the centre of the clearing, not even in the centre of the lawn, is the tomb.

Flowers are scattered throughout, flowers almost as though independent of their supporting plants: arum lilies, fuchsias, cannas, plumbago, and hibiscus climbing fifty feet up into the firs. There are ferns, and mosses and lichen on the low terrace walls, a bougainvillea festooning two of the Norfolk Island pines. It is the peace of a shaded lawn, with busy-lizzies growing round the base of the wrought iron railings of Napoleon's tomb. Plain black painted rails, and a plain, cracked cement slab, not even a plinth.

There are geraniums and peach trees, and a white olive planted by Prince Philip, but there are no weeping willows. Originally there were, but early on they and their successors were removed piecemeal by souvenir hunters. It is impossible to picture this as a bleak, wet hillside, the freshly turned earth trampled by the feet of troops and pall bearers. For now it is a scene of gentle beauty, the plants so deftly, maybe almost subconsciouly, arranged, it never enters your head that it isn't perfectly natural, and a perfectly correct, location for the tomb.

It is an extraordinary setting to lay to rest an Emperor, the man who shaped Europe, king-maker, great general, a man with an immense range of interests, the wielder of ultimate power. It was bizarre enough putting him on this remote island, but this place is unusual even by island standards. It is hidden, strangely secret, the peace is heavy, tangible, like the still air.

Yet I could get no real feeling for Napoleon, and certainly none of a tomb. You wonder at this mixture of nature and the past, of complete stillness, yet the canopy of trees high above is perpetually stirred by the winds of the South Atlantic. It is away from everything, there are no passers by, you must come specifically to visit the tomb. And once here, the natural calm spreads through you.

In the collection of paintings at Longwood House, is a most beautiful watercolour by Sèze, of three French ships in the Road, their sails furled, flying huge tricolours. A barge with oars shipped flat, flying another vast tricolour, is leaving the waterfront of Jamestown. Behind is a small town, and the hint of a valley, exactly the right shape. This is the record of October 15th 1840, when the French came to collect the mortal remains of their Emperor, and take them to their final resting place in his capital.

*La Belle Poule* was the flagship, a frigate, under the command of the Prince de Joinville, son of King Louis-Philippe. Several of the original French party returned, too. General Bertrand and his son, Arthur, born on the island, Emmanuel, son of the Count de Las Cases, General Gourgaud, and Louis Marchand, Napoleon's most loyal valet. The fleet had arrived on October 8th, and the exhumation of the coffin, and solemn transfer to the waiting ship, was on the 15th, the twenty fifth anniversary of Napoleon's arrival at St Helena. The inhabitants of the island were invited again to pay their respects to the island's greatest visitor.

The coffin was lifted from the vault, and briefly opened. The official record states that the face and hands were surprisingly preserved, as though mummified. Marchand exclaimed at the youth of his face. The silver decorations were tarnished, and the leather of the boots was mildewed. And in those few minutes in the air, the face started to crumple.

The coffin was resealed, and taken in slow procession down Side Path, through Jamestown, the entire route lined by troops of the garrison, their arms reversed. On the wharf it was transferred to the barge and taken to *La Belle Poule*, to lie in State, in a specially constructed chapel, until it reached the Seine. French and British ships in the Road fired salutes. On October 18th, twenty five years to the day that Napoleon rode with Admiral Cockburn to look at Longwood House, the French flotilla sailed.

So the mortal remains of Napoleon were gone from the island. But 160 years later his memory is still strong. One of the great joys of the island is the way its remarkable history is woven through the texture of its character and everyday life. The threads of no one are stronger than those of Napoleon Bonaparte. They are there for all to see, to weave their own conclusions, to add to the endless patterns of those already woven.

# CHAPTER 12

## FIVE MILES : THE LONGEST STREAM

*Jack Mason's at the bottom of Fisher's Valley, below Polly Mason's apple-garden ..... Of all the rude, uncouth, rocky, barren, untempting situations for a house this is the strangest and most remarkable of any I have yet seen. The house is placed on the very end of a narrow promontory of rock, and below, on each side, the water runs through a garden which notwithstanding all yield in proportion to its size abundance of Figs, Grapes, Guavas, Apples, Melons, Cucumbers etc.*

William John Burchell, journal for Christmas Day, 1807

Waterloo and St Helena are geographically remote, but Napoleon brings them side by side. An incident of time changed their relationship. Edmund Halley and William Bligh, one's comet the other's mutiny, are remote too, but St Helena brings them side by side. St Helena for centuries was a point, a beacon, a place where you knew where you were, guiding you to somewhere where perhaps you didn't. It was a place where so many ships called, going or coming, to or from quite literally every corner, known or unknown, of the globe. It was a place where so many threads of history linked or crossed,

St Helena loves to juggle with this ambivalence, this admixture of time and place, of its history and its present. To complicate things, or enhance them, such time shifts are superimposed with shifts of its own special geography. Fisher's Valley, running behind Longwood House, is a good example of this cocktail of time and place, and the quotation above was what got me thinking about it. A little bit of background can bring an apparently irrelevant quotation into surreal life.

In Napoleon's early months at Longwood, he went out riding and occasionally met people. He hadn't yet started to feel, or imagine, the intrusion of the British garrison, his guards. And to be fair he had a decent sized limit within which he was free to ride. Just on the edge of this boundary, past Hutts Gate and across Fisher's Valley, onto the end of Bonfire Ridge, lived an Englishwoman of mature years.

Miss Polly Mason was sympathetic to Napoleon and his changed status, treating him with the respect she felt he deserved. She was considered eccentric, not because of this, but she lived alone, and she knew, and spoke, her own mind. She also rode round on a large black bullock. Perhaps that's what they thought was a bit odd. She claimed it was much cheaper to maintain than a horse. I assume that Jack was her brother. Lieutenant Read's map of 1815 shows he had two pieces of land, one just below Hutts Gate, and the other which Burchell referred to.

William Burchell was an interesting man, indeed his sojourn on the island merits a chapter all to itself. But this is about Fisher's Valley, not just Burchell. In August 1805, a British fleet, under the command of Sir Home Popham, was despatched via St Helena to seize the Cape from the Dutch, before Napoleon's navy did. The fleet sailed from Cork, and one of those ships was an ageing East Indiaman, the *Northumberland*, which ten years later, on His Majesty's Service, would transport Napoleon to the island. On board the vessel in 1805, listed as a midshipman, was one William J Burchell.

He came from Fulham, where his family ran The Fulham Nursery and Botanical Gardens. Burchell was a talented botanist, and had been made a Fellow of the Linnaean Society at the age of 22. But in 1805, to the annoyance of his family, he announced he was sailing to St Helena, leaving the family business to pursue an independent career as a naturalist.

How a young botanist got a place with a military force asks a number of questions. Even before they sailed, Burchell may have had contact with a certain William Balcombe, of Balcombe Traders. Balcombe was also going to the island, to set up a business, and he certainly had contacts in high places. There were some who thought he might have started life on the wrong side of a royal blanket. But that apart, these two disparate souls spent three months together on the *Northumberland*.

Perhaps it's a more straightforward story, and Burchell had a recommendation from Sir Joseph Banks, President of the Royal Society. The wealthy Banks had been botanist on Captain Cook's first voyage on the *Endeavour,* and had called at St Helena on their homeward run, so he knew the island. Whatever it was, Burchell's passage on the *Northumberland* adds a few more serendipitous pieces to the island's story.

If getting on the ship was suspect, getting off was illegal. When he arrived, Burchell is listed as having been left there as invalided, the only way he could have been allowed to land. If he had some kind of 'agreement' with Balcombe, it remains obscure, for Balcombe was yet to establish any kind of formal link with the East India Company, and once on the island, the two men went their separate ways.

In due course, Governor Patton learned that Burchell was *a gentleman of very superior qualifications, whose capacity and character have been vouched for by the most reputable authority.* So Burchell was offered the appointment of *schoolmaster to teach ancient and modern languages, and the science of mathematics in its various branches, and the art of drawing ..... to the young men of the island who are to bear military commissions.*

In January 1807, Burchell's appointment was confirmed by the Company, in London, at £80 per annum. His letter of appointment ended with a reprimand for his having landed on the island without permission. He was listed in the Company's annual Register, as *William Burchill Schoolmaster and acting botanist.* Following a long and acrimonious correspondence with the Company, Burchell became *Company's naturalist* in 1810. He considered the salary of £200 too low because they wouldn't let him stay on and draw the salary as schoolmaster as well.

I will digress one tiny bit more, for there are elements of the island's character in this. Before he left England, or perhaps through correspondence, Burchell had conducted a courtship with, and become engaged to, a Miss Lucia Green. He sent her £200 for her passage out, a year's salary he could ill afford.

The islanders heard of his plans, and knowing he was a little short of the necessary, made all the wedding arrangements for him. This spontaneity of hospitality was an island feature. But William's popularity with the locals failed to extend to this particular good lady. For when the ship arrived, Miss Green called the engagement off, and married the ship's captain. Not long after, Burchell left the island for the Cape, and his travels in southern Africa. It is for his studies there, especially his watercolours of wildlife, that he is best known. Indeed, the common zebra (*Equus burchelli*) is named after him.

In one capacity or other, Burchell covered the island on foot from corner to corner, and made a large number of wonderful drawings of plants, buildings and of scenery. And on one early day he visited Fisher's Valley and found the farm of Jack Mason. Today it isn't Jack Mason's, it's marked on the War Department map as 'Bradleys (Ruins)'.

The track out from Longwood, goes down the long slope of scruffy marls towards the distant sea. It leaves any hint of trees behind, pretty well at Longwood House, and drops through the memory of the Great Wood, past a bush or two, some splendid aloes, and the start of the ubiquitous succulent 'creeper'. This is *Carpobrotus edulis*, a member, with the attractive ice plant and endemic Baby's Toes, of the Hottentot fig family. Only the creeper remains as the track drops down the side of Fisher's Valley, which has broadened and flattened into dusty nonentity.

At the bottom there's a sort of crossroads. One track wends out on the other side onto the even dustier Prosperous Bay Plain, the other heads off upstream, towards the fertile bit of the valley bottom. Downstream an expanse of lank grass, three feet high, fills the valley floor, and Bradleys (Ruins) is no more than a rocky promontory striking downstream, with a bit of carefully masoned wall reinforcing one side of it It was that scrap of relic wall that had first caught my eye, but on top there was nothing, except an evocative hint of something I could never identify.

Here is a fine example of the island's impossible to define character, perhaps another part of its special composite soul. This little promontory, surrounded by featureless rocks and marls, has attracted me from that first climb up one side to see what rock it was made of. Maybe it affects me because the rock type is special, or at least different. The promontory is a fine example (Turk's Cap and the Bell Stone are others) of the particular group of lava flows which spectacularly flooded the east of the island, after that huge chunk of the volcano slid into the Atlantic. Perhaps it was the first time I thought I knew what might have been happening to the volcano.

Whatever it was, Bradleys Ruins' character had taken its hold on me. I asked around, but nobody knew where the name came from, nor what, if it was indeed a ruin, it was a ruin of. Every time I went out that way though, I was attracted across to the little promontory and sat, thinking perhaps, absorbing some to its atmosphere perhaps. And then, reassured by something I knew not what, I would walk on, one way or the other into the emptiness.

Then thirty years later, I came across that entry in Burchell's notebook. So, it had once been a fine farm, above its stream, flowing then, and growing proud fruits. Even then, Burchell says its surroundings were desolate, dried out, bleached and wind-blown, lifeless. So it seemed I'd stumbled across some kind of essence of Jack Mason and his painstaking work, nearly two centuries later. Maybe I'd found another ghost, of a farm this time.

I couldn't explain, even to myself, why I've always found it so emotive, but on Christmas morning 1998 I went to the promontory. If you look very carefully there *are* traces of the house's footings, a narrow house surely, but its masonry was good, you can see that from the side of the promontory. And sitting there, the grey overcast morning adding to the grey bleakness of the setting, I waited to see what might come to me.

Well something did. How many times I'd been there, Lord only knows, but now I could see remnants of perhaps a dozen aged retaining walls, for tiny plots for his fruit trees, tiny terraced bits barely bigger than window boxes on the other side of the promontory, and just across the bed of the non-existent stream.

And if you watched and waited, and perhaps had faith in something or other, it was all there, the fruit farm that so impressed

Burchell, the plant man from Fulham. Wonderful. OK, William Burchell himself wasn't there, as I'd half hoped, and no farmer, no water, no fruit, no flowers. But the sun tried to come through, and the farm, ghost or not, was there. Yes, live for ever, Jack Mason.

Let me not get this out of perspective, for Bradleys (Ruins) is already half way from Fisher's source to the sea. Fisher's Valley is the island's longest 'single' valley, its stream running a fraction over five miles from Diana's Peak towards the sea at Prosperous Bay Beach. It is a weird and wonderful five miles. And don't mock the five miles. If you consider St Helena in terms of continents, then Fisher's is no less than the Amazon, the Nile, or the Mississippi. It's serious stuff.

Above about 2000 feet its headwaters are indistinguishable from the other steep valley headwaters, verdant and humid. High up, there are relic patches of tree ferns and cabbage trees, but mainly the sides are clothed in flax. Then as it drops, there are plantations of high, thin eucalyptus, pastures with cattle and patches of gorse, and a scattered handful of white-washed cottages. Bonfire Ridge is on the southern side of the valley, and close to its top was the house of the eccentric Miss Mason.

By the time it crosses the road which scallops round the island, the valley bottom is stocked, almost blocked, with wild ginger and yams. The other side of the valley is separated from the Devil's Punch Bowl by the narrowest of ridges, barely wide enough for the road, yet the rich agricultural green on one side, and the dry headwaters of the Bowl on the other, are continents apart. These central reaches of Fisher's formed the limit of Napoleon's free perimeter.

On his early rides, Napoleon discovered a cottage or two here in the pleasant greenery below Miss Mason's house. One of them housed a settler called Robinson, and his daughter, Mary Ann, a young lady not devoid of feminine attributes according to General Gourgaud. Napoleon chatted on several occasions to the Nymph, as she was quickly nicknamed. So Miss Robinson achieved a shortlived fame, and in Longwood House, there is a highly improbable picture of *Napoleon et la Nimph de Ste Hélène*. Napoleon is in full uniform on a white horse, and a flower girl, like a porcelaine figurine, stands in front of a splended portico. I don't think Mr Robinson would have recognized his daughter, certainly not his poor cottage.

Gourgaud was single, and complained incessantly to his diary, to his Emperor, indeed to almost anyone who would listen, of the aridity of his love life. His proclivity for the *black women of town* was an element of Longwood House chatter. And it was Gourgaud, not Napoleon, who took a fancy to Miss Robinson, though his diary never reveals just how active his fancy might have been.

But eighteen months on, it reveals how cross he was when she became engaged to a young officer of the 53rd. And a few months later the young officer was positively furious, when out of the blue, she married the captain of a ship passing through, and sailed off with him into the sunset. Perhaps the Nymph was the subject of the syndrome described by Napoleon's Irish physician, O'Meara: *Young ladies, some of whom are very pretty, and very uneducated, do not require a long courtship, or much persuasion, to induce them to quit the rock where they had their birth.*

This part of the valley is strangely closed, hidden from roads, hidden from views of ocean. It has a rich infilling of trees and flowers, and small fertile fields. But it doesn't last, and although the floor is filled for a while with plots of vegetables, the valley sides have become straggly scrub and coloured marls.

From the valley floor you can see the trees around Longwood House, though its next door neighbour, the St Helena Golf Club, is hidden. No apologies for a diversion here, for the boundary of the golf course, along one entire side, is Fisher's Valley, making it a haven for mis-hit balls. The nine holes of wind and sun dried grass and clay, dust and loose chippings, test innovation as much as skill, sense of humour as much as patience. The golf course is like island cooking, it has few embellishments but considerable character.

For a start, the grass is a hazard. It doesn't form delicate greens, or compact fairways. Instead, individual tussocks, small medium or large, deflect the ball, bouncing it in directions dependent as much on when it last rained and the laughter of the breeze, as when the cattle were last driven this way.

Conditions vary from hot, still and humid, to driving mist, and rare chilling cloudbursts. The wind is probably the key factor now, though there was a time when hitting donkeys incurred penalty strokes. And wirebirds still slow down play by running along the fairway, or sometimes by just standing and not running anywhere. But these are mere hints of the true joy of the course, for every hole has a spectacular view of a different element of the island's scenery. Course fees are barely noticeable, and guests are warmly welcomed, on the course and in the club house.

Back at Bradleys (Ruins), the setting is bleak. South, away from Longwood, are the flat wastes of Prosperous Bay Plain, a hazy expanse of white dust and rocks. Prosperous Bay Plain is conceptually a bit like the Cape of Good Hope, better an attractive than an accurate name. It is a grim area, apparently almost devoid of life. You can see the distant Signal Station on the cliff tops, but I shall leave that for later. This is about Fisher's Valley, and its character is about to change again.

Downstream is a dusty scratch of path that will finish this journey down Fisher's. All the changes in the valley so far are as nothing to what lies in store. Upstream, behind you, Fisher's has the strip of lank grass 'flowing' from the trees and the green interior. Even the tattered end of Longwood plateau is welcoming with its subdued inhospitability. But as you move towards the sea, the low sides of the valley close in, and suddenly the rest of the island disappears as the valley drops into a canyon carved through massive, flat-lying, stepped lava flows.

One moment Fisher's was a nondescript broad valley, the next it is a chasm, its walls dropping shear, as waterfalls jump a hundred feet at a time down from the head of the gorge. The path clings to one side, and far below, the bottom of the gorge is a bright green line. Broad leaves of yams, insipid looking thatching grass, and stagnant pools, form a green cleft between the stark, monstrous sides. The air is still and hot and it's getting hotter, the rocks reflecting and radiating the heat. It will be even hotter on the way back up in the afternoon.

The cliff of Holdfast Tom is the formidable buttress on the

other side. On the path side, the valley opens slightly, and a ragged side valley rises to King and Queen Rocks, topknots on the cliff next to the Signal Station. Our path has dropped into a broad valley bottom, full of mud, some of it whiteish, which was once guano from a bird rookery. Assorted bones, skulls and beaks, poke out of the surface, gradually being exposed by the elements. Welcome to Prosperous Bay Beach, the end of Fisher's Valley.

It's a flat triangle of dust and sand and cobbles. The stream went underground so didn't quite make it, but the lank grass and lanky wild tobacco did. In the dust are bits of broken bottle and fragments of blue china, the fingerprints of the island's military past. The battery and a fine musketry tower are on the start of low cliffs towards Turk's Cap.

There is more recent debris too, donkey droppings bleached white, and ash from fishermen's fires, crab claws and limpet shells. Crabs are used for bait, but the limpets I'm not so sure about. It is possible that they are popped on the fire - a bit like potatoes on Guy Fawkes Night in England - providing a tasty snack. The main meal cooked up by the fishermen is a rough and ready version of plo - they bring the rice and potatoes, and catch the fish. Next time I go back I must remember to ask what they do with the barnacles, copious shells of which occur too.

It was here in 1673, that Keigwin and his 400 merry men landed, anxious to get back at the Dutch. The landing in itself was no mean feat, but if Keigwin was pleased with surviving getting ashore, he must have been daunted looking for a way out. The gorge of Fisher's must have put him off, as did, in the other direction, the inaccessible stretch of rubble cliffs up towards Turk's Cap. He chose the great cliff facing him, and it became an island legend.

The actual cliffs look almost vertical, no less uninviting than the gorge in Fisher's, but the lower half of the thousand feet wall is a relatively easy scramble. So, lured on by this, Keigwin and his band got half way up, to the bottom of the near-vertical five hundred foot bit, and that must have seemed like the end.

But no, up steps Tom to volunteer his services. With a length of twine attached to a rope at one end, and his ankle at the other, trail blazer Tom, set to to climb the cliff. Exhorting him in his endeavours, his colleagues shouted "Hold fast, Tom, hold fast!" And Tom's bravery and skill was engraved for posterity.

Brave it certainly was, foolhardy it may have been, but in the end it was all a bit of a waste. Captain Munden had sailed into James Bay with the rest of the force, and the Dutch surrendered, pretty well just like that. Keigwin's men didn't know this, and spent the night apprehensively on the clifftop. Then in the morning, they girded up their loins and set off, only to be stopped somewhere in the Great Wood by a runner with a message from Munden. It's all right lads, it said, I've got the town back, now don't rush across causing damage to anything, there's good fellows. So they walked to town, their job well done. Munden's ship was put on the island flag and he got a knighthood, Keigwin got sent to Bombay, and Tom got a cliff.

All the time I'd spent on the island, I'd never tried Holdfast Tom. Then in '98, I'd been down to the beach with Basil on an organised walk, and they decided to go back the short way, up Holdfast Tom. One of the group wasn't feeling too well, so I volunteered to accompany him back the long way. It's called social responsibility, or cowardice. Basil came too, and as we slowly went up one side of the valley, we watched these ants scuttling up the cliff on the other.

A month later, Basil and I were down there again. Let's go back up Holdfast Tom, says Basil. No excuse this time. The bottom five or six hundred feet are all right, bit gritty, but OK. Then we're at the bottom of the sheer lava pile, and the bottom flow is a good fifty feet thick, straight up and down. No problem says Basil, we go up this little chimney, look, there's a fishermens' rope here somewhere. Basil's got a severely arthritic knee. I look up the chimney, I've got severe sweating. I turn and look round the fantastic cliffs, maybe there's a lift.

"It's all right." It was Basil's voice, and I turn back and there's no Basil. Well, it's one thing to lose half a volcano, it's very different to lose a walking companion. "No, up here!" And there he was, thirty feet up, offering encouragement. I won't say Saints are good on verticals, but if they'd been called in to redecorate the

Sistine Chapel, you wouldn't have had to pay rental for ladders.

But I'm concerned. The chimney is fine, it's just that the first step is a good six feet off the ground. Bruce Lee couldn't have got his foot up there. It's OK says Basil, easy on from here, tell you what, I'll pull you up the first bit on the rope, just let me get comfortable. And he wedges himself into the cliff, and down comes the end of the rope. Well, I grab it, what to do? It would be a three hour detour to meet him at the top. Basil tugs, and I rise gracelessly upwards, eager to put foot on first step.

What he hadn't said, and I hadn't noticed, was that the first step was on a corner, to the right of where I was standing, so as I rise I swing out, away from the face, describing an arc some considerable way above the musketry tower at the beach. Even at the time I remember being impressed. The entire coastal cliff system up to The Barn as a backdrop, me arcing like an irregular plumb bob, and the two bounces I would make onto the tower several hundred feet below, all etched on my retina.

Twice I did that, before I realised I'd have to stop playing around, as Basil's face had gone deep purple, he did after all have all my weight on his line. But he got me up, and the view of the wild cliffs now had a distinctly personal component.

There was no real feel of 1673, and Keigwin and Tom at Prosperous Bay Beach or at Holdfast Tom. But there is massive respect, that Keigwin should have got his party successfully ashore, and that Tom should have led the way up the nightmare cliffs, and for the men who followed him. I have special sympathy for the last man to go up. But they are not discrete feelings for those specific, sort of founder's day, memories. There is more an empathy for the soldiers of a long line of later garrisons, who sweated down here building and manning the fortifications.

So all these bits and pieces are a compendium of Fisher's Valley, and none of what you've seen is more than a quarter of a mile from the bed of the barely existent stream. It covers a lot of ground, from the endemic tree ferns of the mist swept Peaks, through Napoleon and Burchell, golf and maidenly assignations, signals and seagulls, to the brave reclamation of the island from the Dutch.

There is a lot of the island's different geographies and its lively history, a lot of island character and some wonderful atmosphere.

All of that in barely five miles, as the myna flies. It's only the myna that is prepared to take on all elements of the extraordinary diversity of Fisher's Valley.

# CHAPTER 13

## FURTHEST REACHES OF THE EAST

*And besides that, two light blue eyes held me fast, the eyes of Ann Mira. They made me forget father, brothers and sisters, the City with the proud gabled houses and the crowned tower near the stream of the Elbe, and held me fast on the remote island with its contrasts of nature and peoples.*

Georg Wilhelm Janisch, letter from St Helena, 1843.
(from a collection of translations by Hudson Noel Janisch,1998)

Georg Janisch came from Hamburg. He was 21 when he came to St Helena on the *Phaeton*, as a secretary working for Sir Hudson Lowe. He wrote to his cousin on April 17th, 1816, five days after arriving on the island:

*How grateful was I, therefore, to kind fate that I found a new home in the house of the widow of a former government official, William Seale. In spite of the bad weather the worthy lady, in a plain dress, received me at the open door. A touching picture because, clinging to her side, laying a delicate arm round the mother's waist, was Ann Mira, her only daughter, half a child still, half a budding maiden. And when the mother bade me heartily welcome, the delicate features of the young girl were also lit up with joy.*

Georg Janisch had fallen in love. So when Lowe left in 1821, Georg stayed on, and became a ship's chandler. He bought the house where Polly Mason had lived on Bonfire Ridge, and named it Teutonic Hall, largely as a dig at the British. Later, further along this story of the east, we shall meet up again, with Georg and Ann Mira.

That was a bit of a digression perhaps, but a love story like this brings a touch of warmth, should one be needed, to the east, the most remote, most isolated, part of the island. And Bonfire Ridge, the southern side of Fisher's Valley, forms the edge of Prosperous Bay Plain.

The Plain is a great emptiness. In the late sixties, it sprang to life when it was covered with yet more aerials for the short-lived Diplomatic Wireless Station, but virtually all traces have long since gone. It stretches nearly two miles, at a pinch, east to west, and up to a mile north-south. So, as the only real patch of flattish ground, it will be where any airstrip materializes.

Most people can live without the Plain, they find it dull, hot and monotonous. But I've always enjoyed its emptiness, just me, dry zone plants, dust and rocks, the wind, distant clifftop skyline one way, distant Peaks the other, and its immense silence. Trudging across its dusty surface brings a warmth of solitude, an isolation not felt elsewhere, a bit like farewell to the inhabited island. So an inquisitive fairy tern, fluttering three feet above your head, is welcome. Its tiny body and wings provide the only shade you'll see anywhere on the Plain.

You can blame the goats and man for despoiling many areas of the island, but here its barren coat of white dust and acid-eaten rocks is natural. It's flat because it sits on a great pile of flat lava flows. It's white partly because of dust from altered lavas, and because part of it was once an enormous bird rookery. Bird droppings over countless millenia turned its surface into a phosphatic desert, part dust-bowl, part solidified into rocky slabs.

The Plain is one of the more bizarre elements of the island's extensive collection. After Fisher's Valley, and particularly after the empathy of Bradleys Ruins, the sudden introduction of such bleakness, comes as a shock. The creepers thin out, the odd prickly pear disappears. Probably the only thing that attracts anyone to the Plain, apart from its incredible seclusion, is what was once the island's most remote habitation, Prosperous Bay Signal Station.

On the seaward end, the concept of plain falls apart, into flat hillocks or mesas, and wadi-like features filled with cracked mud. The overriding colours of the marls, the dust, even the relic lava flows themselves, are ochrous maroon, faded grey-blue and pinkish grey, reminiscent again of dirty velveteen public house wallpaper. The white 'puddles' are dusts mainly of gypsum washed in and dried out.

It is amazingly desolate, it is hot, very hot, and airless. Large tracts have more the look of long abandoned spoil heaps. Vistas might be out of *One Million Years B.C.*, and *Lawrence of Arabia*. Or where large scale rusting rubbish has been dumped, *Mad Max* might just feel at home.

Prosperous Bay Signal Station overlooks the desolate entirety of the Plain. The path to it used to be solid, with little walls on the zig-zag bends. And the cottage was built solidly too, on top of the cliff opposite King and Queen Rocks, with a back door step a thousand feet high. It wouldn't do to come home after a few pints, and forget which way to go for a widdle if you woke in the night.

There's a narrow chasm, though you can't lean out far enough to see its bottom, between the Signal Station and the abstract, sculpted rocks of the King and Queen. You can't see which is which from here, but coming up from Prosperous Bay, with the eye of faith, you can see the king seated on a throne, but I'm not sure that the crumpled figure, perhaps doing abeyance at his feet, is really the queen.

The views are monumental, along vast cliffs towards Turk's Cap and The Barn. Flagstaff Hill stands proud on sunny days, but disappears in the mist, hence the need to shift a signal station here. It can look fifty miles out to sea for shipping, then signal to Deadwood, and let them pass it on to Ladder Hill and the Castle. You could also tip the wink to the tower, seemingly miles below, at Prosperous Bay. In days of sail, you gave several hours warning to the batteries, so no excuse for a shortage of sponges or lack of shot.

The silence is amazing, you find yourself straining to locate the steady grinding of the distant sea, for a bit of company. I would have thought the isolation, and some of these bizarre views, might, on mistswept days, be seriously depressing. If you like the independence it's a treat, but not for very long for most of us. But the Gunnell family lived happily here for years. Robert Gunnell took over as signalman at Prosperous Bay aged seventeen, when his father died.

His gravestone, by the side of his father's, is in St Matthew's churchyard at Hutts Gate. *Robert Samuel Gunnell (1883 - 1904) There remaineth therefore A rest for the people of God.* You can see the Signal Station from the grave.

On November 2nd, 1904, Robert Gunnell's body was found at the Signal Station. He had been killed the afternoon before, as he sat in his chair, by a 12 bore shotgun blast to the back of his head. The house had been ransacked. The murderers had helped themselves to bits of food, leaving glasses and plates on the table. Field glasses had been stolen, a watch, and a hairbrush.

In her evidence, Angelina Gunnell, Robert's mother, stated: *I think deceased had an Enemy, he told me it was Richard Crowie, the ill feeling was caused through a donkey. Richard Crowie worked my son's donkey without his permission.* She identified the watch and its gold chain, recovered from the accused, as her son's. It had belonged to his grandfather.

On February 2nd, 1905, Richard Crowie, aged 17, and his cousin Louis Crowie, aged 20, from Tobacco Plain on the southern side of Fisher's Valley, a little way below Teutonic Hall, were hanged in Jamestown. It was a public hanging, almost next door to the gaol, *at the Customs back shed,* at the back of what is now the PWD warehouse on the square, at the foot of the Ladder. *And there buried in coffins in quicklime.* The Crowies were the last people hanged on the island, and the murder was the last for some three quarters of a century

I said the cliffs looked impressive, and the long one south of the Signal Station, is dramatically sheer. It made such an impression on Charles Darwin, he described it in *The Voyage of the Beagle*:

*One day I noticed a curious circumstance : standing on the edge of a plain, terminated by a great cliff of about a thousand feet in depth, I saw at a distance of a few yards right to windward, some tern, struggling against a very strong breeze, whilst, where I stood, the air was quite calm. Approaching close to the brink, where the current seemed to be deflected upwards from the face of the cliff, I stretched out my arm, and immediately felt the full force of the wind : an invisible barrier, two yards in width, separated perfectly calm air from a strong blast.*

With an arm that would stretch two yards, I can see now how he could throw a stone from his lodging at Hutts Gate, onto

Napoleon's tomb. No, but here is a splendid example of the magic of St Helena. I was standing exactly, exactly, where Charles Darwin stood in the second week of July, 1836.

Coming from inland, it is a staggering feeling after a mile or more of dusty plain, suddenly to reach those cliffs. Flat, the plain is, rocks and dust, solid as a dug-up motorway all the way. And then, Kerpow! it all disappears. One stops suddenly when that happens, leans the head forward a bit gingerly over the edge, to look *about a thousand feet* straight down to the dark blue ocean. Impressive.

I'd first been there in January, 1966, and at the time I hadn't read Darwin's account. I was on the cliff tops about midway between the Signal Station and Gill Point. The South-East Trades come a few thousand miles across nothing but waves, and then whack straight into this vertical cliff.

Coming over the Plain, it was breezy, but here there was nothing, not a tweak, not a breath of wind. I'd realised there might be something odd. I'd watched a myna flying from behind me, perhaps twenty feet up, and as it crossed the edge of the cliff it just shot vertically upwards, whirling untidily in a cacophony of ruffled feathers and ego. But unlike with Darwin, the full realisation of *why* it was doing that, hadn't dawned on me. It was a glorious day, barely a cloud in the sky, me enjoying a banana and a rest, and a myna raucously disappearing skywards, whatnot over wingtip. Serve it right, I thought, very full of themselves, mynas.

Before I continued on my way, it seemed, since a call of nature was scheduled, quite an imaginative thing to do, never having tried it before, to pee off the top of a thousand foot high cliff. I had watched the plight of the myna, and it *still* hadn't dawned on me.

Now, if the *full force of the wind* could cause a tern to *struggle against it,* indeed my myna had been positively battered, then you can imagine, or perhaps it is better if you cannot, what such a wind does to a frail stream of liquid. It would certainly be difficult to design a fountain to do that. But that's the magic, isn't it? I had discovered the same phenomenon that the mighty Charles Darwin had done, at the very same spot, a hundred and thirty years apart. Though perhaps one of us rationalized it rather more eloquently than the other.

The Plain is a link with the changing topography of the east, but you might have been aware that the character was changing even at Hutts Gate. It's actually a contorted cross-roads, when you sort the bits and pieces out, with St Matthew's not quite in the centre. One road from town, one turning right, back into the interior, one turning left to Longwood, and the middle one heading out east.

On the ridge above the church is where Halley carried out some of his observations in 1676. Lower down that same ridge are the remains of the observatory that Dr Nevil Maskelyne, another Astronomer Royal in the making, set up in 1761. Maskelyne's visit, to witness the transit of Venus, was to say the least ill-fated. Clouds obscured the event, his equipment malfunctioned, it was a disaster. In fact his visit deserves mention only because it was part of a larger scientific venture, and two other observers stopped at the island on their way home to collect tidal and gravitational data, and pick up Maskelyne. They were his assistant, Charles Mason, and one Jeremiah Dixon.

Mason and Dixon had had a more colourful time. Destined for Bencoolen on Sumatra, they had just sailed into the Indian Ocean when they were attacked by a French warship. They lost 44 men, and had to put into the Cape, where they successfully completed their Venus observations. It took a lot to dampen scientific determination in those early days.

And yes, they were the Mason and Dixon who were sent to the American Colonies, two years after St Helena, to resolve the question of the common boundaries of Pennsylvania, Maryland, Delaware and Virginia. Their east-west line, principally separating Pennsylvania and Virginia became the Mason - Dixon line, traditionally dividing the slave-owning South from the non-slave-owning North.

It's probably just as well to get most of the island's claim to astronomical fame out of the way, for there's an odd feeling at Hutts Gate, as though you're turning a corner, which you aren't, and leaving the rest of the island behind, which maybe you are.

The changes come in slowly at first, then with more of a rush.

After Fisher's Valley, and Teutonic Hall, there is the barren greyness of Prosperous Bay Plain, and then start a series of increasingly deeply incised valleys, and long ridges slowly descending to spectacularly sheer cliffs. The road contours at around 1600 feet, zigging up one side of the valley, zagging down the next, sticking pretty close to the feet of the Peaks. Below the road, there are up to three miles of the barren outer fringe. It's marvellous rough walking, with some great, oddly different, scenery.

But from the road, take a detour into a field of flax. Funny stuff, flax. It has flame orange flowers on stalks, and seed pods that might be cockroaches, or crab claws. Odd, but pretty. And walk on. The plants reach for you, their long leaves, like tendrils poking at your head, clutching at your back, tying round your feet and tripping you. But it's helpful, very strong, you can pull yourself up by it if you fall down or get stuck on a steep slope. Locals cut the long blades and use them to tie up bundles, secure things to their donkey, or keep bits from falling off ageing cars. It's a very hands-on plant, flax.

What used to be the flax mill at Woody Ridge is a point of reference. North, to the left, green pastures, cattle, a donkey or two, stretching into Longwood, Flagstaff and The Barn a distant end-drop. Longwood Plateau gets increasingly threadbare seawards on that side, but as you cross to Prosperous Bay Plain the serious desolation comes in. Turning right, east, and the plain, while no less barren, is a palette of ochrous colours from the weathering of the hard dark lavas.

Then a chasm, Sharks Valley, and the grey misshapen hillocks of Stone Tops, Great and Little. To your right, south, it's the green rural landscape of domesticated ridges and fields and colourful houses. And turning fully west, new woodlands reaching back to The Peaks. Even standing on the same spot, that's a lot of geography to take in,

Woody Ridge is a good starting point. Keep on the road, and it's into, and through, Levelwood. But go down the track, branch into the ochrous landscape, and discover yet another different world. Across the coloured marls, and they really are an extraordinary range of colours, like one of those cases of different eye-shadows, is a low, flat-topped hill of solid rock, seemingly close to the edge of the island. It's called Bencoolen, though why the EIC's great centre in Sumatra, should have given its name to a mile long nondescript hillock here, is anyone's guess.

Very few people go into this area, a few fishermen go down Dry Gut to Gill Point, or someone might go after rabbits. The area is made up of thick lava flows, very thick, and way down the ochrous plain, beyond Bencoolen, it has the habit of dropping out of the blue fifty or a hundred feet in one step. Do watch where you're walking. Makes for impressive waterfalls, except they're almost always dry.

So although it looks like it Bencoolen isn't the edge of the island, and beyond it and onto Gill Point, there's a square mile of lost island, which almost nobody knows is there. Remote, windy, the sounds of the sea, and views onto the seaward face of Great Stone Top, eight hundred feet of Landseer lion face. It doesn't look much like a lion from elsewhere, but it does down here.

It's a landscape of vast gentle waves of ancient lava, those dry waterfalls, straight up and down cliffs, like the ones that so impressed Darwin. And it's not dizzy terns, but white long-tailed tropic birds that know about these things, patrolling the cliffs, and the four - five - six notes of their shrieks, like a tortured referee's whistle. There are no tracks beyond Bencoolen, but the fishermens' path to Gill Point is perfectly recognizable. It even takes you down a couple of the waterfalls.

If you like isolation, there are plenty of places on the island to find it, but there are few places better than this. It's all yours, no one else's, nothing else's. The crags of Bencoolen hide the rest of the island, but you can see round its ends, huge empty vistas of the multicoloured ruff of half the island. In the right mood, this is an area of wonderful strength, of extraordinary natural beauty, at all scales. In the wrong mood, its heavy, uncertain silence can make it perhaps a little brooding.

But if you stayed on the road, then this is Levelwood. Wooded it might have been, but level, it never was. Maybe it started off as 'levelled wood'? The Trades certainly come in pretty strongly on occasions. It was always a distant part of the island, and more a collection of scattered cottages, over the sides of two valleys, than a settlement as such.

It has grown a lot since I camped in the field of what was then the school and is now independent flatlets for the elderly. And today Levelwood has stores, a thriving bar, a mobile fish 'n chip van, a community centre, and a clinic named after the Medical Officer, Ian Shine, who helped build it. Most of the people living in Levelwood are Jehovah's Witnesses, and for years attended their faith's original Hall in Half Tree Hollow. Only recently have new Halls opened in Levelwood itself, and at Longwood Gate.

If you want to go down Sharks Valley, and it's well worth it, a very different walk, a path starts at the bar and Solomon's Shop at Silver Hill. Bright and breezy at the top, the valley closes into a chasm, and the bottom is full of wild mango (*Schinus terebinthifolius*). Their branches are so tightly knitted, or perhaps knotted is better, that the path becomes a tunnel cut with 'swords' by the fishermen. Then the path gives up, breaks out, and continues as a scratch on the lava wall above the treetops.

This infilling by the plant has happened in no more than a generation, there used to be nothing but thatching grass and a few yams. But now with the goats gone it is growing back everywhere on the barren outer reaches of the island, very often it's the only thing that will, as a first step back to some form of vegetation. And give it plenty of water and Wham! it's in like Flynn, impenetrably choking the bottoms of many of the narrow valley bottoms.

Lower down the valley yams appear. They were brought in originally to feed the slave population, huge, yard long triangular leaves on their high purple stalks, deep green, with little balls of crystal water collected in them. There are waterfalls, and the path scrabbles round boulders spalled down the side. Some idea of the size of Great Stone Top overhead, is given by the size of these boulders, some of them fifty feet across. Pretty fearsome, one of those, breaking off the lion's mane a thousand feet above, and bouncing down.

Two islands come into view, Shore and George, glistening guano white, from the colonies of boobies, gannet family, heavy birds, a yard long and two yard wingspans, they make the tropic birds look anorexic. Tradition has it that the gypsum for Napoleon's (second, the first fell apart) death mask came from George Island.

The stream ends up threading down a low cliff, a dozen white runnels braided with algal ribbons, dotted with ferns and tiny plants. At its base there are yams, and stream pools where you'd expect to find watercress, at the back of a little boulder beach. Sixteen hundred feet of cliff face and the power of the ocean is a powerful meeting, but then you have this completely incongruous, miniscule haven, hidden from view from anywhere, poised on the edge of insanity.

It's worth taking a closer look at Stone Tops from the top, much brighter, more airy. You start from what is signposted The Bell Stone, a large discoid slab of rock which earned its name because it rang sonorously when struck. Phonolites, the rocks of Lot's Wife and the Asses Ears, get their name from the Greek *phone*, meaning sound. I found that much out in the library in 1964. They are supposed to ring when hit, and a lot of island ones do, often quite dramatically.

But the Bell Stone isn't a phonolite, which is a pity. If you want to be technical it's a trachyandesite, the stuff of Bradleys promontory and so much of the younger lavas between here and Turk's Cap. In any case the Bell Stone doesn't ring much at all now, probably because someone tried to move it. Some souvenir. But it's a handsome sylvan setting, and a sort of *Boinngg* Stone is better than nothing.

Bencoolen and the Stone Tops are recognizable as some of the last serious flows erupted from the volcano, and they're very odd to boot. The Stone Tops oozed out, a bit like toothpaste, but a thousand feet thick, to form enormous viscous domes. The way the eruptions reached the surface was very different, and other strange things that were going on at depth cracked and split the sides of the volcano in very odd ways. Older lavas have even been bent almost through a right angle by this subterranean pressure. A problem or two here all right, but don't worry about the rocks, just enjoy going through them to the summit of Great Stone Top. It's another great spot to wonder at the enormity of these eastern cliffs or half the island you can see inland.

After Levelwood, there are no more than a handful of houses in the south-east until you get into Sandy Bay. The road contours sedately on, the Peaks on one side, chasm valleys between high ridges on the other. It's a sort of wildly rural road to ride. On one ridge a Norfolk Island pine has been beckoning you on. At its foot, the flax mill that was there has been made over into an outward bound centre for the Duke of Edinburgh awards. Good thinking, a great base for exploring this side.

Behind it is Rock Rose, a two storey white-washed ruin, its windows gaping eye sockets. It was not a big house, but then with the exception of Plantation, none of them were, but it had a simple grace. And here's the tenuous connection. At one time, the Seale family, one of the oldest families on the island, lived in Rock Rose, although I must confess I don't think Ann Mira ever did.

Having fallen in love at first sight, Georg Janisch waited seven years before he married Ann Mira Seale, on her twentieth birthday. They had thirteen children, of whom only eight lived into adulthood.

In fact when Georg wrote that letter in 1843, he knew he was dying. *I have not yet reached the fifth decade but the dreadful contrast between tropical heat and icy storms makes all those who are driven here by fate become prematurely old and pass early away.* And he passed on a month later. Ann Mira lived on till 1866, and sadly never saw their firstborn, Hudson Ralph Janisch, become in 1873 the second, but certainly the more famous, island-born Governor, a position he held till his death eleven years later.

Rock Rose today is just a shell, a shadow, its massively thick walls unconvincingly solid. It looks big, but it was only one room wide and three rooms long, with huge fireplaces and great chimney work at each end. There are traces of a staircase, said to have been of magnificent ebony, marked on the rotting plaster, with the reinforcements in place for a landing. On either side of the house are views onto the deeply entrenched headwaters of its neighbouring valleys. Probably the most isolated major house on the island, its natural setting was striking, with barely another habitation in its fields of view.

Long Range, behind the house, has Deep Valley on one side, and Powell's on the other. Make a note of Powell, we'll come across him in Sandy Bay. I've never managed to get into Deep Valley, but it's accurately named. There is a scratch of path squiggling down the cliff end near Stone Tops, but even the fishermen rarely use it today. There's a half decent track down the other valley, passing Powell's Battery at 1000 feet a.s.l, certainly the least used fortification on the island. It was handsomely built in 1804 by Governor Patton, to *close the back door to the island,* though in reality it was here more a cat-flap than a door.

So the east is rather different. Even on the long, big sky slope of Long Range you're still only two miles, as the myna flies, from Hutts Gate, but there is a staggering amount of island on the way. Even if you stayed on the metalled road, and saw only the broader spread of this side, you'd be glad you made it, and it prepares you, as much as anything can prepare you, for Sandy Bay. And if you couldn't make any of the other diversions down valleys or ridges, then you have to go out to Sandy Bay Barn, on the eastern end of the rim of the southern ampitheatre.

It's another of the great walks. But I'll keep it brief, for I'm saving Sandy Bay. Start from the picnic table at Green Hill, then go along the rim, with Powell's on one side and a rocky hillock called Billy Birch, after the lad who in looking after his goats fell to his death from its crags. Go over White Hill, where the winds from two sides meet and cause dust devils, sometimes spinning almost stationary near the hill's summit. People who regularly look across at White Hill believe it is still erupting, quietly of course, "You see White Hill smoking?" Nobody gets worried, it's a kind of mascot for the region.

From a distance Sandy Bay Barn looks like a huge grey slug lying along the end of the rim. But the closer you are, the more it's just rocks blocking the way. But there's a way round and up, a scrape that a rabbit might think twice about, and a Saint would think was a dual carriageway. It skirts below one slug eye, on a slope I'd rather not let on about, picks over a series of rock steps and gains access to the sloping roof of this other, smaller Barn.

Up to the crest and along to the end. Cheat now, for this is the full wonder of Sandy Bay. You're looking right down the southern coast, and no coast on the island is as wildly beautiful. Behind the shores is the ampitheatre of Sandy Bay, its columns and pillars looking different from here. Lot's Wife is flatter, more solid, Frightus Rock is gaunter and less simian, the Asses Ears are broader, and Castle Rock which is usually hidden is like a ragged fairytale cathedral.

It's like being on the roof of the world. And have a look over the end of Sandy Bay Barn. But remember the tale of Darwin's cliff, so best to lie down on your stomach and inch forward. Fourteen hundred feet straight down into the sea. You couldn't get much higher than that with drugs. It has impact, that's for sure. But it's Sandy Bay that draws you back.

This is one of St Helena's most spectacular views, one of those where you can't stop turning again and again, knowing you will never be able to take it in completely, it's just too enormous. It is a wonderful way to see at least one aspect of the totality of Sandy Bay, which it never reveals when you're inside. So there you are, I started this chapter with Georg Janisch's love story, and I've finished on Sandy Bay, one of mine.

# CHAPTER 14

## A BACKWAY UP COUNTRY

*Little glens and dells, from whose beauty one would almost be tempted to pronounce them the favourite haunts of fairies.*
James Johnson, visiting in HMS *Caroline*, around 1800 (in Teale)

The Barnes Road is the quietest way to go up country, a hidden short cut out of town, but you can only walk it. A good way to find it is to use the other way through town, the Run. That's hidden, and you can only walk that too. Main Street, running up the valley from the seaside to the hospital, is peaceful enough, although one old lady complained to me that the pollution from so many cars was getting out of hand. But tucked away in the bottom of the valley is a sort of country lane, well, for for part of its way.

Chapel Valley was the obvious place for the early navigators to anchor, because of the permanent stream. All the water that drains off the north-western end of the Peaks is channelled into James Valley. So although Jamestown settles for ten inches or so of rain a year, the more than forty inches that fall on the Peaks ensure the year long supply in town. The stream flowing through town was known as the Run, and for long has been channelled in a stone and cemented 'bed'.

You can see bits of the Run when it appears from under the Market, and flows along the side of Narra Backs, until it runs into the sea close to West Rocks. The dog-leg in Main Street, the plain bit of road with its shops outside the Market, is called The Bridge. With not even a hint of water in sight, you may have wondered why. It's obvious when you know that the Run is hidden underneath. And you find the start of the almost private, shaded walkway through town, from the little passage behind The Standard.

But this stretch is a bit 'urban,' lots of concrete and stone retaining walls, so further up Napoleon Street, you can take the side lane down towards The Haven. The lane crosses the Run, over a bridge to join Main Street at Seale's Corner, which is the nightime locale of the town's best known white lady.

So the pleasant backwater bit of the Run is from the haunts of Free Molly up to the Hospital. Hidden from town, there are trees and shrubs, the succulent samphire, a few bananas and papayas. Above are cottages and the rubble brown sides of Munden's Hill, the wall of Side Path, already high above skirting its way out of the valley. And here the character of town comes down a bit to join the Run. Houses are a mixture of all styles, or none, original stone buildings with corrugated and wooden extensions. Houses after all are for living in, not for any civic display.

There are some council flats, balconies festooned with plants and washing. Patches of space are higgledy-piggledy fenced for vegetables and flowers, fuchsias, ferns, green chilis, even domesticated lantana would you believe. There are some big trees, mangoes, a banyan, and a mighty one is "Mahugamy, Sir," says a small boy as I stand there looking puzzled. These are the remnants of the old Botanic Gardens, though not necessarily the one looked after by Mr Porteous.

The Run is very mixed in its messages, one minute it looks a confused northern Mediterranean, oleanders, acacias with bunches of small pink berries, the island's 'pepper tree,' patches of pumpkin creepers, wattle, patches of yams.

Then there's Brick House, two storeys turn of the century desirable residence, straight out of the Home Counties. They say it was built from bricks left over from the desalination plant in Rupert's, but the colour seems wrong. They say the original house at Kinghurst, near the Cathedral and now a Community Centre, was also built of bricks from the same source. It's also said that Kinghurst was the only, or the first, house built (rebuilt?) entirely by Boer prisoners-of-war; the date's right and the bricks are the right colour. It's not only The Run that's very mixed in its messages.....

Palm Villa was the house where Governor Hudson Ralph Janisch lived. Because he was island born, they wouldn't let him stay in Plantation House!

Climb out of the Run by the hospital. Its services, and medical provision in general, are very fair, with four doctors, a fully trained nursing staff, and a resident dentist. Most districts have their own clinics too, twice a week or so. Serious cases must of course go to Cape Town or Britain. Provision of home care for the elderly or disabled appears good too. It's odd in the early morning, walking along some half lost stretch of country lane and finding a young, smartly uniformed, health worker getting out of her car for her daily visit on old Mrs So and so.

Up the lane and across New Bridge is 'the dam', haunt of a motley variety of ducks, a cement pond partly overgrown with yams. Years ago it was emptied once or twice daily to flush the Run. After all, the Run was then the only drain for a crowded town, full of people and cattle and horses. Lucky the town was so narrow. The dam was also where town kids used to learn the rudiments of swimming, before they took to the sea.

You're now on the road that goes up Constitution Hill, a quick way to The Briars. Nice road, broad, airy, birds and assorted flowers, fine view of the sheer valley side under High Knoll. With the town all but disappeared downstream, it's like a lane along a country valley, with vegetable gardens and mango orchards in the valley bottom, and relic stone walls, even terraces, of the gardens that much earlier fed the town.

Perhaps the best known of the old houses is Maldivia. It may have started life as the town's first hospital, and it may well have had the town's best gardens for close to two centuries. It earned its present name in 1735, when a group of Maldive islanders were brought to the island. They'd been rescued from an open boat drifting in the Indian Ocean. That's very kind, thank you, they said and then were put to repayment work building the gardens, and so left their name behind.

In 1815, it was the Town Major's town house, Major Hodson, and during Cockburn's few months in charge of Napoleon, the Council meetings were held here. It was cooler, breezier, than the humid town, and a lot less smelly. Its gardens are still reknowned on the island for their flowers, fruit, especially mangoes, and vegetables. In season the jacarandas are brilliant, and there are night blooming Cereus, too.

The Barnes Road really starts above the tanks holding the town's water supply, at Chubb's Spring. You're immediately below The Briars, so be patient with the racket of the mynas as they strut their stuff. Their ancestors, five of them, were released from The Briars in 1885. They are the common myna of India (*Acridotheres tristis*). Hill mynas from India had been introduced in 1829, but these darker birds, better known as talking cage birds, never bred. So the island settled for the common variety, which became a pretty dominant inhabitant. They're also great mimics. They can't do humans very well, but they're remarkably good at other birds, and goats, and they confuse and infuriate cats and donkeys.

You have to keep your wits about you, for at a bend an overgrown side track, marked only with a large rock, disappears into the foliage and clinking of frogs of a little valley on the side of Peak Hill. This is Barnes' Road *pukka*, the fifth way out of James Valley. There was no way out of upper James Valley, because the valley is terminated by the spectacular Heart-shaped Waterfall, and the walls are vertical, and several hundred feet high. So although there was a track up the side of Peak Hill, a proper way was needed. But when the Barnes Road was built is open to question.

The road wasn't there when Napoleon was at The Briars, and it must have been after 1816, for it's not on the beautifully detailed Admiralty map of that year. An archival trawl suggests it is after the island passed to the Crown, possibly as late as 1849. Apparently there was a Major Barnes as island engineer, but the restricted budget of those decades doesn't offer much support for such a beautifully engineered and finished right of way.

At the start the Road probably followed the line of the Peak Hill Road, using Black Bridge which long predates Barnes. On March 20th, 1809, in a duel fought here, Lieutenant Stephen Young, aged 31, was killed. Lieutenant Robert Wright fired his pistol hitting Young, who *expired after breathing two or three times and never uttered a syllable.* Wright was unmoved and went up to the fallen combatant: *Young, speak - are you dying? Young, you must die, you ought to have known me better.*

The Reverend Jones refused to conduct a service for one

killed in a duel. So Major Hodson *read the Funeral Service over the deceased* in Church, and William Burchell, schoolteacher and accomplished naturalist, who was also the church organist, hurried there, *to be ready with some melancholy piece of music.* Young was buried the same day. Burchell was also in on the inquest, at which a charge of *wilful murder* was levelled against Wright. At the subsequent trial, legal technicalities resulted in Wright being found not guilty.

The road, much overgrown at the start, gradually reappears. It runs initially through low old trees, their canopies closing it into a humid tunnel. Built with retaining walls and stone 'paving', it winds steeply up the side of Peak Hill. As the vegetation thins and the views open out, it leaves the flank of Peak Hill to climb proudly round the exposed edge of the next ridge.

High Knoll is high above, and buried in thick foliage below is Cat Hole. Thc Heart-shaped Waterfall, three hundred feet high, and looking much less like a Valentine card close to, plays hide and seek with the ridge, aloes and prickly pear. The Briars is now behind and below, with a lovely view onto the Pavilion. Sections of the reassuring protective wall of heavy basalt blocks, have started falling away.

Barnes Road, its left over flowers and plants, and its striking views, was the quickest way up country, on foot or horseback. Above the severe lava cliffs, it went quickly into pastures, woods and farmlands. More importantly though, it had brought you onto Francis Plain, then very much a military area.

But once the military passed away, its meadow became the main focus of the island's cricket and football. It is a magnificent setting for sports, as indeed it is for the island's modern Prince Andrew Secondary School. Sportsfields with panoramas like this, the north of the island from High Knoll right across to The Barn, don't come too often.

From here, that view puts High Knoll into perspective for its massively undeveloped potential. A fort sits on top of a stark conical hill, with a precipice on one side. It overlooks the approaches to the island, its main landing, its capital, and huge areas of its interior.

Militarily it had major drawbacks, in that it couldn't come into action until invaders had landed and wished to deal with it in their own time. It's odd how little is generally known of High Knoll's early years. There is even one school of thought that suggests the fort might have been more for protection from internal island strife - there were enough mutinies to offer some support for this.

What a setting for one of Ludwig II's fairytale castles! But none of the Governors had Ludwig's romantic creativity, and they certainly didn't have his money. No, a *Neuschwanstein* on High Knoll would have been wonderful. Maybe a Disneyland version, if tourism really picks up .....?

Francis Plain, at almost 1500 feet, had a long military past. It was the home of the St Helena Militia, founded in 1673, becoming the St Helena Volunteers in 1802, and only disbanded in 1874. The Militia had been inspected annually for generations on the Plain by the Governor, as Commander in Chief of the island's armed forces. It was a great ritual. The event was followed by a large celebratory lunch, for the entire island. It may well have been the event on which the Island Sports was later modelled.

The Annual Schools Sports Day, traditionally held on January 1st, was certainly the event that brought together the largest collection of the population. People were there in strength from early morning, for an action packed day of parental culinary celebrations, and the catching up with people and gossip from all over the island. The Governor was there, chatting to all and sundry. His wife was there, presenting prizes and medals. The Bishop was there. It was a good day, and usually a warm one. People could get quite exhausted sitting, drinking beer, eating substantial quantities of curry and plo, and, should time allow, watching energetic children racing round the Plain. For reasons certainly unclear to me, the great island get together has joined the Plain's long military role as history.

The Plain is now flatter than it was, it used to be noticeably domed. But a major earth moving project in the late 1970s, part of the construction of the Prince Andrew school, undertook a spot of levelling. This improved the facility, certainly for cricket, though not necessarily for the technicalities of local football. The original curvature had been such that parts of the pitch were almost invisible from others. So in those olden days, great advantage could be gained from 'coming over' or 'playing up the hill', after luring the opposition into a carefully choreographed ambush.

Prince Andrew's is a school anyone anywhere could be proud of. In fact the school system, for a population this small, and geographically dispersed, is rather good. Prince Andrew's serves the entire secondary school population of the island. Outlying schools are primary, and are closing gradually as the school-going population declines, and many children are bused to and from school each day. Local mixed age schools with local teachers are long gone, and the Environmental Centre in Sandy Bay, and some of the Community centres elsewhere, are re-cycled descendants.

The facilities in Prince Andrew's provide a fitting establishment for the young people, and they and the island are justifiably proud of it. But it's what happens after that is increasingly worrying the young people.

In spite of strenuous programmes of overseas training, there are still a significant number of expatriate teachers. Salaries for teachers on the island are also low, compared to Ascension or the Falklands, or compared with other jobs in the UK. This is a similar problem with nursing staff at the hospital. So there is a steady, and costly, erosion of numbers, especially in overseas trained staff.

For the students, there is only a limited range of A-levels on offer. There is also a reduction in numbers of students staying on for them, and it's hard to say which is chicken and which is egg. If young people are to stay on the island, they require training, much of which is only available overseas, so another chicken and egg dynamic is established. And in spite of professed commitments to vocational training, there is little offered and very few youngsters doing any.

The future of the entire educational structure is a major problem now that the population is decreasing rapidly through migration. The number of births has been falling for some time, and today is barely a third of what it was fifteen years ago.

Encompassed within Prince Andrew's is the older Francis Plain House, now the Teachers' Building with work rooms, kitchen, and staff common room with its original fireplace. It's worth a moment, for in the last decade of the nineteenth century, this was briefly the home, and hearth, of the exiled Chief Dinizulu and some of his entourage.

After the Zulu War, Cetewayo, the last great Chief, was replaced, and the Zulu nation broken up. In 1890, his son, Dinizulu, with a family group including two uncles and a number of his wives and children, arrived on the island. He was an easy detainee, a popular one with the islanders, who unlike his uncles, rapidly adopted western ways. He learned English, took to western food and clothing, he studied the latest fashions, and music, even learning to play the piano.

The party was originally housed at Rosemary Hall, which Dinizulu claimed was too wet. Then it moved to Maldivia, which his uncles liked but he didn't, so he ended up at Francis Plain House. It was here that he entertained the Bishop of Zululand, visiting the island in 1896, to tea and cucumber sandwiches on the lawn. In December 1897, the entire party were packed up and returned to Africa. Several of his children were born on the island. Two of them died here, and are buried in the cemetery of the Cathedral. And there was at least one child born from liaisons with island women.

Forget the striking seaward view from Francis Plain, you came here to get up country and the rest of the island is yours. You can make for the east, or go over The Peaks to Sandy Bay, or head for the west road. You can go anywhere from Francis Plain, and it so easy to get to. But there's no real need to go very far at all.

All round the Plain, west to Plantation House, behind to the slopes of The Peaks, and east to Hutts Gate, is a long domesticated countryside. I'm not sure about Mr Johnson's fairies, but he got the feel pretty well, and that was two hundred years ago. It still has little farms, lichened stone field walls, duck-ponds, the ever changing mix of flowers and trees, chickens and vegetables, black and white cattle, and glades, even hillsides, of arum lilies.

Somewhat subdued, a bit British, this scenery is so soft compared to the wilder outer fringes, that you don't think to question that the boundary fences are of giant thorn trees, break off a branch, stick it in the ground and it grows. You accept distant skylines of tree ferns, you accept fairy terns puzzling over you, cardinals and canaries. It's a land of winding lanes, copses of pines and bananas, chinking frogs and yams, sheep and hibiscus hedges. It's so easy to get lost in time on the island, and this is the best place to get lost in somewhere else's geographies.

And yes, it *is* a chapel (Baptist) with a bell-cote tower up on that slope. It's Knollcombes, and close by is the Boer Cemetery. Unlike the irregular graves of the older cemetery at Knollcombes, those in the Boer Cemetery are laid out in rows with military precision. They are maintained by the South African war graves authorities. They are in two plots on the steep hillside, 40 above the path, and 121 below. The graves have concrete surrounds and their precision is sprinkled naturally with golden everlasting daisies, originally sent, it is said, by Lady Holland as a gift to Napoleon to remind him of his time with Josephine at Malmaison.

At the bottom of the rows of graves are two granite obelisks, the first inscribed in Dutch *Gedenksteen Ter gadachtenis aan de overleden Republikeinsche Krygsgevangenen opgerricht,* lists 109 dead, their ages from 17 to 68. The second is English: *In Memory of the prisoners or war whose names are inscribed hereunder who died at St Helena. Erected by the Government of the Union of South Africa 1913. They that sow in tears shall reap in joy*, and 71 names are listed. The totals don't tally, one with the other, or with the graves, of those who died on the island.

Down the valley, you can see the dark bulk of the fortress of High Knoll on one side, shutting off the views of sea and freedom. High Knoll was where the more violent, more truculent prisoners were kept, when the majority were in the two camps, many even working and travelling within the community. It's odd but the fortress appears out of place in the short story of the Boers' imprisonment on the island. This gentle rural setting seems that much more reasonable.

Below the fence of the cemetery, there are pastures and fields, and a line of thorn trees. It is so quiet, you can hear the cows tearing the grass as they feed. There are little wooden fences, painted white, and you expect a small child on a pony out jumping them. It is very peaceful, trees and flowers abound, doves walking everywhere, their incessant cooing interspersed with the farmyard noises. If the dead can indeed rest in peace, then this rural peace is a fitting setting for those from the largely farmers' army.

# CHAPTER 15

## INTERIOR TREASURES

*When the sun had somewhat subsided, I .... went with the Governor up the road to Ladder-hill .... About six we reached Plantation house, a neat, thoroughly English house .... As I have been driven in a Cape of Good Hope Wagon, eight in hand, and dragged up Ladder-hill in the St Helena Government coach by six bullocks, I may flatter myself that I have known two of the most singular conveyances on this planet.*

Sir James Mackintosh, late Recorder of Bombay, visiting in 1812

It's so much easier now, going up to Plantation House, the journey may not be as distinctive, but it's still full of surprises. It's a continuous climb from town, Ladder Hill, and Half Tree Hollow, until you breast the col which leads to High Knoll.

It is the first really sudden change on the island. One moment, indeed several rather long moments, through barren volcanic dust and rubble, then the road side falls away into a valley of fields and farms, gardens and hedges and coppices, everything green and domestic. Pastures stretch up towards the Peaks, and the intensity and variations of the greens increase. You've left the barren volcano behind you, you may even have left the island behind and arrived somewhere else.

This is now temperate hill country. Perhaps the upper reaches are too lush for it to be Scotland or Wales, possibly it's the Pyrenees or north Italy. Before you can make up your mind as you drive on a few hundred yards, it has completely changed again. Pine woods have closed in on you, and the two white, red-roofed cottages, are the White Gate to Plantation.

Continue along a lane tunnelled through the trees, then the blinkers are suddenly removed and the world spreads wide again, from wooded hillsides, past the facade of the house, across lawns, over gardens and trees, and onto the vast ocean. Plantation House certainly has a theatrical setting. Melliss described it as *a mansion with its undulating and well-wooded park.*

It is a lovely two-storey Regency house, stone-built and stuccoed white and green. It is large by island standards, but not in terms of 'plantation' houses you might conjure from *Gone With the Wind*. Governor Brooke started the present Plantation House, at the end of the eighteenth century, after endless fights over costs, with the Court of Directors, and it was substantially enlarged by Sir Hudson Lowe.

It has thirty five rooms, and the *heart of the house* is the library, which was one of Lowe's additions, with 2000 volumes, many from the Company days. There is lovely furniture, beautiful woodwork, paintings of royalty, and old prints. The large chandelier in the dining room was made from two smaller ones, one of which came from Longwood House. Hudson Lowe removed some of the better pieces of furniture from Longwood, and although they may have gone temporarily to Plantation, most left with him to go back to England.

The house stands in some hundred acres of grounds. There are lawns and gardens, but most is wooded. Old prints and maps show various features which have disappeared, a house for the Chinese masons, a dairy, a bakery. Below the vegetable gardens, in a steepish valley, was Plantation Square, originally known as Black Square, for the barracks there for the Company slaves. There was a tiny gardener's house, known as Garden Cottage. In 1816, it provided lodging in his first few weeks on the island, for Major Gorrequer, Lowe's Military Secretary.

Then, much against his will, Gorrequer was moved into the house, into a room which he described as little more than a closet. He missed the privacy of his cottage in the garden, for in the house he was permanently at Lowe's call. Gorrequer moaned incessantly about his personal circumstances, and Lowe's dictation and demands for drafts, drafts and re-drafts. *There was not a black man, not a slave on the island who had not more relaxation than I had.*

Gorrequer didn't like Georg Janisch, usually referring to him as *Teutonic*. He didn't like it that Lowe liked Janisch's work. In 1818, he wrote: *He* [Lowe] *appointed young Janisch to a situation of clerk when he could not work,* adding a little later that he *wrote ten times more like a clerk and not the twentieth part so well.*

But to be fair, Gorrequer didn't really like anybody. His secret diary was in a private code, and everyone had nicknames, often more than one. Lowe was *The Chief*, the head of the Engineers was *Old Brick and Mortar*, Colonel Nicol was *Constipation*. Saul Solomon, the founder of Solomons, was *Sapient King of Hebrews*, and Sir William Doveton, pillar of island society, was *Weeping William*, or *Old Yam Knight*. The diary makes entertaining, outrageous on occasions, obscure on others, and generally rather bitchy, reading. Gorrequer certainly had little time for Napoleon. The entry for May 5th 1821, is one of the longest in his diary, yet Napoleon's death is not mentioned. But the next day, it is mentioned when he refers to him as *defunct Neighbour*.

On the lawns are a number of giant land tortoises, brought in originally from islands in the Indian Ocean. The first arrived in about 1860, but there have been top-ups several times since. Collectively or individually, they are still known as Jonathan, a name given to an individual, later discovered to be female, in the 1930s, by governor Sir Spenser Davies.

If Plantation House is lovely, its woods are a glory. From earliest times, the Governor's land received trees and plants introduced piecemeal for one good intention or another. But from the arrival of Governor Beatson, the first of the great agricultural and forestry experimenters, in 1808, Plantation became for a while an intentional repository for an extraordinary mix of trees from all corners of the world.

The forest grew with one of these from here, half a dozen of those from there, a small trial plantation of this, and a collector's item of that, from somewhere else, no matter. Bring me this, couldn't we develop that? Requests went out, gifts from visitors came in. Try this, try that, grow more, bigger, better, faster, hardier, tastier, and end up with two, nearly three, centuries of botanic trial and fancy.

There is an old track, broad enough for a carriage, heading west from the house into the thick trees. It was almost certainly the one used by the ghostly carriage that night in 1890. It is slightly humid, shaded, warm and restful, it is almost breezeless, but not quite.

There are trees of all heights, shapes, colours. The floor is a battleground for leaves, needles, cones, fungi, beetles, ants. There are thickets of wild ginger, rolling humps of ferns and mosses, conifer saplings, trunks so thick and high you forget they are trees, lowest branches so far above your head they couldn't possibly belong to the trunks.

There are tree stumps large enough, and high enough, to lay the table for lunch, or dinner. Drag up a log, rays of sunlight on crystal glasses and Napoleon's Sèvres porcelain, not at all out of place in this dream of the eyes and the mind. It is very, very beautiful. Paths and stone steps are half buried in the detritus from the canopy, hollows and shaded groves, overgrown water gardens, and sounds of streams and frogs, averdevats tinkling unseen in patches of dappled sunshine. There is even the fussing of fairy terns, fluttering through the branches of the high canopy like slow albino bats.

There are so few signs or sights or apparent hands of humans. Away from and below the track are groves of bamboos, some over fifty magnificent feet high, huge elegantly curving 'poles' dappled golden in the sunlight, and leaves shimmering in so many shades of silver. There is natural light of half a dozen textures, filtered through one canopy, scattered by the false ceiling of fronds of the next. So many different leaves and seeds, where do they all come from? This is truly a setting from the Fairie Queen, and like the poem, it is phantasmal, even before you find the two graves.

Or at least you find the soft honey coloured, imported stones, one with a skull and two bones either side, not crossed, with an arrow through each. The writing has all but disappeared, worn away so delicately by two centuries of falling pine needles, and mist. *Here lieth the Body of Margaret Wife of Francis Butcher Who Departed this life November .... 1777.* The other stone is headed with a scroll, a cleaver and two knives (or could one be a bradawl?), their handles crossing, and no script left. These are the Butcher graves, apparently from their name, not necessarily from the cleaver.

Who they were, why they are here, nobody knows, but the setting is amazing. It's a gigantic dell, if such can exist, like the inside of a cathedral, you can hear the leaves dropping. Curtains of bamboos under the higher canopy of massive conifers, the wide roots of cork oaks fingering across the deep litter of leaves and fallen flowers. One moment the skull is at the end of a long straight sunbeam, the next it is resting softly shaded, in the dappled filtered light. It is a wonderful piece of forest, truly magical. This is indeed a place of elves in its softly scented silence.

A forestry consultant at the Agriculture and Forestry Department told me it would take months, maybe a year, to do a proper inventory of the trees in Plantation's woods. I can believe that. And wouldn't it be something special? But sadly there is still a real world out there, and we must return.

On the road, a couple of hundred yards beyond White Gate, or the same distance on the Governor's private path from the back door of Plantation, is the Cathedral. It was started in 1850, on the site of the earlier Country Church, in a rural wooded setting, pastoral in every sense of the word. If the woods of Plantation House are a history of the British Empire's global botanic quest, the Cathedral cemetery is a history of its people and their everyday lives.

Not all of the island's first settlers and later 'planters' lived in such home county surroundings. Many, especially into the nineteenth century, were in lands where the island's more rugged character was all too obvious, in views and in the paucity of trees and fertile soil. So here was a place suitable for laying their mortal remains to rest.

Suitable too, for the soldiers of the garrison, sailors from the ocean vastnesses, and those who would have been visitors en route to India and further east. Or more usually those en route home on furlough from sickness, or on retirement at the end of long years in the tropics. Here was the essence of the island and her people, the isolated rock in the ocean offering food and shelter, and for many travellers, this almost English churchyard, offering the succour of a final resting place.

In those early decades of the colony, and its disparate collection of settlers, the moral fibre was hopefully held together by an equally disparate collection of clergymen. Gilbert Martineau, ever the succinct reporter, summed them up: *God moves in a mysterious way, and it is impossible to explain the succession, uninterrupted for a century, of reverends who were for the most part rogues, crooks, fornicators and quarrel-mongers.*

Probably the best known of the chaplains was the Reverend Richard Boys, who spent more than a decade from 1812, trying to preserve, or instill, that moral fibre. But Martineau felt that Boys' eccentric, irascible, vitriolic even, behaviour, *bore the stamp of that intransigent absolution commonly seen in a tiny community where mediocre minds quarrel over crumbs of power.* Martineau knew the situation all too well, having spent more than thirty years on the island. It says a great deal for the excellence of Frances Partridge's translation, in that I can hear Gilbert Martineau's voice as I copy those sentences.

Although Boys and his exchanges were colourful, I have a lot of time for the earlier figure of the Rev John Jones, who arrived on the island in 1719. Perhaps he was the start of Martineau's century. Rev Jones kicked off pretty sharply, for in the Council records that same year, we learn that : *Mr Tovey complains of Parson Jones who peeled off his gown and struck him, the said Tovey, with his fist in one of his eyes which is now swollen.* Mr Jones explained that Tovey had called him a *Scoundrell,* admitted striking him, apologized and shook hands. But Parson Jones' behaviour, starting badly, clearly got worse, for within months, he was confined to his quarters to await a suitable ship on which he could be 'transported'.

The records are lengthy and it would seem that Rev Jones had little time for the government of the island, for people, indeed perhaps for the workings of Christianity in general. But he had his supporters, and the Council didn't take kindly to them either. His defenders were taken into Custody, some were bound over, two men were fined £5 each, and a man and a woman were sent to the pillory, specially set up in the centre of town. The lady was a Mrs Southam, who later in the records refused to take delivery of letters from the Marshal, shouting that *if he left them there she would make Bumpapers of them.*

The cemetery is large, having continued from one church building to the next. It stretches over a large tract of hillside, in several ill-defined sections, this one in use, that one older, those bits older still, overgrown with brambles, nasturtiums, ferns, buddleia, dandelions, even the dying remnant of an oak tree. There are firs festooned with lichen, new paths in places, wallflowers, thin dark green cypresses, roses, yews, ankle-deep leaf mould and tangled undergrowth. There are fresh flowers on many graves, even nineteenth century ones. There are simple graves, child-size graves, ornamental mausoleums, and fenced family plots. Just wander, dip into so many personal histories.

In the section in use are all the present island names. In the older bits are more of the early settlers; Bagley 1793, de Fountain, Mason 1817, Pritchard, Harper 1762, Greentree, Robinson, Torbett, Lambe *Planter of this Island*, and Seale. Henry Porteous is buried here. Sir William Doveton, who died aged 90 in 1843, is in the family plot, with his wife, who died in 1807, aged 33. Which is why his married daughter helped him entertain Napoleon to breakfast.

Many regiments are remembered here, First Punjab, Coldstream Guards, Royal Field Artillery, St Helena Volunteer Rifles, Royal Marines Light Infantry, St Helena Home Guard, Imperial Yeomanry, Gloster, Royal Sussex, and the Royal Engineers. Selecting just one, a composite, cracking sarcophagus to six of those engineers, one *accidentally drowned bathing,* another was killed by falling over the West Rocks at Ladder Hill Barracks, one corporal died of *Typhoid fever,* and a second was killed in the quarry at Half Tree Hollow.

An old man guides me to the graves of two of Chief Dinizulu's children who were born on the island. They are almost lost, a rare demonstration of the remarkable democracy of death, in a small simple grave: *In memory of Unomfino, died May 8th 1891 aged four months, also Umohlozana died March 17th 1894 aged three years. Children of Dinizulu. Thy will be done.*

And what an unfortunate event is recorded on another: *In Memory of Henry Yates Weston High Sheriff of this island Died 26th February 1862, from the effects of an accident when he was on his way to the consecration of St Matthew's Church at Hutt Gate aged 52 years.* What was the saying that Gilbert Martineau so liked, about God behaving in strange ways?

This central area is 'old' land, cooler, with adequate rainfall and rich soils. It is a small area, compact yet open at the same time, with innumerable fields on the hillsides, little valleys, copses, pastures, old boundary lines of trees. Although small in area, it is easy to get lost. For the visitor, it all looks the same, or rather it all looks quite different, because all its bits and pieces, of up and down, brook and tree, field or hedge, are mixed in an infinity of ways. So you are sure you have seen this before, been here already, and you haven't. Long before you know it yourself, you are lost, or puzzled, or both.

In the outer circuit of the island, there are no trees, so you have long lines of sight. You might be lost, but you can see where you are, if you follow my reasoning. But here, with so many trees, you only have time to settle on a particular rock, or tree, or patch of grass with a cow, as a landmark, when it disappears or changes its appearance because you've walked half a dozen paces. But you can't be lost for long, and there's always the cathedral to fall back to.

Hidden away in the middle of all this is Scotland, the headquarters of the island's Department of Agriculture and Forestry. Does it look like Scotland? Well it might. But it's more mundane than that, the house was built on land purchased by one John Scott in 1834!

The open fields and experimental plots, for vegetables, flowers, trees, grasses and endemic species, of the Agricultural Station roll round the slopes. It's warm, sheltered by the higher ground crowned with the Cathedral. The sawmill is close by, and there is a beautiful photo of it, from the early part of this century, with a caption: *The sawing of timber is undertaken in the field called the Laundry, where the Department's donkeys graze.* Were there really such times ... ?

Along the edge of the sheds of stored timber, someone will show you a hole in the fence. A stumble or two down the bank finds a path, gloomy in its thick, forest cover. Somewhere along the path is a rocky crag on the valley side, and by a process of trial and error you find it, and break out of the gloom into the sunshine on the crag. It's the finest view of Plantation House, surrounded by its forest. It is a beautiful view, one that would stand with the finery and character of such buildings anywhere in the world. And you ask yourself, as at so many other places, how can so many views so utterly different end up on this one small island?

It is hard to believe that a few hundred yards down the ridge, had you kept going, you would have arrived at the island's outer fringe of rocks and dust and prickly pear. You'd have found the road round from Half Tree Hollow, which connects all kinds of places I hardly know, because the good soil, and all that grows on it, completely hides the geology! New Ground, Cleugh's Plain, and further on to Guinea Grass, Terrace Knoll, Crack Plain, Rosemary Hall and Plain, Rural Retreat, and Farm Lodge, which is now an hotel. The place names are such far calls from the barren island fringes.

It is from Crack Plain that you can go down Lemon Valley. There is a reasonable enough path down, which starts in rural greenery, but steep brown rock sides quickly close in. For a very short while there is a bit of shade from trees, spoor, pepper, and silky oak, but then the path is bare, the traditional scratch in the lavas, broken rocks clattering and clinking as you make your way down.

Lemon Valley has a permanent stream with excellent water. For centuries, ships filled their casks here for the next two month leg of their voyage. Edmund Halley is better known for his observatory and his mist-interrupted viewings of the southern stars a quarter of a century earlier, but he anchored here in Lemon Valley in 1700.

He had returned to the island, commanding the *Paramore* pink, supposedly the only civilian to be given command of a Royal Navy warship. He was on his way home, having led a scientific expedition sailing as far south as it could get (they reached latitude 52 degrees). He took in water at Lemon Valley, and a few days later found it murky, because it had been raining up country. So he diverted to Trindade to get clean water, and while he was about it he claimed the island, temporarily, for Britain! There's so much more to Edmund Halley than his comet.

Close to the bottom of the valley, are the ruins of two or three stone buildings. The old quarantine station was down here, and from 1840, the valley was used for sheltering liberated slaves, mainly women and children while the men were kept in Rupert's. With part of the garrison down here, and gunners for the batteries, it must have been congested as well as damnably hot.

But it's very pleasant on the shingle beach, beneath the wall, another good spot for a picnic. Very peaceful, just the sea to watch, mynas in the valley behind to listen to. The wild mango has bunches of little berries. At the top of the valley they were green, here at the bottom it is so much hotter they're already red.

Lemon Valley is a popular place to visit from Jamestown, but most people come by boat. You can bar-b-que, and swim and use the rough landing stage to dive from. There is even an excursion to build up your appetite, to another Half Moon battery, which is in fact almost a complete circle. Beautiful basalt masonry and views along the coast from Sugarloaf one way to Horse Pasture Point the other.

The valley may be hot, but it grows good prickly pear, the fruit of which, tungies, are refreshing in season. Choose the yellow-green ones, carefully brush off the tiny, soft as velvet looking spines, peel the skin off and eat the pale grey-green flesh. It's packed with black seeds, so you start by spitting them out, but it's a waste of time, and you just swallow the rest. The flesh is sweet with a delicate flavour, not at all cloying or watery, but fresh and clean.

There's a path here, so it's all right, but moving randomly through prickly pear is best avoided. The big spines are bad, but they're so horrid you automatically recoil. Infinitely worse are those hair-like little tufts, on the fruit, or new paddles. They are as insidious as they are invisible, once they are in whatever part of your anatomy they've selected. Tweezers and patience, and perhaps a close friend, can remove a lot, but weeks later newly emergent pimples remind you of the longer term effects of your fleeting brush with nature.

A bug (*Cactoblastis cactorum*) was introduced in the 1980s to attack the prickly pear, and its impact is skeletally evident all over the island. For a while the prickly pear may have been worried, but it quickly held its own again and is now extending its cover, making some less accessible parts even more difficult to get through. Another bug, brought in earlier, against lantana had almost worked, and in the '90s the bushes had almost disappeared. Ten years on though, and it's making a colourful if aggravating resurgence.

Back in the greenery, just above where the path started, is the pine-covered knoll of Mount Eternity, one side of which was used as a slave cemetery. And here starts Friar's Ridge, the straightest and narrowest ridge on the island. Lemon Valley is one side, and Friar's Valley is the other. In places it is only a few feet wide. It gets its name from a natural rock sculpture, not far below the hillock. It is the stone figure of a cowled friar, standing on the razor edge of the divide. Melliss gives a lovely account of how he got there.

Where this rock now stands, there used to be a chapel with a Franciscan priest who was the epitome of piety and humility. He carried out acts of charity and benevolence, he administered to the sick and the oppressed, he interceded between harsh masters and threatened slaves.

Not far from the chapel was a cottage wherein lived a beautiful young woman. The first time the friar saw her, she had been tending goats on Goat Pound Ridge. But the animals had scattered, and she was at a loss to know what to do. The good priest knew just what to do, and collected them all up, and as she dried her tears she smiled her gratitude. In time, the priest's *senses became enthralled by the surpassing beauty of a mountain nymph*, and he sought her out as she wandered the hills with her goats.

Eventually he told her of his love, and asked her to marry him. She agreed, but her father insisted that he renounce his creed and become of her faith, and until he had made up his mind he forbade the two to see each other. The conditions were harsh and hard, but soon the priest broke his vows, and love triumphed.

The wedding was arranged, and the father-in-law-to-be insisted the ceremony be conducted in the priest's own chapel. The bride, more beautiful than ever, and her attendant maidens, stood by the altar. The service was read, and just as the priest clasped his bride's hand there was a terrible crash.

The rocks were rent asunder, and the chapel and all it contained disappeared down a crevasse for ever. *In its place stands the gaunt image of the grim friar, an example and a sad warning to those who suffer their evil passions to prevail over their better judgement.* I imagine that the Reverend Boys would have welcomed such a display of righteousness.

PLATE 17

TOP LEFT: SPORTSDAY ON FRANCIS PLAIN BELOW HIGH KNOLL

TOP RIGHT: GRAVE OF DINIZULU'S DAUGHTERS, THE CATHEDRAL

BTM: UP COUNTRY AND THE PEAKS BEYOND HIGH KNOLL

Plate 18

Top left: The Butcher graves

Top right: Friar's Ridge and the Friar

Btm: Plantation House

PLATE 19
TOP: THE BOER CEMETERY, KNOLLCOMBES
BTM: ENDEMIC SMALL BELLFLOWER (*WAHLENBERGIA ANGUSTIFOLIA*)

PLATE 20

TOP: ENDEMIC TREE FERNS (*DICKSONIA ARBORESCENS*) & BLACK CABBAGE TREES

BTM: ENDEMIC BLACK CABBAGE TREE (*MELANODENDRON INTEGRIFOLIUM*)

PLATE 21
TOP: HIGH HILL AND AREA ROUND BLUE HILL
BTM: BROAD BOTTOM

PLATE 22
TOP LEFT: LUFFKINS AND RIM OF SANDY BAY
TOP RIGHT: LOT AND SANDY BAY BAPTIST CHAPEL
BTM: MOUNT PLEASANT

PLATE 23

TOP: FRIGHTUS ROCK, ASSES EARS, MAN O' WAR ROOST, LOT'S WIFE

BTM: SANDY BAY BEACH FROM HORSE'S HEAD

PLATE 24

TOP: BATTERY BELOW THE BAPTIST CHAPEL

BTM: FORTIFICATIONS AT HORSE'S HEAD

Plate 25
Top: Sandy Bay: Lot and Riding Stones Hill
Btm: Lot and Lot's Wife

Plate 26

Top: Centre of the volcano from Lot's Wife's Ponds

Btm: Man o' War Roost and inland cliffs

Plate 27

Top left: Lot's Wife's Ponds towards the Asses Ears

Top right: The back of Frightus Rock with Gary Stevens

Btm: Frightus Rock

PLATE 28
ENDEMIC OLD FATHER LIVE FOREVER (*PELARGONIUM COTYLEDONIS*)

Plate 29

Top left: Endemic Salad Plant (*Hypertelis acida*)

Top right: Speery Island and Manati Bay from Botley's Lay

Btm: Regrowth of endemic Scrubwoods (*Commidendrum rugosum*)

PLATE 30

TOP LEFT: BLACK ROCKS, COAST BELOW CASTLE ROCK PLAIN

TOP RIGHT: MAN AND HORSE CLIFFS FROM MANATI BAY

BTM: SANDY BAY BARN AND SOUTHERN COAST FROM SHARKS BENCH

PLATE 31

TOP: CASTLE ROCK AND SPEERY ISLAND

BTM: MAN AND HORSE TOWARDS HIGH HILL

PLATE 32

TOP: ENDEMIC BABY'S TOES (*HYDRODEA CRYPTANTHA*)

BTM: CALCITE STALACTITES, MANATI BAY TOWARDS DEVIL'S HOLE

# CHAPTER 16

## TREE FERNS IN THE MISTS

*The island of St Helena has many claims to rank as one of the most interesting botanical stations known; almost the whole of its native flowering plants and several of its genera being peculiar.*

Joseph Dalton Hooker, *Erebus* Expedition of 1840

Hooker was good at many things, and understatement was clearly one of them. If I hadn't been so set in my ways in the sixties, I might have been tempted to shift from geology to botany. I'm hopeless with plants, but I was almost overwhelmed by the range of what grew on the island.

Over a thousand species have been introduced, and these completely dominate the island's own flora. But I didn't know that. I'd never lived with semi-tropical plants, so the introduction was stunning. The bougainvillea that then dwarfed the Castle gateway, brilliant hibiscus hedges, jacarandas and flame trees, there was plumbago, canna, oleanders and strelitzia, in each and every direction, and that was just the town square!

And the fruits! Not only had I not tasted them, I'd never heard of most of them. In Britain of the mid-sixties, supermarkets had just begun appearing. They certainly hadn't done away with the concepts of geography or seasons as they have now. Now here I was faced with guavas, Cape gooseberries, half a dozen different kinds of bananas, rose-apples, tree-tomatoes, figs, pineapples, cumquats, loquats, peaches, grenadillas. St Helena clearly hadn't really recognized geography or seasons, either. I couldn't keep up, I was sold. I can't remember their names, relationships, provenance, anything, but I do like flowers and plants of all sorts. And St Helena certainly had all sorts.

Approaching on the RMS in 1995, I was struck by the apparent greening of the island. Nothing too dramatic from several miles out, but the outer fringes, the bottoms of the valleys, were undoubtedly greener. Perhaps this was an optimistic start, but no, it was fully supported once ashore. That was also to do with introduced species, but it was a kind of herald, for so much that was now happening with the, infinitely more important botanically, endemic flora. I was still amazed by the profusion of plants, but it was the endemics that I now found the special attraction.

I was pretty late in the queue. It had impressed Sir Joseph Banks, then only Mister, the wealthy botanist accompanying Captain Cook, on his first great voyage. The *Endeavour* stopped at the island for only three days on its homeward voyage in May, 1771, but Banks collected material for what would become The Royal Botanic Gardens at Kew. The official account of the voyage records: *We stayed here till the 4th to refresh, and Mr Banks improved the time in making the complete circuit of the island and visiting the most remarkable places upon it.*

Hooker visited the island while on the *Erebus* and *Terror* expedition to, and from, the Antarctic in 1840 and 1843. He was so captivated by St Helena's flora, that he would describe them later as *fragments from the wreck of an ancient world.*

There were others too, William Burchell of course, of Fulham and zebra fame, and Dr William Roxburgh, Chief Botanist of the East India Company, come to mind, and of course John Charles Melliss. It is interesting that what impressed Darwin most was the number of *imported* species, *and most of them from England, [so] we see the reason of the British character of the vegetation.* British character? You have to remember that Darwin had been away at sea for five years!

Yet any major description of the endemic plants had to wait till 1875, when it appeared in the remarkable volume by the island-born Melliss. This remained the standard available work, until Quentin Cronk's volume appeared for the new millenium. In the nineties, Michel Martineau, Gilbert's successor as French Consul, and a talented artist, produced two sets of prints of his watercolours of the endemics. These, and the lovely illustrations by Lesley Ninnes in Cronk's book, are wonderful introductions, on paper, to the magic of the endemic flora. On the ground the real plants can be breathtaking.

The terms used are 'indigenous' meaning all the flora that was on the island when it was discovered, and 'endemic', meaning species which are found nowhere else. Indigenous species can occur elsewhere, but endemics are unique, lose one and it's lost from the planet for ever. I seek no forgiveness for spending this time on the great botanists' interests in the St Helena flora, for it is a truly remarkable collection of plants, and a remarkable story. And it has a real life island hero, in George Benjamin.

George Benjamin started off as a donkeyman in the flax industry. He became a forest guard with the A and F Department in the '60s, and developed an eye for, and deep understanding of, the endemic species. He is perhaps best known for finding the last two specimens of ebony, in 1980, on a cliff on the western edge of Sandy Bay. From the cuttings taken from them, several thousand ebony 'bushes' are thriving again across the island. But George found several other species, some thought to be long extinct, the She Cabbage Tree, the St Helena Olive, and the False Gumwood.

Another great traveller of the remote places, with a good eye, is Stedson Stroud, who found the Bastard Gumwood. Then in November1998, he thought a plant he saw in the detritus of giant rocks behind Lot's Wife looked unusual. He was coming up from fishing at Sharks Bench, so he detoured. It *was* unusual, it was a St Helena boxwood, thought to have been extinct for more than a hundred and fifty years.

That the conservation and regeneration of these species, believed already lost, has been possible, was in no small part thanks to George Benjamin. He's retired now, though is as active as ever. He lives at Pounceys, opposite St Paul's School, in the very centre of the island, and his back garden contains some fine examples of his role in conservation. He was awarded the BEM for his outstanding contribution to preserving the endemic flora, and there is now a small garden at Cason's Gate named after him to commemorate his work.

The endemic flora is like so much on St Helena. It is a miracle that it is still there, it is scientifically staggering, it is very beautiful, and you never know when or where you'll come across it. There are 49 endemic plant species, 13 of which are ferns. They cover all the island's geographic variants, though the largest collection of them is on the high ground, particularly The Peaks. But you find plants in the wildest areas, and you can even find them unexpectedly in easy walking areas.

When the island was discovered, it had a flora of all kinds, from succulents in the harsh waterless areas of Sandy Bay, through grasses, ferns and shrubs, to the strange trees and tree ferns of the misty peaks. St Helena boasted a flora that was a time capsule, of plants largely lost on the mainland millions of years ago. Whatever it had received from the continent, had been saved from the depredations of climate change there. Then five hundred years of man were let loose on ten million years of nature.

But how did the flora get here in the first place? Seeds or spores could be washed in by the sea, drifted round the South Atlantic from the shores of southern Africa, theoretically even South America. They could be blown in by the heavy South East Trade winds, again from southern Africa. Exceptionally, they might be brought in by birds visiting the island, in their guts, stuck to mud on their feet or feathers, improbable but not impossible.

Volcanoes are pretty inhospitable when active; molten lava, incandescent ashes, boiling ground waters, acid vapours. But eruptions take place only in certain locations, leaving large areas free of the threat of instant extinction. And eruptions may be separated by hundreds or thousands of years of inactivity. So, more than ten million years ago when the island had established itself above the ocean surface, plants would have started growing on the nutrient rich rocks and ashes. Having got there, these gatecrashers from their different world set about finding their most suitable ecological niches.

The island's position provides it with plenty of rain, and a warm but not searingly hot climate. So, remarkably quickly, a rich vegetation, in numbers of individuals if not necessarily numbers of different species, would have taken over those bits of volcano not actually glowing red hot, ie most of it. Once activity ceased, the vegetation had free range. Seeds and spores would have continued to come in, but that resident population, developed in the first few million years, would be dominant, the lords of the isle.

Almost by chance, we can be sure that they really have been on the island for so long. We have to return to the north-east of the island, to Turk's Cap Ridge. When that huge slide took away the flank of the volcano, it left a broad, saucer-shaped depression behind. Detritus from the higher slopes washed down into this, and was buried under the lavas that filled the broad hollow.

Today, exposed in the valley side, in the material that was washed down, are thin, just a few millimeters, dark brown layers containing pollen and seeds and uncertain bits and pieces from the flora growing on the island at that time. The lava flows lying immediately above the deposits have been dated at 8.6 million years, so the flora is older than that. Once suitably treated and studied under assorted microscopes by a specialist, the material shows a predominance of ferns and tree ferns, but several other species are there, some of which are still on the island, some of which had disappeared before man arrived.

This Late Miocene flora was preserved in whatever niches it had found. Climatic conditions changed on the planet over those millions of years, wind speeds and directions, rainfall patterns, temperature etc. But St Helena had so many microgeographies that plants could move the small distances required. And its position in the middle of the ocean buffered it against extreme changes, so they could adapt to climatic effects that were cataclysmic on the continents.

So Hooker's words were correct in a way. What was on the island were fragments from an ancient botanic world, and the ancient world was destroyed. It was a bit like the Titanic, and St Helena was a lifeboat. There it was, an island in the middle of the ocean with a flora all but lost elsewhere. Yes, a kind of fossil, but very much a living fossil, that was able to develop in its isolation, a magnificent relic, a collection of orphaned children growing up on their own, without the constraints that had wiped out their parents.

In the early years after its discovery, the island was described as extensively covered with *forest*. It impressed the early navigators, but they couldn't eat much of it. But if the soil and water and climate were so good, they reasoned, what a marvellous place to bring their own plants. So fruit trees and vegetables were quickly introduced. And as for the local stuff, well the pigs and goats, that they brought in for fresh meat, could eat it. That was how we treated it for the next few centuries.

And of course, from the very beginning trees provided fuel, for ships' galleys. Once the island was settled, demands soared. Any decent timber, and there was some, was used in building. Of course the needs for fuel rose. With the discovery of calcareous sands in 1708, demand for wood to burn it to produce lime, added to the demands for distilling arrack, and for tanning. So with an increasing population of wild goats and pigs, and with slash and burn clearing of land for agriculture, you had an accelerated rate of devastation of the native flora.

Some Governors tried to slow down this destruction. Attempts were made to preserve The Great Wood, not because it was a unique flora, but because it was a natural resource in terms of wood, and it was recognised that the resource was finite. Preservation of the forest cover, where some still remained, was probably also recognised for soil and water conservation. But devastation was rapid. Coal as a fuel had had to be imported in the eighteenth century, as were trees for building and for fuel. Gorse made its first appearance not to reduce homesickness, for a countryside most of the islanders had never seen, but as a quick-growing fuel wood.

By the start to the nineteenth century, some species had already disappeared. And so it continued, destruction either directly by man and goats, or by imported vigorous aliens. Other Governors cleared the native vegetation away to try other imported varieties, coffee, mulberry, cotton, *cinchona*, bamboos, pineasters, an endless chain of largely random good intentions.

A closer look at the *cinchona* experiment is salutary. On the southern face of Diana's Peak, in the area known as Newfoundland, a plantation of Peruvian *cinchona* was started in

1866/67, in an attempt to earn money from the production of quinine. The suggestion appears to have come from the redoubtable Dr Joseph Hooker at Kew.

Hooker had commented after his second visit in 1843, how in only three years at least two endemic species had disappeared, and several others *held a very precarious tenure.* He knew the plants of the island well, and had great respect for their remarkable character. Yet here was a scheme which necessitated the cutting back of thousands of endemic plants, many of them cabbage trees, to make way for this alien.

It might have turned into a successful economic venture, but Governor Elliott's successor couldn't see its promise, so it was left to die. Five years later Melliss reported that only 300 of the trees were left. It was doubly tragic for the endemic flora, not only were so many individuals cut down, but such clearing allowed rapid access for the invasive blackberry, *buddleia* from Madagascar, and the bilberry from central America, to challenge what was left.

Then starting in 1874, flax was seen as a miracle cure to the island's economic ills. And up to the Second World War, endemic vegetation of the Peaks was cleared to plant the New Zealand crop. The island couldn't live on its endemics, but it could earn money from flax. In 1966 the flax industry died abruptly, but for the better part of a century it had provided the island's only industry.

In the twentieth century, and particularly its latter half, policies of reforestation have made substantial inroads into the destruction of those first four centuries. One of the main results is seen indirectly, in the improved availablity of water throughout the year. That, with the eradication of goats, and control of sheep grazing, has all been for the island's benefit. But it was almost exclusively in terms of imported species.

Then at the Rio Summit on Biodiversity in 1992, St Helena was designated a Site of Special Scientific Importance (SSSI) by the British Government, a welcome declaration, but one more of political expediency, than serious financial intent to do very much significantly constructive with this floral jewel.

Finally in March, 1996, Diana's Peak National Park, the

island's first, was declared to be in existence, 155.89 acres of the crest of the island, *being an area of land which contains representative samples of features and scenery with plant and animal species, geomorphological sites and habitats of special scientific, educational and recreational interest and that also contain one or several entire ecosystems that are not materially altered by human exploitation or occupation.*

This statement spells out too, the importance of the other endemic species on St Helena. We know of the wirebird, its single endemic land vertebrate species, but we tend to forget that there are a host of endemic land creatures (insects, snails etc). Here at last, with the work started earlier on endemics by Agriculture and Forestry, was serious progress.

The Peaks form the crest of the island, the culmination of innumerable ridges reaching higher and higher to the final serrated central ridge over 2000 feet high. It forms a sort of curved backbone, and the rest of the island slopes seawards from it. It is an exceedingly rugged backbone, with its most precipitous slopes, on the Sandy Bay side. The northern side is more subdued. The actual area of the Peaks is not large at all, stretching in plan little more than a mile north to south, three miles east to west. It may be tiny, but it is both strikingly beautiful and fascinating, and a mile on the map may be a couple of hours of humid warmth, or cold wet mists.

When you look up to the Peaks, it is the flax that probably strikes you first, or perhaps second. For the Norfolk Island pines on Mount Actaeon and Cuckhold's Point are even more distinctive, although the one on Cuckhold's is dying. Diana's Peak, in the middle, doesn't have one.

Who named the three peaks is lost, perhaps in the Archives, perhaps forever, but their classical names are from the earliest days. Diana was the Roman goddess of the hunt, of wild animals, but originally she had been merely a woodland goddess. Actaeon was a hunter from Greek mythology. Ovid says Actaeon saw Diana bathing, and was turned into a stag to be killed by his own hounds. As a stag, he became representative of men whose wives were unfaithful, hence presumably the third peak of Cuckhold's Point. I can't work out the logic in that. And why there is an 'h' in Cuckold's is lost in time, or at least since it appeared on the 1902 War Department, map.

There are a number of ways you can get onto the Peaks, but Stitch's Ridge at the western end is one of the best. One reason is that it's the start of the Cabbage Tree Road, laid down by Hudson Lowe, just too late to have been used by Napoleon. It is also the highest point at which you can start, *and* get there by car.

For the opening of the National Park, the Endemic Section of A and F had laid out three signposted trails, aimed at all comers. They offered 'The Snail Circuit' (two hours) for sluggish souls, like the endemic 'blushing snail'. Then 'The Weevil Walk' (three hours), St Helena has 77 endemic species of weevil for those interested. And for the fleet of foot, 'The Spider Sprint' (four hours), where you can *chase the golden sail spider* (one of the island's 48 endemic species of spider), and visit the parts of the Peaks that most other people don't reach.

These paths are a great boon. They not only ensure that part of St Helena's natural heritage is accessible, but they make useful, if somewhat energetic, short-cuts for getting across the island. The Peaks provide wonderful views of all parts of the island. If you add up all the views from the various vantage points, you have an unforgettable journey.

The Peaks receive over 40 inches of rain a year, and the temperature can be ten or fifteen degrees Centigrade colder than town. Even if it's not raining, low cloud levels are common, and mists can come in very quickly. So, even with the paths you can get lost, and you can get very wet and very cold. You can lose your view, and your way, for minutes, even hours if you decide to wait.

It's difficult to guarantee that particular days, or parts of days, will be fine and clear, so it's best to ask locals what they think of the weather conditions. Mind you, as with most things on the island, you may get more points of view than people you ask. So take a waterproof most days, and water and food any time, for you are bound to spend longer up there than you planned, there is just so much to see.

The Cabbage Tree Road begins with views down wide swaths of the upper pastures and woods, the sunlight picking out High Knoll as a distant point of reference. Up through the flax and ferns and grasses, disturbing clouds of small grey-brown moths, and the island starts unfurling.

As you go into tree-ferns and cabbage trees, you realise you need a local who knows his or her plants, to get the most out of the Peaks. Descriptions, and even pictures, on paper can be confusing, and it's not as though the names do anything but mislead. The pamphlet produced for the Park is helpful, but what is really needed, for here and for the other endemics, is a proper illustrated pocket guide, especially for those like me, who are botanically challenged.

Having said that, I'll venture a few words on the extraordinary endemics on the Peaks. In general, the 'trees' are dependent on the availablity of rain, as well as on altitude. From the top downwards you have : Tree ferns - Black Cabbage Tree - Dogwood - Whitewood - He Cabbage Tree - She Cabbage Tree, and Redwood, on the fringe of, or just outside, the Park. If you go outside it, you get into relic gumwood areas. The island ebony, which has been extensively replanted, and the scrubwoods (what I first knew as 'daisy trees'), grow in areas of substantially less rainfall and greater range of altitudes. Most of the trees are mist-interceptors.

All the trees listed for the National Park are very old. The Black Cabbage Tree was specifically identified in the plant bed material found under the 8.6 million year old lava flows of Turk's Cap, so were some gumwoods. The tree-ferns occur elsewhere in the southern hemisphere, and are all relics of more widespread forests of the Miocene.

Cabbage trees appear to get their names from their fleshy leaves looking like cabbage (Black), or when flowering they resemble caulifowers (He). She Cabbage Trees are very rare, and were thought to be extinct until re-discovered in 1976, and are now being re-planted across the Peaks. To confuse things further, all three cabbage trees are only very distantly related to each other, their nearest relations being in Australasia or on Pacific islands.

The Endemic Section, widely referred to by other islanders as 'the epidemics', began working in earnest on the Peaks on the restoration of species and their environment only in 1995. It is a small, dedicated group of islanders, several of whom have received specialist training in the UK, and one or two expatriate specialists. The work has been painstaking, sorting and establishing the population numbers and the great range of their individual and collective problems.

Only when you have to exert yourself a little do you realise just how high the humidity is on the Peaks. And in winter, just how cold you can get. The work is backbreaking. Invasive plants are cleared from small plots, and endemics are re-planted into them. Great care is needed on these upper reaches, slopes are so steep, and rainfall is high. Remove too much too fast, and hundreds and thousands of years' worth of 'soil' is flushed into the gullies. Too little, and the invasives, which are extremely vigorous, grab the land back in a couple of seasons, endangering again the hardy, but slow to settle down, endemics.

Flax may be a lost industry, but its cloak of the Peaks and upper slopes is essential for retaining soil, run off and groundwater, until it can be slowly cleared and replaced by endemic regrowth that will be equally strong for these tasks. Rush it, and you could see the Peaks denuded, their essential habitat lost and the island's precious water supply endangered. Do it carefully, as Endemic Section is doing it, and a priceless resource to world science and the island's day to day living, is restored. It promises to be a slow job, the budget is still very small.

The islanders are proud of their plants. George Benjamin's early work was invaluable. Now there is the endemic garden, there are programmes promoting the planting of endemics in schools, and they're even made available for home gardens. There is too, the highly successful idea of the Millenium Forest at the bottom end of Longwood Plain. Pay a contribution, get your name in the 'book', and an endemic (usually gumwood or scrubwood) is planted and looked after. Only four years on, there is already an impressive coverage of the island's original trees.

Perhaps the extreme fragility of the plants in nature needs a little more awareness, and with the potential for increasing numbers of visitors, there will be the need for more stable long term access paths on the Peaks. Much more work is required on endemics from other environments, the barren outer fringes for example. Some of these appear more vulnerable to rabbits than other 'predators'. But that said, what is needed is a word of substantial gratitude to the 'Epidemics'.

That is it in writing, now for the real thing, a walk and scramble through this ten million year old top of the island. The paths offer three choices: stick to the Cabbage Tree Road, contouring round the north side; go to the right and skirt the headwaters on the Sandy Bay side; or go over the top. Whichever way you choose to go will be memorable, but if you only have one chance, go over the top, along thc spinc of the island, and get the best of all three worlds.

The geometry of the island changes slowly, like a complex kaleidoscope, the interplay of the closer ridges and distant landmarks, the changing light from sun and clouds. You walk, it changes. You stop, it continues to change. Spend all day up here, and you'll never see the same view twice. The path closes in along the very crest of the island. Views disappear, and suddenly, so may you, into a rich mix of earth, trunks of cabbage trees, roots, the hairy debris of tree-ferns. There is a wonderful sense of isolation, alone up here on top of the island.

Sit for a while in the hot sunshine, in the grass on top of Diana's Peak, and there's a little wooden post-box with a rubber stamp, 'Diana's Peak Highest Point on St Helena 823 m'. It's a new one. In the '60s the elevation was still in feet. And now there's a sheet of Plantation House note paper pinned inside the box

*Dear Visitor* *Ref FP 200/5 10 May 1985*

*This new stamp-pad and cachet from Diana's Peak have been kindly provided [as before] by an island private person and I feel sure you will agree that it is to be hoped that all who*

*make use of it will do so carefully, leaving it in good condition for the many who will follow after.*

*2 Thank you for your consideration and I hope you enjoyed your visit to this beautiful place*

*Yours sincerely*
*F E Baker*
*Governor*

Have you ever been wished 'Have a nice day' more eloquently than that? In anywhere even half as beautiful, come to think of it?

It takes a little longer through the tree-ferns to reach Mount Actaeon. Their hairy orange-brown trunks are reminiscent of orang-outangs. They can be ten or more feet high, with heavy, classic fronds, the boles are heavy and hairy too, but they are soft if you fall onto them. They shed hairy bits like matted lumps of giant confetti. Lichens are mixed with the 'hairs', and occasionally on the trunks are epiphytes, of other endemics, and even flax.

They are handsome, these tree-ferns, primeval, exotic. There are tunnels through them, humid and airless, narrow with their hairy trunks brushing you, and the floor of richest soil and plant debris. They are bizarrely and beautifully friendly. Even the small patches of hill sides which are covered with them are emotive, and they'll be staggering when the replanting has really taken hold.

This then is the island of so many millions of years ago. There are other ferns, the young ones rising from the floor like suede covered Bishop's crooks. There are the waxy-feeling, scale stemmed ones, almost like snake skins, and ones that look as though they are made of plastic. There are mosses of all kinds, even an endemic lycopodium. Another clubmoss, the buckshorn, grows a foot high, and looks like a miniature monkey puzzle tree. The fuchsias and some other exotics seem to blend into this primordial 'jungle'. But not the buddleia. The buddleia is hated, the buddleia can take out decades of growth of the endemics in months.

And don't forget, as you walk damply and happily back, the many other endemics which grow in other environments. The bell-flowers, large and small, the St Helena tea plant, the boneseed, salad plant, old father live forever, the scrubwoods and baby's toes. Most are rare, most are unusual or extraordinary, all are unique, found nowhere else on the planet. They deserve tremendous respect for their diversity, and above all for their contribution to the web that is the special character of this island.

# CHAPTER 17

## BLUE HILL SCHOOL : THE SOUTH - WEST

*Climbing High Hill is a pleasant way to spend half a day ..... Having reached the summit there is then a short walk along the crest of the ridge, from which vertiginous drops and spectacular views compete for attention.*

Exploring St Helena: A Walker's Guide

The run out west is almost straight by island standards. From town to just beyond the Cathedral, you climb up half the island. Barren and dusty at first, then the green valley on your left, with cows and sheep, and cottages, pastures running up towards the Peaks. On the right the woods that hide Plantation.

You stay more or less on top for a while, a few wiggles with old pines, bamboos, hills, glimpses of distant clifftops, an arboretum, a garden of endemic plants. Then, at Cason's Gate, you're almost on the rim of Sandy Bay on one side, and on the other the wide pastures of Broad Bottom, where the second Boer camp was, and a former flax mill. In front are the pyramidal High Peak, with most of the remaining donkeys, and beyond it, the imposing grey bulk of High Hill.

Unless you stop you don't see Sandy Bay at all, because the road is just below the rim. Instead, down to the right, you see the collection of houses of Headowain, 'head of the vein', but vein of what? Fool's gold at best, though a couple of clerical adventurers in the eighteenth century arrived swearing "Here be gold." Of course there wasn't, and there's no record that the Governor locked them up for their baloney.

It's always windy, blasting across the road as it saunters along, past the little church of St Helena and the Cross, and the turn off right to Blue Hill, or straight on a few more yards, till the road seems to end at a tin garage, which someone has emblazoned with *Sex is bad for one - but good for two*. Almost hidden in the trees, the road flicks to the right dropping to the half dozen cottages of

Thompson's Wood.

Although it's long been settled, not many people live in the south-west, their cottages are scattered over those hillsides below the road. There is a small concentration at Headowain, but that is really en route to the south-west proper. It's the later side-shoot road that drops you down to its one true community, Blue Hill, lying at around 1500 feet, on the irregular stepped slopes of the valley headwaters. There are some newly built homes which are not yet hidden, but most of the older cottages are obscured by trees, you can hear family noises rather than see them.

Blue Hill defines the community that lives in the area, much as Levelwood does, rather than any specifically identifiable feature. So Blue Hill is no more than an expanse of hillside, lorded over by the regal High Hill. But why 'blue' must be an informed, even uninformed, guess. Most likely it is from the flowers of the strangely named gobble-gheer (*Psoralea pinnata*), which is a delicate, indigenous little tree, which used to be common in the area.

According to Williams, gobble-gheer might be a corruption of 'goblin's hair'. That's reasonable enough when no alternatives are forthcoming. In December, it bursts into blue-mauve flowers. It was a traditional island decoration for Christmas, and is still used in the south-west. It is said that the slaves, when they saw its distinctive flush of colour, knew they were another year older, so used it as a calendar.

A gateway on a bend opens onto a field of grass, surrounded by high pines, a hint of a knoll or two, and the school. With a little imagination, it's a miniature village green. It's just that the village only appears to have three buildings.

In the '60s, I spent a number of weeks in Blue Hill, in the old school building. To be exact, in the Bishop's room in the old school building. Originally it was built as a Church school, so it seemed logical that a room there should have been set aside for the Bishop, when he visited his flock. Until 1951 when St Helena and the Cross was built, there was no Anglican church closer than the Cathedral. Knowing I was looking for bases in different parts of the island, Bishop Beardmore had very kindly offered me the use of his room.

A few yards away, in a sort of Hansel and Gretel cottage, that had originally been the schoolmaster's, the Peters family provided me with dinners, cups of tea, insights into the area, and warm hospitality. The family consisted of Alfie and Nellie Peters, and two sons, Bert who was a carpenter, and Lennie who worked at the wharf. Lennie played guitar for us some evenings. He was married to Pauline, a local woman, and was building their house lower down the hillside. They had a son aged two, a little shy of strangers. When I came home at the end of the day carting a pack full of rocks, Lynton would be sitting on the step of his grandparents' house. He didn't talk much, but he watched a great deal.

I'm not sure what Alfie's job had been, it might have been with A and F, or possibly with one of the flax mills, but he was a Blue Hill man, a respected local figure. On one of my later visits, Tubby Thomas, Maurice's elder brother, confirmed my reckoning that Alfie Peters had been a real gentleman. "You know, he never called me Tubby." Now I thought, after all these years, I'll find out what Tubby's real name is. "So what did he call you?" Tubby would have been a few years younger than Alfie Peters, "He called me Mister Thomas."

In those ensuing thirty years, Bert had gone to work in England, and sadly, Alfie and Lennie had both passed on. Mrs Peters, in her 80s, still lived in the wooden house, with her sister, but the old school had become the local Community Centre, and the Bishop's room had been absorbed into it. I've got a feeling it was where the bar is now. The later primary school building had already closed, and become a Field Centre. There were too few children for a local infants school, so they were bused out each day to St Paul's. I organised a couple of field trips for trainee teachers, so the Education Dept let me rent the centre for a fortnight.

It feels good to be back in Blue Hill. The building doesn't look, but it certainly seems, old fashioned, somehow like a First World War village school. It has a single room of two classrooms joined, and narrow verandahs back and front. I have a camp bed, not as elegant as Napoleon's, and free choice of the residual half dozen tables and twenty or thirty wooden chairs. There is a little kitchen, and a shower room, with invigorating cold water. Unfortunately the water tank is not a small one on the roof, which would warm up a bit through the day thankyou, but a large one, the water of which I swear got colder as the fortnight wore on.

Evenings are very dark, because the only house I can see is Mrs Peters', and she still seems to use oil lamps. No street lights (no streets), nothing but the night sky and some kind of hint (imagination?) of lightening of the blackness over the sea. It is so peaceful. Other than the wind in the tree tops, the only sound in the evening is the muttering of a fairy tern, or a pine cone dropping onto the roof.

There's a telephone in the room, because it's a school centre, and it rings, shatteringly loud. A male voice says I won't know him, but it's Lynton Peters, Lennie's two year old son of thirty years ago. He'd heard from his gran that I was back. He lives just up the hill, in a house he's building. When I've settled in, he and his wife Tina would be pleased to see me. The empty room is beginning to feel decidedly homely.

Then a set of headlights comes through the gate, and a Landrover parks outside the Community Centre. Lights come on, country and western music starts. I wander across to let somebody know why there are lights in the school. A large man grins, "You the rock man? I thought so. When you stayed at Distant Cottage, I was a kid and used to bring my donkey to take your rocks up to the bus stop. I'm Stedson Francis from Thompson's Wood." If Gary Stevens wasn't around, then Edward Williams summoned Stedson.

Stedson, a lanky lad of about 10 then, now works for Government. [He is now one of the island's Councillors, equivalent to MPs.] He's on the Committee of the Community Centre, and is preparing it for a dance because he's also the resident DJ. We have a cup of tea, chat a bit, and I return to my spaciously empty room. Country and western continues for a while, then the lights go out in the Centre, and the Landrover departs. Silence and darkness.

Through the night, the winds have played with the imagination, running like cats on the sheets of the corrugated roof.

Distant cockerels call through the last hours, irregularly and imprecisely pre-empting the dawn. When it comes, it slips more quietly than the wind down the long slope from the rim of Sandy Bay.

If you're lucky and have time, you can find places like this up country. In the straggly grass at the end of the building, is a mother rabbit and two young ones sitting like little jugs. One sees me, folds its ears, does little hops for three feet, stops, sits like a grey jug again, nibbling the end of a piece of grass. It's like an illustration for a child's book, with delightful (for me) and probably unfortunate (for him in the long run) growing trust and familarity. How long such innocence will last, I know not, I've seen the numbers of cartridge cases veneering much of the island's surface.

Fairy terns, high overhead, fly slowly seawards. Pairs of them dance through the branches of tall trees high up the slope behind, in the clump of trees that hides West Lodge. Across the green, behind the hibiscus hedge of Mrs Peters' cottage, a white cockerel fusses pompously over its wandering harem. The hens scratch away, totally unconcerned. His bark is worse than his bite, or whatever is the equivalent with poultry. Aged firs, lichen dripping from trunks and branches, look after the other two sides of the green, tall and silent, heads bent in the wind.

There are unseen bird calls. St Helena has very few species of birds, especially field birds and song birds, but the few there are produce a confusing array of calls, perhaps by way of consolation. Trying to sort them out is a pleasant, if frustrating, pastime. It is much simpler visually, with colourful manifestations of passing cardinals and canaries, even an occasional Java sparrow.

Birds were introduced for a variety of reasons, and from early on islanders trapped and caged the warmer climate varieties for sale to passengers on homeward bound ships. In 1801 the capture of Java sparrows was banned to try to restore numbers: *Penalty, if a child, to be whipped, if a grown person, fined.*

Different game birds were brought in for food, pheasants and partridges very successfully. Others, like the Mexican turkey, guinea-fowl from West Africa, and francolins from the Cape, never settled. Even peafowl were brought in, but they were killed off in 1820 because they settled too well, and caused too much damage to the crops.

Several attempts were made to bring in English birds, to make it more like 'home' it is said, thrush, blackbird, larks, starlings and linnets. Sparrows were brought in on several occasions, and Melliss records they all moved to town. Some varieties thrived for a time, but none survived for very long. Someone tried the American mocking bird in 1870, but it was clear that the field was unlikely to be widened.

Blue Hill drops in several steps down the headwaters of Old Woman's Valley. The road goes through the community, but cottages are linked by much older paths. Ground is being cleared for a number of new housing lots, perhaps as many as a dozen. It is a pleasant, sheltered setting, and although the road stops, a track contours round towards Headowain.

You come across hollowed bamboo 'logs' left by the Environmental Health Department, filled with rat poison. Occasionally there are orange drums too, marked 'Poison - EHD', and you just help yourself, in a manner of speaking. Rats are still a problem, but there are far fewer than in the '60s. Doing field work then, I could never get rid of fleas, which I'm sure were rat-borne. In the '90s, I spent as much time in the country as before, but I never saw a flea. But rats will be a harder problem to crack finally than the goats.

Below the community, the rural atmosphere changes dramatically at the start of Spyglass Ridge, a narrow divide between Old Woman's and Swanley Valleys and their steep, striped lava walls. The band between inland green and desert island rim is sharp. One minute it's fields and cottages, gorse and pines. Then it's marls and junipers, scratchy wild coffee and everlasting daisies.

You can see the sea, and the guano encrusted Egg Island. You can even make out on its top the semi-circular wall of Cockburn's battery, authorized by the man himself in 1815, to protect these highly inhospitable approaches. But at the mouth of Swanley Valley is Bennett's Point, where tradition has it the traitorous settler Coxe shone his lantern for the Dutch to land in 1673. So perhaps the very careful Cockburn, was just being very careful.

The seaward end of Swanley Valley is hidden by the rock pile of Spyglass, but the sides are worryingly steep, all thousand feet and more of them. It was up this valley supposedly, that Coxe led the Dutch, to High Peak. The British garrison arrived, a quick battle, Dutch the victors, see off the Brits, slaughter a couple of cattle for lunch, and on to Ladder Hill, to watch the English sailing off. It's not a climb I would happily undertake, so hats off to the Dutch, but it's marginally more manageable than Holdfast Tom.

There is said to be good fishing down there, but I've never been able to find a trace of any path. The locals seem to prefer fishing on the Sandy Bay side, climbing over the island and down past Lot's Wife to Sharks Bench. If you add up the footage climbed, that works out pretty well to climbing up and down Snowdon to look for lunch, except here there isn't a path.

I spent a lot of time in the barren areas, and talked about them too much, so one day Lynton took me through the long domesticated, more comfortable parts across to Headowain. Most of the scenery could fit into Wales, without anyone thinking anything amiss. A good half mile from the nearest cottage is a spring, where to the end of the '70s, Lynton and siblings old enough came each morning to fill buckets to carry home. Then their morning chores done, they could walk to school.

Now of course, virtually every house on the island has piped water for bathroom and kitchen. This ready availability of water year round, has been another success story to add to its related reforestation, and to education and health provision. Since the '60s demand has soared, and I was amazed at how good provision and conservation are.

A grassy mound, with outlines of rooms, even outbuildings, is all that is physically left of Swanley Valley House. You can trace driveways, old boundary walls, and old paths. Near a rose-apple tree are the ruins of another once grand house, or houses, Half Moon. An oak, with enormous leaves, pheasants and rabbits and gorse, keep the image of border country going. But the image is corrected, up by Bushes Hollow, where whole pines lying crashed on the floor, have been eaten from within by termites.

Long lost though the physical aspects of the old houses may be, there remains a legacy of ghostly carriages and horses, and babies or mothers crying from the remnant outlines of slave quarters. The wind and the clouds play all kinds of tricks when they pour over the lip of Sandy Bay, especially as we hurry on home past West Lodge.

All week, Stedson has worked getting the centre and his tapes ready for Friday. The evening of the dance, I'd been out to dinner half way across the island. After midnight, with the top of the island and its road obscured in swirling mists, there was a welcoming oasis down below, coloured fairy lights outlining the Centre.

It wasn't misty here, and the green was filled with parked cars, groups outside laughing and drinking, plenty of light, plenty of people, maybe 250, from all over the island, the bar still hyperactive, groups chatting round tables, a snack bar dispensing goodies of all sorts. The dance floor was still packed, music good and steady, not too loud, predominantly country and western, but *Quartermaster's Stores* belts out, and people join in with "I have not brought my specs with me." Music I hadn't heard in years, banjo, even bagpipes - shades of the North West Frontier.

Blue Hill has a reputation for good dances, good bar, nice snacks, good music, and no violence, so tickets are sold out long before the night. One or two people recognize me, "Saw you over yornder yesterday." "That you over top of Old Man's Head other week?." "I came to your talk here in the school thirty years ago." That was a bit of a turn up. "Don't remember what you said." Honest they are at Blue Hill. But at least he'd remembered as a lad being dragged along to an incomprehensible talk. In the '60s that was a bit of a night out in Blue Hill.

Now the dance, the last before Lent, is a good steady enjoyable evening out, late teens to over seventies, old fashioned double-breasted suits to cowboy shirts, even one guy in a great-coat. Dresses from post-war (which one?), shiny dance frocks, through layered petticoats of the '50s, to little black numbers.

At about two the music stops, by half past most cars have gone, by three the lights are all out. Around half four the last vehicle departs, after its driver has had a bit of a doze to clear his eyes. Darkness of drizzle, a sort of afterglow in the mist, no stars (no sky for that matter), but light from somewhere, enough for shapes to swirl if you look long enough, but no galloping horses, nothing threatening, just the end of a good night out.

Apart from dances, one of the great island traditions upheld by the Community Centres is skittles. Concrete lanes, solid ball and heavy skittles, lot of noise. Skittles is a marvellous event, an absolute riot, unless of course it's a tournament match. They take their skittles seriously, islanders, most of them, indeed they do most sports, and their card games. But skittles, if it's not a competition, then for an evening out, good bar, good if largely incomprehensible conversation, good crack of the Irish, is a real hoot.

In the morning, Mrs Peters was sitting inside the open front door. Her sister was making island lace, elegant coasters in the palest yellow, the intricacies of which will only be noticed when the wine stains them. As girls they both lived at Rock Rose on the other side of the island. Alfie Peters, on Sunday mornings, his days off, used to walk over the island, across the Peaks, to pay court to his bride to be, and late in the afternoon he walked back.

When Nellie married and left home, her sister had to go to town for the rations. This was long before there were any shops outside Jamestown. "First you had to catch the donkey," she explained, and saddle him, "but I'd got brothers to help." Then off on the road at the back of Sandy Bay, over the Peaks onto Francis Plain, and Barnes Road into town. Then all the way back, six or seven miles each way, but a total climb of over 3000 feet vertically up and down. Nice to have Blue Hill Store half a mile away now, and the fresh fish van coming round three times a week.

My return to Blue Hill introduced me to elements of island fauna that had hitherto escaped me. Perhaps I was very tired after being out all day, perhaps it was hot in the kitchen. But there was certainly something odd, when I was cooking supper, with the kitchen door open to the darkness of the green.

St Helena has many endemic insects, and its moths are so famous there were those German enthusiasts on the RMS, the yellow-green ghost ones, spending their Christmas holiday collecting some of them. I needed their help, because I found a species of moth in the kitchen, which if not endemic, was certainly odd. It didn't choose candle flames for its ritual death, but the frying pan. Onions just softening nicely, nice pinch of curry powder added, and Splat! The *kamikazes* had started.

I had a dog once that thought it was a cat, and climbed (easy) trees. Now here I had another species of moth that thought it was a cockroach, and rushed (marginally more slowly than a cockroach) across surfaces, like draining boards, or chopping blocks, until squashed (much less messily than cockroaches). Or if chased patiently for long enough, with a ladle or whatever, it reluctantly took off, but only to land on another surface and start running again.

And don't yawn without putting your hand in front, not at Blue Hill, or the moths and their insatiable genetic death wish will be in. They actually settle on you, onto your face, into your hair, moustache, eyes or ears, even onto your fingers as you eat, waiting for you to open your mouth. You stand up from the table and a swarm rises with you, different species, different sizes, like animated dandruff. They needn't bother climbing the Peaks, these moth specialists.

Why most people go to Blue Hill is to climb High Hill. Quite a lot of locals climb it too, for a bit of a walk and a picnic. Although it only stands 500 feet above the ridge on which it is situated, its cliffs and sheeted sides of grey rock drop nearly a thousand feet into Old Woman's Valley, then her sheer sides plunge another seven hundred. Impressive, High Hill, dominant, a very solid presence, a well deserved place in a *Walker's Guide*, and unquestionably my favourite hill.

It's not a difficult climb, more an energetic scramble, plenty of trees, plenty of shade, even a few steps cut into the wiregrass. There's gorse, and surprisingly an odd prickly pear, brambles and relic lantana bushes, bilberry, and wild coffee on the rockier patches. Here too, are little, only six to eight feet high, thin spindly bushes like emaciated conifers. At last, the gobble-gheer.

And at the top, sit in the breeze and drink in the panoramas. To the north you can focus on cottages in Blue Hill, the ruins of Half Moon, the Baptist chapel at Headowain, and the uphill pastures, rucked like a great green cloth. Below them are the desolate valleys and Spyglass. In the distance the immense rim of Sandy Bay and the dark serrated cloud-tipped Peaks. On a clear day, far beyond, you can see Flagstaff Hill and The Barn, nine miles, and almost as many worlds, away.

South is the little collection of cottages of Thompson's Wood, originally said to have been Tombstone Wood, set in pines and the sparsely pastured headwaters of Thompson's Valley, across to Wild Cattle Pound. Beyond, is the final south-west wedge of the island, dropping from the old telegraph station on Joan Hill, through sweeps of ashes, intense oranges, reds, browns, and ochrous gold, towards the final staggered steps of the cliffs of South West Point.

Big country, the views from High Hill, most of the island spread before you. But at the back of the hill, falling towards the sea and Egg Island, is a little valley, hidden from the top, hidden in fact from pretty well anywhere. I found it by mistake one day, climbing by way of somewhere different back up from the sea. I'd picked my way through the prickly pear of a steep slope, and literally tumbled over a ridge and into it. It was a valley, filled with long, pale yellow grass, the colour of the foothills of the Sierra Nevada in California. With that colour and the big sky, I thought I'd found cowboy country.

I was resting there taking it in, just looking, a different view, a delicate little valley, so private, a sentinel pine at the top. And something moved. No, some *things* moved, and I couldn't believe my eyes. A family of wild goats! Big male, two females and a kid, picking their way through the grass, with the sort of ballet dancer's walk that some animals have.

In the '60s I'd seen wild goats, but even then on only a couple of occasions. I was sure that they'd all been shot after that. So I was dumbstruck, it was so unexpected. And slowly, in fifteen minutes perhaps, they picked their way across the valley and disappeared into the rocky bits of one of the ridges, out of my line of sight. Quite, quite wonderful, the sight and the feeling of warmth it brought.

Seeing the goats was very special, but sitting anywhere on the island, there's always something different. A wirebird with young, a feral cat, a long lost donkey, a mouse smaller than your thumb climbing the spines of a prickly pear to eat the orange flowers, tiny plants and flowers in the most desolate desert waste, different coloured lichen encrusting rocks, hills massaged by the mists, and the thrill of solitude, peace, silence so intense you can feel it.

Sitting is a pastime well worth developing, though it may require a bit of effort at first. You need to have the time to look at things, to let things impinge on you slowly. Work on it long enough, and you don't really have to think. Sitting on High Hill, you have it all, and again you get that feeling of being on top of the world. But in keeping with where I started, look back over Blue Hill, at the patch of trees just below the road, just before the turn drops you to the community. Those trees are hiding West Lodge, or what's left of its name and its legend. Stop by on you way back to town.

Standing on a barely discernible platform on the slope, down from the rim of Sandy Bay, two new cottages are built in the grounds of the old house. The main approach from the Blue Hill side, is gently impressive, through what is left of a dark grove of high trees. In a broad, shaded clearing, is one of the new houses, more or less on the site of the original West Lodge. People had talked of building there for many years, but had never actually started, for this is the site of the island's most famous ghost story.

Many of the tales of West Lodge, written, or offered at first hand, are of crashes on still nights as of trees being torn down, of galloping horses, of carriage wheels, even of violins but no violinist. It's particularly round here, that some manifestations are witnessed by two people, yet one saw something and heard nothing, and the other heard something and saw nothing.

There are stories that human bones were found near West Lodge long years before, when ground was being prepared. Lynton said he wouldn't go near West Lodge as a boy, even though he could take a short-cut past it to his house. He remembered stories about a pane left in one ruined window, and at certain times of year blood appeared on it and ran down the glass.

The most striking accounts are probably early twentieth century, and involve a visitor to the island spending the night in the abandoned shell of West Lodge. He lit a fire, cooked something to eat, had a drink, and fell asleep.

He was woken by the noise of wind blowing through the trees, and there are various embellishments. More winds, shadows which moved although there was nothing there to cast them, heavy rain putting his fire out, candles blown out, dancing lights, but they all return to quiet. Then the man was woken a second time, and was drawn by some force out into the yard. In the centre stood a tall mulatto man, with his arms bound, he was well-built and stripped to the waist. A white man, proceeded to lash the man till he was dead. On one side, in old fashioned dress, an older man forced a young woman to watch it all.

They were the young girl, the planter's daughter, and the young man, her young man, the slave. They were lovers in a harsher time. How much is in the Archives, how much is in the mists of the night, I don't know. But there you have it, you've seen the copse of trees, and the place where the house once stood. Now you have the legend, the ghosts, of West Lodge. But Blue Hill doesn't have a lot of time for them. Too much going on with dances, and friendly rabbits, and funny moths, and goblin's hair, for that.

# CHAPTER 18

## HOUSES ON THE CRATER RIM

*The valley beneath Diana's Peak was cultivated and interspersed with cottages, among which our host's, Mr Doveton, is eminently beautiful. The opposite side, naked, as when it arose from the great abyss, with several ragged rocks rearing their heads a considerable height above the red, white, and purple clay, which divides the hills into regular strata of unequal thickness, altogether forms a magical scene, to which the ocean itself, from the point where the valley first became visible, was only a suitable back-ground.*

Lord Valentia, visiting in 1802

I was in the States in the late '60s, and a piece of West Coast cliffside graffiti always stuck in my mind, *Death is the biggest kick of all - that's why they save it till last.* Sandy Bay is like that. Not death, nothing like death, its incredible vibrancy is quite the opposite, but it is the biggest kick, the most spectacular part of an extraordinary island, overflowing with astonishment.

Sandy Bay is a geographical feature, a huge bowl-like ampitheatre carved into the core of the south-western volcano. It has a wonderful rim of hills and ridge tops, containing the highest points of the island. It is also a district, a specific collection of people, their houses spread round the back of the ampitheatre at the feet of the Alpine Peaks, down into the main valley draining through the desert wastes to the Beach

But Sandy Bay is more than that, it is a presence, which elevates. It is hidden from the rest of the island, yet it has a domination like no other part. Wherever you are along the rim, or in the great bowl, its atmosphere is unique. It is an atmosphere that changes constantly, partly changing itself, and partly changing your mood. Sandy Bay draws you, to watch it from a distance, or to go down into it.

It looks different from whatever viewpoint you choose. Its

rim runs from Sandy Bay Barn in the east, through the Peaks, and out along a great ridge of hills to the Asses Ears, where it plunges once again into the sea. With a bit of effort it is possible to walk the length of its rim, and as you do so your surroundings change continuously, and as a backdrop, it too slowly changes.

One of the finest views is from Sandy Bay Barn, where you're standing on the lip of this huge bowl, with an irregular rim of rich greens, of scattered trees, of primeval forest, pastures, sweeps of flax. And the bottom half of the bowl is rugged, irregular, its surface scored into ridges and valleys. It gives a first feeling of reddish brown and yellow, but all shades of the spectrum are there, yes, even to blue and violet. Jagged pinnacles and serrated walls, pale grey, or blinding white in the full sun, protrude and stretch across its tortured flesh like scar tissue.

The southern half of this great bowl has gone, eaten away by the sea, which you can see still tearing into it, even from so high and so far away. White waters thrash into black dyke walls, briefly protecting cliffs of yellow and bright grey rubble. And in the hollow, great sculpted figures dance, a pair of ragged donkey ears, a black gorilla face, the elegant white broken statue of Lot's Wife and the stockier stump of her husband. It is bizarre, unreal, here again you're tempted to say phantasmal. And it appears lifeless, no sign of anything growing, a true rocky desert.

Look at Sandy Bay from the Peaks, and it's so different. The top half of the ampitheatre is green, in places impenetrably overgrown with endemic and imported vegetation. This immense side-drop of the rim is constantly changing too, shades of colour, its relief, its texture, the light of the sun, shadows of clouds. You can hear the wind, and on more distant ridges you can see the wind as it ghosts across it, bending trees, dappling the soft flax wall hangings, bobbing fairy terns up and down like corks in a stream. Up here the lower desert half is no more than a backdrop.

This steep back wall of the ampitheatre is veneered with species introduced over 300 years, an outburst of vegetation. Here are the older houses of Sandy Bay, with later ones clustering in the centre at the back of Riding Stones Hill. Settlers came early into these fertile upper reaches, there was plenty of water, the temperature and humidity were high, and the soils rich and deep. And over the centuries it became a sort of natural equivalent of the glasshouses of Kew.

Below the western rim, starting from Cason's Gate on the west road, there is an ill-defined shoulder which runs to the Ball Alley, a wind gap in the rim. It is a fertile place, decent soil, decent water, and it included in those early days what was called Ebony Plain. It was a fine setting for some of the early houses, and a number of them, intact or in ruins, some present only in residual name, are particularly interesting. Sitting on its own little ridge, just before the shoulder starts, is the most famous of them all, Mount Pleasant, perhaps the most spectacularly situated house on the island.

Mount Pleasant was originally owned by the Bazetts, the first of whom, Matthew, a Huguenot, had arrived in 1684 as a new cadet with the Company. In 1786 Mount Pleasant was owned by a descendant, another Matthew Bazett, who sold it to one William Webber Doveton, Sheriff of the island.

His ancestor, William Dufton, as the name was then, from Dufton on the edge of the fells, west of Appleby in Cumbria, reached the island, aged 20, in 1673 and married one Anne Wild. Their son Jonathan was the progenitor of a prolific Doveton line. William Webber, several generations later, was a pillar of the island community, a devoted and deeply loved family man, a member of Council for decades, and senior officer of the St Helena Militia. He travelled to England in 1818 to receive his knighthood from the Prince Regent.

There is a lovely story in Mrs Abell's *Recollections*, about William Doveton taking precautions before he went for his knighthood: *Thinking that he might never return to his lovely and beloved valley, he had a tree felled from his own 'fairyland',* [not the house called Fairyland, close by, which belonged to another long standing Council member, Thomas Greentree] *from under the shade of which he had so often viewed the enchanting scene around, and had his coffin made from the wood.*

His ancestral namesake, William, had been less successful

in his relations. In 1695 the records show that Robert Exeter was charged for saying that Mrs Doveton's three last children were his. For such a slur he was fined only a dollar, on the grounds that Mrs Doveton was always counted a very light woman.

Napoleon had ridden over to Sandy Bay in 1816, but it's not clear if he called on the Doveton household. After 1817 he rarely left the grounds of Longwood House. But in October 1820, although terminally ill, Napoleon decided he wanted to go out, he wanted to go to Sandy Bay. He would go over to Mount Pleasant to call on Sir William.

Accompanied by the Bertrands and Montholon, who by then were all that was left of the French senior household, Napoleon took his carriage to Stitch's Ridge. Here he transferred to his horse, and the little party, impeccably uniformed, rode down to Mount Pleasant. It was Napoleon's last excursion outside Longwood. Here again you can follow in the footsteps, and the hoofprints, of the Emperor.

I came over the top of Stitch's, thorn trees, flax, pastures, and bright yellow gorse flowers, and in the early morning light the colours of the bowl of the Bay were aflame, the sea, white flecked and rough even from this height. The barren lower reaches might be truly multicoloured, but they are dwarfed by the immense semi-circle of green hills. And on the first little promontory of the western wall is a white single storey house. In the stillness, are the sounds of unseen cattle lowing, and visible men cutting thorn tree branches for fodder.

A drive leads away from the road, tunnelling through Cape yews, an old stone wall, bilberry, bamboos, doves and an assorted mix of high trees, some clearly planted at one time to line the drive, others tumbling down the slope. At a final bend, the trunks of two huge Norfolk Island pines, recently felled, lie in cut lengths down the pasture. They were felled, I think, because of termites, not for the making of coffins.

At the end of the flower-lined drive is Mount Pleasant, an elegantly simple house with a lawn in front. Nothing is visible of the rugged barren lower Bay. Fifty yards of lawn and flower gardens, a riot of species, of colours, of provenances, all the richer for the morning sun, in front of the house. And on that lawn sat Napoleon, in equally brilliant sunshine, more than 175 years ago. Of course details have changed, but the richness of the setting, the house, the beautiful gardens, the calm and tranquility, and the great arc of green hills are timeless.

Sir William had been taking his morning constitutional in the garden, and was puzzled at the group of uniformed horsemen he had seen riding down from Stitch's Ridge. He was considerably more surprised when he realised it was Napoleon and his entourage. Montholon came forward and explained the situation, and he presented Sir William to his Emperor. Sir William invited Napoleon and his party into the cool interior of Mount Pleasant.

He introduced his daughter, Mrs Greentree, and Napoleon gave liquorice to a grand-daughter. They chatted, the setting and the informality, laced with Doveton's rather blunt old-fashioned charm, was a boon for the ailing Emperor. Doveton invited the party to join him for breakfast, but Napoleon reversed the offer of hospitality and invited Mr Doveton and his family to join him on the lawn, where Marchand had laid out a masterly picnic breakfast.

At that time, there were of course many shortages of foodstuffs on the island, and what Napoleon may have described as a modest repast, left Doveton at a loss for words. I have a picture of Sir William, rather like Mole in *Wind in the Willows*, on that first picnic with Rat, for he reported later to the Council, that there had been *cold pies, potted meat, cold turkey, curried fowl, ham or pork, dates and oranges, and almonds and a fine salad.* O my, O my ....

Mrs Greentree placed a huge plate of the butter she had just made onto the table, and Napoleon was offered a glass of *shrub*, which Doveton explained was as famous on the island as his butter. It was rum with orange cordial, and Napoleon was appalled by it. He very quickly, and undoubtedly diplomatically, switched them all onto his champagne.

There was laughter and the noise of children, there were dogs in the background, and faces peering from curtains, uniforms gleamed and decorations sparkled in the sunshine. It was, even by standards of the island, a splendid admixture of formal society and family jollity, in the beauty of the garden and a setting of unsurpassed natural magnificence. And you can relive it, on the lawn, in the sun, with enough visual effects to make it perfectly tangible.

There are a couple of steps to the front door of the house, and through its glass you look into one room and through it into, and across, a dining room. Out of the windows the other side you can just see the end of Hooper's Rock, the end of that sweep of green that has so enthralled you in front of the house. If you go out of the back door, there is a tiny lawn and a low wall against the sky.

Half a dozen steps, still dreaming of Napoleon and the greenery, and Wham! from a garden wall on its floral shelf, the world has dropped, straight down, into the immensity of the desert Sandy Bay. On the right is an extravaganza of cliffs and broken green hills out towards High Peak. Lot is suddenly in the foreground, and below is the multicoloured diversity of the lower reaches of the Bay, lines of huge grey-white rocks of the main dykes cleaving, riding, ploughing across the ridges of reds and browns, oranges and yellows, sweeping into Lot's Wife, or an angry sea at Sandy Bay Beach.

To the left is the rest of that apron, midway below the Peaks and Sandy Bay Beach, the curve of Riding Stones Hill, the lovely simplicity of Bamboo Hedge, and cottages in the valley below, in the last vestiges of green.

Although Napoleon went to the sitting room, he didn't go through to look at this alternative view. The chances are that, like Mrs Greentree's *shrub*, it would have appalled him. The contrast from the two sides of the house could not be greater, but unlike from on high, there is no ambivalence, it is just two different ways of looking at the same thing.

What a house, what a location. You choose your view to fit your moods. I have said how good it is on the island, the chance to choose your walking to suit your mood. At Mount Pleasant you choose your breakfast or lunch or drinks. Which way shall I look? Which of the aspects of this fabulous setting shall I have as a backdrop? Wonderful, indeed almost awesome. Views of such immensity and diversity, constituting your back and front doorsteps, are more the stuff of fairy tales.

I talked of the shoulder, of the old Ebony Plain, and then digressed. But to get onto that shoulder you must go to the rim again, along to Cason's Gate, where once these lands and a no-longer existent house were Mr Cason's. There was a lookout point here, linking the fortifications at Sandy Bay Beach with lookouts in the far south-west, and across to the north of the island and Ladder Hill, via High Knoll Fort. Very military, but it's supposedly a white lady who comes out of the trees and drifts along the slope above the main road, not a redcoat.

The road, and the white lady if she's around, head west outside the rim, but a good track takes you inside Sandy Bay, and drops towards Fairyland. No longer Mr Greentree's house, not anybody's house, but a flax mill, and a dead one at that. In 1964 when I first went down, it was thriving, with the tearing noises of the scutcher and stripper, with ox-carts and women in their gunny bag aprons putting out the lengths of white fibres in strips to dry and bleach on the pasture. Now it's just very quiet, and very scenic.

You don't even have to go down to Fairyland, for the track itself lies above. It more or less contours round the wall of the ampitheatre along the shoulder, out round one ridge, and back into the stream valley, and out round the next ridge and ..... It's a marvellous walk to the Ball Alley, sometimes in avenues of thorn trees, sometimes in patchy endemic gumwoods. They're working on rejuvenating this area into a proper plantation, and it's already impressive.

Closer to the ground there are arum lilies, and it's a great place for blackberries, and pale, ellipsoidal, old world raspberries, if you look very closely, and Cape gooseberries in their Chinese lantern jackets. These, and the ubiquitous nasturtiums, are the garden relics of the old houses. All the bucolic setting you wanted, the majesty of the Bay below, and Lot coming closer and then dropping away. There are very few houses now, a couple on the ridge of Rock Mount running straight into Lot, and Peakdale in the almost Himalayan foothills, with acres of new ebony and redwood high above up to the crest.

Below the track is Old Luffkins. Funny house, Luffkins. It's a two storey stone shell, with its former glories of gardens, run wild a century ago, but the residual grand trees are there. John Lufkin was one of the earliest settlers, he was accused of involvement in the 'rebellion' of 1684, and bits of the shell may stretch back to that.

Even in ruins the house is proud and disciplined, even the overgrowths have an order about them, perhaps induced by the great trees. The character lingers, and although it's not large at all, it says this was a house to be reckoned with. This is the stuff of ghosts of centuries past. But not of ghosts of burning and lashing, of shame and violent death, this is a house full of life. Listen! You can hear laughter and music and dancing, this is where military men and fine ladies came to dance, and to eat breakfast in the magical dawns of Sandy Bay.

You can still hear the music, or perhaps it's only the wind, as you move to Horse Ridge, where its old house has become a little, rather rugged, rather ragged, rather lost, botanic garden. Lot is hidden behind you, but you can see Lot's Wife now, and her dominance will increase steadily. In the wilder parts of the Bay, Lot has very little presence. In front is a little apron, cultivated in part, small fields, round the ruined Horse Ridge House. I wave to the man working there, it's Randy Stevens, Gary's father, who also works Botley's Lay beyond the Ball Alley.

It's really quite theatrical here, with rocks the size of buses, spalled off Hooper's Rock, dotting the slopes, resting before they plunge down into the contorted rockscapes around The Gates of Chaos. I don't know anything about the history of Horse Ridge House, but there is a single dark tree near the house, and that's what switches time again.

*Every joy and blessing attend you my Life, and bless my Dear Herriet, My Dear Mary, My Dear Betsy, My Dear Fanny, My Dear Jenny & my Dear little Ann. I send you all many kisses on this paper & ever pray to God to bless you - I will not say farewell to you now my Dear Betsy because I am homeward bound - I shall lose no time every happyness attend you My Dearest Life and ever remember me your best of Friends & most affectionate Husband.*

Thus wrote one of the best known, if not best loved, seamen of the eighteenth century, indeed of all time. He was writing to his wife, on October 2nd, 1792, from Coupang in Timor. The writer? I'll give you a clue, the tree by the ruined Horse Ridge House is a breadfruit, or what on the island they call breadfruit. Does that help? No? Well it wasn't Cook, it was Captain William Bligh, aged 38 years. The mutiny on the *Bounty* was three years behind him, and having written that letter, Bligh sailed round the Cape and arrived at St Helena on December 17th.

Bligh had sailed with Captain Cook in the Pacific, 1772-74, when they had discovered breadfruit. He was to sail with Cook again on his third voyage, when they discovered the Hawaiian Islands, and Cook was killed. But Bligh was now commanding the *Providence*, a newly built West Indiaman, and this was the second breadfruit expedition. The expedition, which had been prompted by Sir Joseph Banks, and was authorised by the King, was to take breadfruit to the West Indies. Bligh left Tahiti with 2634 assorted plants, including 830 breadfruit, of which he had been instructed, on behalf of the Company, to deliver 23 at St Helena. This he duly did.

After ten days, Bligh sailed for Jamaica. He confided to his wife that he hoped it was to be his last voyage - after all he had a lot of daughters to look after - but it was not to be. Nor was it his last visit to St Helena, for in 1799, in command of the *Director*, he returned to the island to escort the homeward East India convoy. And because of that special link between the navy and science, he collected more botanical specimens for Kew, presumably once again prompted by Sir Joseph Banks.

But there's a sadness about my dreaming. The tree near Horse Ridge House is a *Monstera*, even I could recognise that, and although they call it a breadfruit the real breadfruit trees that Bligh brought were *Artocarpus*, and very few of their descendants seem to have lived on. But you can bend the nomenclature a little, can't you, if the setting warrants it?

So much beauty in the scenery, so much history and so many stories almost hidden, such mixtures of place and time. That's one reason I love Sandy Bay. But another is just in front. It's a tiny ruined shell now, but it was the little cottage where Edward Williams lived in the 1960s. Beyond it is the Ball Alley, and just down from that towards the Asses Ears, is Distant Cottage where I stayed. Sandy Bay is a different world, and it's only just beginning.

# CHAPTER 19

## THE AMPITHEATRE OF SANDY BAY

*... hills rise above hills; the left, clothed with wood to the summit, displays an extraordinary contrast to the wild nakedness of the other side; the downward View consists of a variety of ridges, eminences, and ravines, descending into the sea. The beauty of one part, the grandeur of another, and the horror of a third, cannot fail to astonish every observer. The Island, from this situation, has certainly the appearance of being forced up by subterraneous fire: the abrupt ridges and chasms into which it is split seeming strongly to indicate a volcanic origin.*

G.H.Bellasis, View VI 'Fairyland', in *Views of St Helena* 1815

It doesn't matter how you first see the great ampitheatre of Sandy Bay. Out of nowhere there is a totally different world, indeed it might be a different planet, just a few steps away. It is unlikely that you have ever seen anything like it. Bellasis certainly hadn't. He must have been standing pretty well at Cason's Gate when he wrote those notes, and the effect the view had on him was more accurate than the painting of Lot and Fairyland he finally produced.

And it doesn't matter how often you see Sandy Bay. It always produces this shock. Wherever you cross the rim, it leaves you wondering what on Earth it is doing there. From relative normalcy and green hills, the island drops Boom! a thousand feet and more into that vast barren hollow, rocks of many colours, contorted and mismatched, jumbled in pillars and chasms, cliffs and ruined pinnacles.

Bellasis, like most of the other visitors of his time was confused, even repulsed, by the wildness of the great hollow. Henry Salt, Lord Valentia's travelling painter in 1802, was ahead of his time, in getting some of its character and grandeur right. Turner would probably have done justice to some of the intensity of its impact, and its special light.

Sandy Bay didn't stop early settlers getting their farms into the higher fertile ground soon after 1659, but it disturbed them. Its wild and beautiful rock formations were anathema to them and passing observers. They equated them to Hell rather than to anything on the Earth. Such names as The Gates of Chaos and The Devil's Garden did not help, and calling two of the most dramatic rock pinnacles Lot and Lot's Wife, gave a somewhat ambivalent biblical colouring to the contents of the Bay. But they enhanced its theatrical image, and it was probably shown off to visitors with some degree of pride mixed with the horror.

From the rim, the size of the Bay, it's three miles from Sandy Bay Barn to the Asses Ears, tends to flatten the true enormity of some of these rock sculptures. Lot's Wife is twice the height of Nelson's Column, and Lot, from the south, is three times the height of Big Ben. But that means very little when you watch the Bay from the rim. It looks majestic, no doubting that, but it's walking into it that teaches you the respect that grows with familiarity.

Welcome then, at last, to Sandy Bay, once the heart of the great south-western volcano, and now the core of the island, the least hospitable part and one of the most welcoming. Each time I leave the island, I take my last walk in Sandy Bay, the only problem is choosing which particular aspect of its splendour.

It's very easy to say, Sandy Bay, Wow! So different from the rest of the island. And forget just how extraordinary it is as a feature. We saw the variations along the five miles of Fisher's Valley, well they pale in comparison with here. You start at the Peaks at 2697ft, vegetation so thick you can hardly move, you can't see the ground, more than 40 inches of rain, temperature up to 60° F or so. In a fraction over two miles, you are at Sandy Bay Beach, totally barren, negligible rainfall, and temperatures in the nineties, sometimes well over 100° F. Visually it is spectacular. For condensed geography, it may well be unique.

The back wall of the ampitheatre is awesome. From the Peaks its cornucopia of vegetation falls, folded and rumpled, like a huge disturbed curtain. It is wondrous. As the slope steadies, the profusion of the stream courses is mixed with small pastures, which can't make up their minds where they are

Any wrinkle or fold has water running, dribbling, or percolating through. Streams are buried in monstrous yams, great jumbles of plants. Their sides are carpetted in nasturtiums, threaded with chow chow (christophine) creepers, or morning glory. There are rice paper plants, brought in from China, twenty feet high with their crowns of fronds on long stalks. Loquat and cumquat, flaming canna and glimpses of pasture, with arum lilies and assorted dairy cattle. There are hugely convoluted trunks of thorn trees, yards across, their even more contorted branches overhead, so close they shut out not just the sky but the light.

Bends in the road reveal cascades of fuchsias, banks of cream flowered ginger, or the pendulous white blooms of *Datura suavolens*, variously discribed as Lady's Petticoat, Moon Plant or Angel's Trumpet. There are bamboos and poinsettia, aloes and bottle brush and Barberton daisies, so much hibiscus and plumbago that their reds and blues are no more than background, eucalyptus and avocados, passion fruit and red hot pokers. Its warmth and humidity wrap around, its sounds the clink of frogs, the murmuring of doves, and raucous squawks from startled mynas.

This mix of tropical and temperate, fruits and flowers, stems, berries, stalks, blooms, sprays, creepers, leaves, bells, tendrils, trumpets, firebursts or whatever, is a cross between Victorian fairy paintings and an exotic *Sound Of Music*, all of it in just a few a hundred yards. These small patches of Alpine meadow, with tiny flowers, bitter wild strawberries, and weeds from God knows where, are a part of Sandy Bay you don't expect. But then Sandy Bay has something of almost everything, from everywhere.

As you have dropped, any evidence of barrenness lower down has disappeared behind the trees of the spread-out 'settlement' of Sandy Bay. Very few of the numerous cottages are visible, well glimpses of them are, but you can hear people talking, radios, dogs and chickens. Then you find a couple of shops, a bar, the clinic, a community centre and the old school building. You can see neither sea nor desert, nor can you feel them. It is rural makebelieve, with cool temperate patches totally confused with warm, humid, tropical floral extravagances.

It's not only the vegetation that is confused. On the edge of a meadow is a two storey house which has been extended at some time to produce a church, and a school in between. The half porch half verandah has wooden pegs for coats, and benches to sit and put your wellies on. Simple it is, white-washed, the old sash windows of the house, a piano, a small stone font, and a painted St Peter window with its colours almost lost.

But from the porch it was clearly a school, before they built the new one a little higher up. That one was clearly a school, several class rooms, football pitch, kitchen, staff room. But it's now a modestly used field studies centre. Not enough children, so they bus them out to schools in other geographies. Chequered lives these buildings, their function changing with local needs.

That is a social development to match something of the geographic confusion of Sandy Bay. From the rim, the Bay is dominated by harsh colours and rocks, the rugged desert confusion. And here we are, half way down, and not only have we seen no hint of barren desolation, we've got a mix of tropical and temperate splendour, and thriving rural calm.

This is courtesy of the lie of the land. As you move round the rim, the overall character of the Bay keeps changing, but as you go into it it gets worse, or rather it gets better. Not only are things hidden from the rim as you look down, but from within as you try to find your way around. There are all kinds of paths and tracks down here, leading who knows where. There are more lost corners in Sandy Bay than in a geodesic dome.

Maps don't really help, not as you get into the detail. A good example, a significant track, ie originally for horses, is marked, starting from near the shop, wiggling round to Fairyland. That would be interesting, I thought, a rather natty shortcut. It starts out wide enough for a carriage, lined with great thorn trees, till it almost reaches Bay House, an old, extended cottage, and stops. You can look straight down onto this from Mount Pleasant, though you probably miss it, concentrating more on the spectacle of the lower reaches of the Bay.

The lady of the house very kindly shows me her garden. In terms of content it's a bit like Burchell's account of Jack Mason's, or William Doveton and Napoleon's breakfast menu. There are bananas, loquats, plums, apples, figs, peaches, guavas, rose-apples, mangoes, coffee ("Grows like a weed, coffee does"), and a rose garden all round. This is the fecundity that attracted the early settlers.

Behind the proliferation, several great rock ridges rise sheer, monumental crags, towering three, four, five hundred feet behind your back door. One of them is Coles' Rock, named after settler Coles who was murdered by his slave. Not only was his death recorded in the rocks, it was recorded in the Cathedral, where a stone once set in the floor said here lies John Coles murdered by his slave Sultan on 9th April 1721. No secrets round here.

Nothing to do with Coles, or Sultan, but the lady of the house says they have a medal, that was issued to certain slaves for good behaviour, by Governor Patton in 1806. She doesn't show me that, but she does show me the continuation of the old track. It was completely invisible, buried in vegetation within ten feet of the approach to the house. In truth it is an old bridle path, cut stone surface and a little wall, only today it's lost and inaccessible. Although wide enough to walk comfortably, it tunnels, still and humid, through the verdure beneath the invisible wild scenery.

Oh it gets you there, except at the end it disappears completely, and you're left to climb up a slope which is so steep you have to drag yourself up on the flax, until suddenly, like Mole again, you pop out propelled by your enthusiasm, disturbing rabbits on the pasture below Fairyland. And that's just one of so many of these old, hidden by-ways.

The configuration of the half bowl of Sandy Bay, is disturbed by the rounded bulk of a hill, pretty well dead centre. Riding Stones Hill partly protects the fertile higher tracts, partly extends them out, as on a promontory, into the barren colourscape of the lower Bay. Its top is left clear as pasture, and in the days of flax this was a huge drying field, geometrically spread with white patches of fibre, which was central to any view, or photo, or indeed postage stamp.

Here is Bamboo Hedge, a lovely Georgian two storey house

in red and white, recently restored. Its flax mill is now a piggery. In the sixties, the metalled road stopped at Bamboo Hedge, and the old, military track down to Sandy Bay Beach was only for feet and donkeys. Then twenty years ago, the Public Works Department made it vehicle-worthy. No mean feat, as it drops a thousand feet in about the same number of yards.

Just below Bamboo Hedge, wrapping round one side of Riding Stones, is the old Coffee Grove, now revived into a coffee 'plantation' that produces some of the most expensive coffee in the world. It's warm and very humid, with sprinklers going much of the time. *Arabica* coffee was first brought to the island from Mocha in 1732, and this plantation is said to be a descendant. One young man, David Henry, rebuilt it in the nineties, and now there are several other plantations and growers.

Riding Stones and cattle lying on the grass, the coffee grove, flower gardens, you could well have forgotten what's in store. But as the track breaks from the vegetation, there are hints of the Bay yet to come, coloured marls and a ring of grey crags, and in the middle of this sort of hollow is a Baptist Chapel.

It may well be the only chapel in the world built entirely of phonolite, the rock of Riding Stones Hill and Lot. Lot is half a mile away, but it rears up behind the chapel, the strength of its presence depending on the weather. It is white and bright and friendly in sunshine, but on overcast days, it is higher, brooding darkly.

The new, to me, road drops past the Chapel to the floor of Sandy Bay. I prefer to go round, bearing right, into another of the Bay's lost valleys. There are one or two new cottages on the edge, lovely location, grand views. Downstream is Virgin Hall, with a lengthy history long before Napoleon's time. But The Rosebud, Charlotte Knipe, lived there then, and Gourgaud thought himself much enamoured of the fair lady. Whatever it did, or most likely didn't, all amount to, Gourgaud left, and in 1820 she got married, while still living in the Hall.

Below the Hall, the valley runs tight under the great cliff of Chapel Rock, and today it's wall to wall bananas. Sandy Bay is famous for its bananas, and all of the island's eight varieties are found somewhere around. So wander your fill of these fascinating plants, groves and groves of them, and then regain the road, at a pair of cottages marked on the map as Lemon Grove.

As you clamber through the foliage, keeping your eye on, and your ankles away from, the local, viciously spined aloes, you might just make out a black stone built into the corner of one cottage:

Rob. Jenkins Esq.,
December 16th AD
1741

And that stone introduces another story of the world stage, revealed in a cottage dwarfed by its surroundings of great fertility and cliffs of phonolite.

Yes, that's right, Robert Jenkins. And the date's about right. Wasn't he the War of Jenkins Ear man? In 1731, he was master of the brig *Rebecca*, sailing from Jamaica for London. Off Havana, he was boarded by Spanish *coastguards* led by one Captain Faudino, *who had a widespread reputation for cruelty.* The ship was plundered, and one of Jenkins' ears was cut off, but the *Rebecca* and its one-eared Master managed to make it back to the Thames.

The British Government protested rather weakly to the Governor of Havana, but the matter was ignored until 1738, when the political climate was more suitably agitated. Under examination before a House of Commons Committee, Jenkins, being a dramatic story teller, even produced an object he claimed was his ear, to add to the mounting public indignation with Spain. War was declared in 1739.

Check the *Dictionary of National Biography*, and it's not a fable. Jenkins really did have his ear chopped off, confirmed by the Commander-in-Chief West Indies, no less. And he showed it, or something, in the House of Commons, and yes, they went to war of sorts. And at that point the account ends: *Nothing more is known of Jenkins.* Well it is, and there's this rock half way to Sandy Bay Beach to prove it.

In 1739, the East India Company had a problem, involving

the island's most colourful case of fraud ever to reach the surface. It also had Mr Duke Crispe, who although second in Council, in fact controlled the Governor. Crispe was *a man not deficient in talents, but possessed of no common share of knavery and cunning*, according to the island historian T.H.Brooke. And when Governor Goodwin, with whom Crispe had had all kinds of clandestine dealings, died in 1739, he succeeded him.

Perhaps needing a bit of moral support, Crispe entrusted some degree of collaboration in his assorted nefarious activities to George Gabriel Powel, also on Council, and a man, *still more artful than himself, and equally devoid of principle.* We came across Powell's Valley in the east, well that was family rather than him, probably his great-grandfather. But after a promising start, Powel pulled Crispe's plug out. Either Powel thought he had got in too deeply, or Crispe wouldn't let him get in deeply enough. So Powel wrote to the Court of Directors telling them that Crispe had his hand, or more accurately a shovel, in the Company coffers.

What to do, thought the Court of Directors? What they needed was a tough and honest man to sort out what appeared to them, so far away, a bit of a shambles. So they found one. Captain Robert Jenkins, temporarily unemployed, possibly declared medically unfit for the war he'd helped to start, was despatched as governor for eighteen months. Immediately on landing, in May 1740, Jenkins went to the Castle, demanded the keys to the Treasury in the presence of Duke Crispe, and his current side-kick Bazett, and counted the island's cash reserves. They totalled £6 19s. Short by a number of zeros.

That was just the start, for Jenkins uncovered a veritable cauldron of worms in the Company's affairs, but ever resourceful, he sorted everything out. He even found time for substantial repairs to the fortifications. He had noticed something amiss, when the guns firing a salute from the Castle brought parts of its walls down.

When the new Governor, Major Thomas Lambert, arrived, Jenkins departed, his job well done. Crispe had had a short spell in gaol, and was out and about, and back in the thick of things. Sadly, after only four months in charge of his new, 'clean' Council, Lambert died and, wait for it, George Gabriel Powel was appointed Acting Governor! Gosse provides a character reference:

*Governor Powel ruled St Helena for two years .... During this brief period he embezzled the Company's money, stole their brandy, wine, beef, pork and other property from the store, which he sold privately, and he leased their lands for his own use, and their timber, lime, purbeck-stone and other building materials to construct a commodious dwelling-house on his estate in the country ...*

Isn't this where we came in? Complaints again went to London, and Powel was removed. He sailed off into the sunset, to America, where it is said, he did so well for himself he became a Congressman.

Below Jenkin's Cottage, close to the delicate Blarney Bridge, all the waters of the catchment beneath the Peaks, have come together and gurgle busily down to Sandy Bay Beach. I use 'gurgle' advisedly. To hear streams, particularly as they cross the barren outer fringes, is a great joy. All too often water, if there is any, has gone underground, or all that is left dribbles invisibly seawards, or evaporates stagnantly, if colourfully on occasions.

Note that, a finely masoned bridge. Sandy Bay is probably the most easily accessible part of the island from the sea. And Sandy Bay Beach is actually a bit sandy and shelving, and that, with its broad approach, makes access relatively simple. All right, it's not an all weather landing, no way, but this obvious ease of access meant the Bay was fortified before the end of the seventeenth century. Blarney Bridge is a reminder, just like the gun battery below the Chapel, of the military origins of the road down Sandy Bay.

The stream 'valley' you follow to the sea though, is another oddity. It looks quite hospitable, indeed it is quite hospitable, with its ribbon of vegetation hiding the stream much of the time. But it is like a linear oasis, a sharp line defines growing from barren. One side of the line is a green strip of bushy trees, lethal looking and feeling aloes, a vegetable plot or two, yams, and prickly pear. The other side of the line looks as though it was carved, or adzed might be closer, out of a spoil heap.

As the valley opens, the impression of dryness increases. Broken walls of dykes cross from side to side, some of their remnants rising a hundred feet or more above the rubble. Off the path it is *gritty*, this desert combination of altered cinders and rocks broken down into chippings and dust. The scratch-like traces you can see are rabbit tracks.

There are a very few cottages along the valley bottom, only two inhabited, the others in varying stages of ruin. But amazingly, this stretch down the floor of the bay along the stream is so much greener than it was in the '60s. Then, I'd pitched my tent in the middle of a fine field of dust, near some aged date palms. The only green then, this far down, was a strip of grass, a few feet wide, forming the stream's banks.

Now I couldn't recognize my 'camp'. The whole stretch is planted with vegetables by the one active farmer, known as Pickaxe. He uses the stream to irrigate the area, and the lower end of the valley bottom. His achievements are a splendid example of what can be done with hard work and dedication - and of course a permanent and plentiful stream to oneself.

Past a couple of banyans, bent over at right angles by the wind, the track terminates at Beach Hill, a hillock in the centre of the little bay. On its top, is a ruined battery and a chance to look round and see what you've reached. Here, very much in its centre, you still can't grasp Sandy Bay in its entirety, maybe that really is possible only from somewhere on the rim. Under White Hill and Sandy Bay Barn it's a rugged mess of ridges and precipitous cliffs, crags and rubble slopes. The jagged ridges on the western side block much of the view of the rim beyond Lot's Wife, but you can see it's getting wilder in that direction.

The fortifications are much eroded, but once you get your eye in you begin to set them in place. The sea wall is almost intact on the left, and the arch for the stream is quite beautiful. There are still cannon, and Dartmoor granite plinths for the guns. But the longer wall on the right, which was here in the sixties, has completely gone. Burchell's drawings, and later photos, show a line of low stone buildings along the top of the wall, but they didn't make it into the twentieth century.

But on the side of the bay, close to a rock called Horse's Head there is a barrel-roofed magazine, and remnant batteries. In fact, hidden away around the Beach are scattered bits and pieces of the military past, solid picquet huts, the detailed masonry of culverts, tiny bridges above waves creaming into gullies. There's even a lime kiln, currently being restored by The National Trust.

In 1708 calcareous sands were discovered in Sandy Bay. This was a discovery of major importance, because there are no white sand beaches on the island, not like on Ascension. So that was good news. Even better, though less believable today, were the *huge quantities of dead ebony wood for burning the lime* that were lying on the hillsides. You can see some of those sands on the White Hill side, where they constitute part of the Devil's Garden. But the main 'dunes' are a mile or so west, below Lot's Wife. So the kiln went into production, and continued for many years.

The other main valley of the Bay is Broad Gut. 'Gut' is normally only used for tributary streams. But Broad Gut comes into the sea at the side of what is left of the parade ground. It is bleak, Broad Gut, even though now its stream bed is filled with lank grass, and the frenzied intergrowth of wild mango. This is a change since the '60s, when there was quite literally nothing growing in the valley bottom, except in patches of sand you could find gypsum roses. Oh yes, and there was a feral donkey, very much on its last legs, waiting to die here, teased by mynas braying in imitation.

The groundwater conditions down here are amazing. Don't be put off, I mean it. Amazing. Those gypsum roses were fed from the groundwater. But in the side stream coming from the Gates of Chaos, under Lot's Wife, the rocks of its so called streambed are eaten away almost as you watch. The bed's only a few feet wide, and on the edge the rubble is solid, perfectly normal, you can only break the rocks with a hammer. A foot or two away the rocks look almost the same, lying in the dry streambed, but you can poke your finger into them! Just a couple of hundred yards from Sandy Bay Beach, are features they'd be proud of in the Sahara.

Starting from the Beach is one of the island's most dramatic paths, to Lot's Wife's Ponds. On its way it reveals a hidden side of Sandy Bay, normally only seen by fishermen. Part of the way, you follow the 300 year old track to the white sands. The need for lime was so great, they built a roadway for horses and mules, through the inhospitable crenulations of the southern coast.

The path scrapes over one little ridge, and up a valley and the side of another, hiding Lot's Wife. The rocks clink and clatter and slide as you struggle 700 feet up towards a col, still with no real indication of the character of your destination. There seems not only no view, but no air, but each time you pause and look back, more and more of the green of the distant Peaks is revealed, bringing at least a hint of surrogate cooling.

There's a refreshing breeze at the col, and an astonishing view along the south of the island. The ridge you are crossing rises precipitously to Lot's Wife, and as you continue, the pale grey pillar will change shape, into a buxom torso, into a mittened hand. And beyond Lot's Wife, down to the shore, any hint of order breaks down, into a savage display of cliffs and pinnacles, distorted towers and an enormous black gorilla's head.

It is a Martian landscape, of gashes clawed into its garb of many colours, over which white sands have then been dumped. The sands cover the slopes up to nearly 800 feet above sea level, in places 25 or 30 feet deep. They are coarse shell sands, bedded like sand dunes in a desert. They originated as beaches when the water was warmer, and like the ones at Banks they got blown inland when the sea level was lowered during the Ice Ages of the Pleistocene. Now they're the 'fossilized' remains of beaches smeared across the hillsides instead.

Going to Lot's Wife's Ponds is like following a rainbow to find the pot of gold at the end. Leave the sands, leave the traces of old mule track, leave the endemic baby's toes, drop down the low cliff, go round the hundred feet high rock pillar called The Chimney, and there they are. Lot's Wife's Ponds, on the black lava platform, are seawater pools deep enough to swim in.

The coast is controlled, and protected, by the black dykes,

forming walls against the constant pounding of the sea. But treat the sea with great respect, for when it is 'naughty', it can thunder across the wall scouring the platform, dragging all and sundry with it as it swirls and foams back.

On a gentle day, the pools are palest shades of turquoise, with fish of many colours swimming through curtains of sunlight. There are sea urchins and star fish and little brain corals, and wonderful black crabs that don't walk on the water, but run across it. Sit very quietly for a while and then stand and walk towards a Pond. Crabs scurry away across the lava, and then race, skittering across the water's surface to the other side and climb up the wall.

Here is peace, smell the sea, feel it moist and salt on your face, hear it roar along the dyke walls, feel it thud into the lava platform, and duck its foaming curtains hissing into the sky. Sit and watch golden sequinned fish in the turquoise pools. Here on the platform the rest of the island is hidden. Lot's Wife's Ponds is one of the spots on the island when you can feel time standing still. Wait long enough, and it may even go backwards.

But walk across the platform, rest on the dyke wall of the sea, and look inland. There are no real cliffs, not the monsters of elsewhere, just rocky platforms or boulder beaches behind which the land rises steeply, in yellows, golds, browns and blacks of dust, scree, crags and boulders, pinnacles and stumbling steps, all traversed by black or grey or white dykes, rising hundreds of feet, the rock fantasies of the south-west, vast contorted cliffs, the brooding Frightus Rock, emaciated and less simian, and the huge fluted faces of the Asses Ears.

If a theatre director was looking for ideas for a production of Dante's Inferno, he couldn't believe his luck at what he'd found, for it is like a gigantic stage setting. It is awesome, feelings of immense isolation surrounded by a majesty of rocks turned into stone curtains, ripped and shredded, flapping in your imagination in the Trade winds. It is impossible to look at this setting without hearing orchestras, choirs, Wagner, their wonderful sounds soaring skywards with the rocks and your imagination.

It depends on your mood as to how threatening you find it,

how wondrous you find it. But whatever you want it to be, it will be spectacularly that. Overwhelming, peaceful, satisfying, reassuring, massively stimulating. It is primitive, mightily so, it creates a feeling of uncertainty. There is no trace of man, no trace of vegetation, very little of life in any form. There is an enormity of presence here. The rocks seem primordial, you can sense that, and they are, for you are looking into the very heart, the entrails, of the ten million year old volcano.

Here you sit, on a stage of beauty and tranquility, and there, no more than another of Darwin's lusty stone's throws away is the Underworld. Listen to it. Relish it. Tomorrow, you can climb into it.

# CHAPTER 20

## HEART OF THE VOLCANO

*Of some of the largest of these dikes, three or four are very remarkable features in the structure of the Island, striking, as they do, in parallel lines from the north-east to the south-west right across the crater; and, when viewed from its edge, much resembling the trail of some great serpent or monster which had wended its way across it.*

John Charles Melliss, 1875

Close to the end of the western rim of Sandy Bay, beyond High Peak and its donkeys, beyond where the high green slopes stop in Hooper's Ridge, beyond the graceful hollow of the Ball Alley, where the rim is just wind sculpted rocks, and before it falls into the Atlantic at the Asses Ears, there is a final diminutive patch of green. Long ago this was known as Lot's Wife's Wood, though it must be many decades since it saw anything resembling a tree.

At the end of the eighteenth century, there were two cottages here, one named after the Wood, and a further one, Distant Cottage. But with time, the further cottage seems to have disappeared, and the remaining cottage by the relic greenery became known as Distant Cottage. Unusually for a small house it was two storeyed. There was a low extension for a kitchen, and an oven, built into a step in the earth bank of the ridge behind. The cottage had fertile soil around it and panoramic views of the changing patterns of sunshine and moonlight and mists, over Sandy Bay.

In the '60s, nobody lived in Distant Cottage, though its owner, Lioney Yon, grew vegetables there, much the situation as it is today. I rented the derelict cottage for a month or so, as a base for handier access to the rocks of the south-west. It was a strange building. Downstairs was empty, but habitable, if you had a camp bed and some candles. The ceiling was low, and its beams were round, made from the masts of a wreck washed up on the shore far below, Lioney told me.

It was L-shaped. The living room was the longer bit, with a sort of ante-room in the angle, and in the short bit was what had once been the kitchen, so ramshackle it was left alone. I slept in this ante-room, which seemed to consist largely of doors, one through to the living room, one to the kitchen, and a third behind my head. This one, tied closed with a bit of flax, was at the foot of the stairs, to what was the former bedroom upstairs. The floor of the bedroom was unsafe, so nobody went up there, Lioney told me.

Beyond the cottage, there was no definite path to anywhere, only open access to the wilder parts of Sandy Bay, and the extreme south-west, places where you went if you were after wild goats or rabbits, or strayed sheep, or if you had business with the entrails of the long deceased volcano.

So the one path from the cottage led back to the inhabited parts of the island, the civilized world. It went into the Ball Alley, a bizarre little notch in the rim, carved by the wind in a patch of softer rocks. Its floor is of rich fire and flame reds, oranges, golds and autumn bronzes. These ashes are cut by altered dykes, patterned in yellow and black, standing proud but lopsided, wandering across the gentle slopes like unsteady walls, or the fossilized skeletons of prehistoric beasts.

At the Ball Alley, the path divided, one branch staying in the Bay to continue round to Fairyland. The other branch turned away towards the Churchyard and Thompson's Wood, to Botley's Lay and Man and Horse. The only water at the cottage was in the rain butt. So I went for my drinking water along this second bit of path, across the Churchyard, to a tap by a cattle trough, next to the fence which stopped them stumbling over the edge, fifteen hundred feet into Manati Bay.

The Churchyard was a flat apron, sheltering just behind the rim of the Bay. Its grassy surface was scattered with large boulders, looking a bit like gravestones, which accounts for its name. In daylight it was peaceful, a haven for wirebirds, running, sometimes half flying, in and out of the boulders. At night, mists blasted through the Ball Alley, racing across this patch of erstwhile calm, swirling round boulders, chasing the ghostly sow and piglets which ran there, or so I was told.

About a mile from the cottage, on the path which stayed in the Bay, at the foot of the slab faces and slipped blocks of Hooper's Rock, was the cottage where Edward Williams lived. Edward was in his later sixties. He'd been a Government shepherd for decades, and there's a photo of him and his family in Gosse's book of 1938. He'd done a spell on Ascension in the 1950s, and now spent his time working a patch or two of potatoes, on a flat piece of ground below Distant Cottage, watched over by Lot's Wife. He kept his cats there.

It was Edward who arranged the donkeys that met me at the end of the west road, to bring my stuff down to the cottage. Friday afternoons, the donkeys carted my week's collection of rocks back the same way. A boy always came with the donkeys, his grandson, Gary Stevens from Wild Cattle Pound, as it was called then, or Stedson Francis, from Thompson's Wood.

Edward was a quiet man of great character. He told me a lot about the wild rocky places, and the ways of paths which only the goats and runaway sheep used, or the men and boys who went after them. Twice a year, Edward was still involved with the ritual district sheep pounding. Someone, I never knew who, had an aged white horse, and as Edward had become less fleet of foot, the horse was brought over. So Edward, wearing the khaki sola topi he saved for special occasions, stayed on the horse, on the higher, quieter ground, marshalling his troops into the wilder, lower places.

A hundred and thirty years earlier, Darwin had described how during his few days on St Helena, *My guide was an elderly man, who had been a goatherd when a boy, and knew every step amongst the rocks. He was a very civil, quiet old man.* That could well have been written of Edward, every rock he knew, and he was a gentle man, in the fullest sense of the word.

Dorothy, Edward's good lady, provided me with my dinner every evening. Just before it got dark, I would walk along the hedged approach of Distant Cottage, I could hardly call it a drive, across the ashes of many colours of the Ball Alley, and drop down the grassy track to the cottage, two small rooms and a kitchen outbuilding. As I ate my meal, joined by Edward to talk, for he ate earlier, I learned much about this end of Sandy Bay.

After supper, I had to walk back in darkness, in the whistling, sometimes howling, wind, and driving mists. And for light, Edward loaned me a St Helena bottle lantern. Simple to make, he told me. You dipped a piece of string in kerosene, tied bits round the bottom and shoulder of a bottle, and lit them. The bottle cracked, and you were left with the glass cylinder. A base with a socket for a candle, and an angled hood, were made out of flattened tin cans. A ring (and I never knew what that had been in any previous life) through the hood, was for carrying the lantern. Light the candle, close the hood, and I was off.

The light it cast was disturbed. The shadows of your hand, trying to stop the Trades extinguishing the candle, danced over the track. And when the wind got the better of you, which it usually did, re-lighting it was impossible. The wind was strong enough to blow the bottle away, not just the match out of your hand. In the darkness and mists in the Ball Alley, the contorted dinosaur rocks danced surreally, and almost invariably I finished the walk unsure of any differences between real objects and my imagination.

And the entertainment was only beginning. Evenings and nights were never quiet at Distant Cottage, because of the rats. They didn't come downstairs, at least I never saw them downstairs. But then, if island lore is correct, you wouldn't see them, you wouldn't even feel them. They wait till you're asleep and blow on you first, softly, and then nibble the tasty bits (ears were very popular, they said, and noses and toes) without waking you. The blowing was a sort of rodential anaesthetic.

They made a distinctive noise, the rats, as they chewed the floorboards upstairs, or the wood of the joists to the side of my head. There was nothing odd about this, it was exactly the same in those days in the Consulate Hotel, before it was so splendidly rebuilt and re-fitted. It provided a regular scraping, sort of crunching, noise, and the occasional patter of tiny feet across the ceiling was a welcome diversion.

But about once a week, the night became bedlam, with tiny

footsteps, now racing in terror, magnified several fold by the sounding box of the upper floor. There were outbursts of shriekings and squeakings, such as could never have been envisaged when Badger and his companions recaptured Toad Hall from the weasels and stoats of the Wild Wood. "My cats," explained Edward, when I was sufficiently traumatized to recount the adventures.

And then one evening, John Bailey, the newly arrived dentist, paid me a visit. His growing reputation as a great walker was matched by another, as a teller of terrifying ghost stories. As the wind blasted the cottage, shaking the hedge and loose bits of the roof and outbuildings, as the rats tip-toed about their business upstairs, and the candles cast wicked shadows into bare corners, John recounted the story of the ghost of Distant Cottage.

A long time ago, the owner of the cottage was a widower, who lived there with his twin daughters. They were about twenty years old, very attractive, with long dark hair. One evening, father told the girls he had to go out, he would be late, possibly not returning till the next morning. Under no circumstances were they to go downstairs and open the front door, he ordered. They must stay in their room, with the door locked, until he returned, was that understood?

It was, and the girls dutifully said goodnight to their father, and closed and locked the door. They heard him creak down the stairs, walk through the living room, and go out of the front door, locking it behind him. For a while they talked, then growing tired, they blew out the candle and went to sleep.

Some time later, they were woken by the sound of heavy footsteps coming along the path. Then there was a solid knock on the front door. One of the girls was more independently willed than her sister, and decided to go downstairs. In spite of her sister's pleading, she lit the candle, unlocked the bedroom door and went out, telling her sister to lock the door after her. In the darkness, her sister turned the key, and heard her disobedient twin start to go down the stairs. Then there was silence, broken only when the front door was knocked again, loudly. After a while, the footsteps went away, and heavy silence settled for the rest of the night.

In the morning, the father returned, unlocked the front door and came into the room calling to his daughters. But there was only the echo of his voice. He opened the door at the foot of the stairs, and just inside, on the sort of landing, was the body of one of his daughters. Her neck was broken. The room above was silent.

Deeply shocked, he scrambled past the body of one daughter, and raced up the stairs. The bedroom door was locked, and not a sound came from within. He panicked, and broke the door down. In the corner of the bedroom, the light from the little window fell on his other daughter. Her long hair was white, her eyes stared unseeing, and she endlessly repeated "Don't go down, don't go down."

Even thinking where the dead girl had supposedly lain, just behind my sleeping head, didn't bother me at the time. No one else had mentioned the ghost, so perhaps John had made it up. But on other evenings, walking back from Edward's, with the lamp guttering and casting disturbed shadows on the half mists half rocks, it provided food for rather jumpy thoughts.

Then in the middle of my very last night in the cottage, I woke suddenly. But there was only silence. I put it down to the moonlight, which was not something at all usual, coming through the broken window in the kitchen, through the broken door frame, down on the foot of my bed.

Then I heard the first sounds. Were they feet, moving through the grass? No, there was only silence. Then there was the faintest scrape of something brushing against the hedge, and slow scuffing noises. Yes, they were feet, coming closer, uncertainly, furtively. I slowly rose on the wobbly bed, and picked up my geological hammer. It was reassuring, though even at the time I realised how useless it would be against such ghostly tread.

The feet, for I was now convinced they were definitely feet, came closer, and the moon was snuffed out by a cloud. The darkness in the room was heavy, solid, I could almost touch it. The feet stopped moving. They couldn't have been more than a yard from the front door. Silence. Even the rats were quiet. I was sort of frozen, like in those childhood games of statues, half out of the bed, half crouching. And clutching a hammer. I didn't know what to do, except continue to feel rather stupid.

Then the moon shone free of its cloud into the tatty kitchen. I moved, and was almost standing, when it broke through the window - the tortured, lung-draining, rasping bellows of a moonstruck donkey.

I think what was so special for me about Distant Cottage was living in such isolation, with those unbelievable views over Sandy Bay. When I'd camped down below at the Beach, it hadn't been the same, there were no immediate views, so you didn't live with the wonder, almost magic, of this setting. At Distant Cottage, all this, the most spectacular half of the island, was mine to absorb, as and when I wanted.

Behind the ridge behind the cottage, the island is if anything even more striking, and completely devoid of man. Back through the Ball Alley is Manati Bay, and the nearly two thousand feet high, monstrous cliffs of Man and Horse. They were called that because one day a man and a horse, one of each, fell off. Appropriate, concise, that name. And Manati Bay was named after a manati that was found there. But it wasn't, it was a southern elephant seal, but that didn't roll quite so easily off the tongue.

Manati Bay is wild, no doubt about that, but it has greenery at the top, and bits and pieces growing inside it. But move south, along the ridge behind the cottage, and it becomes more and more savage, Devil's Hole, Devil's Cap, Narrow Ridge. That was where I had seen wild goats in the sixties.

Now I was back, and the goats were all gone. This was very good for the island, and the gradual return of vegetation. But it was a loss if you wanted to travel in these places. Before, goat tracks a few inches wide were an invaluable help in getting about. Now they were gone, all you had were the even narrower, fainter, rabbit tracks. With the fishermen's tracks also less and less used, travelling was getting trickier, especially in these outer edges of Sandy Bay and round the Asses Ears.

But I have digressed again. For my final quest is into the centre of the volcano, and that is inside the rim of Sandy Bay, not outside. It is time to move along the ridge. The air is wonderful, thousands of miles fresh, the immense horizon clearly curved, a brilliant sun bringing out every shade of Sandy Bay's multicoloured wilderness. The ridge itself is quite ordinary, narrow and ragged, a mess of altered lavas, ashes, dykes, all the colours of a rather dull rainbow. On good days, you can wander from edge to edge, contrasting the wildness of one side with the savagery of the other.

I found a lovely thirty year difference. Now, on the Sandy Bay side, with a backdrop of Lot's Wife, endemic scrubwoods are returning with a vengeance, reclaiming their own. There are dozens of full-size, and younger, bushy trees, sticky green leaves and daisy-like flowers. But look more carefully down the side a bit. Lift the tendrils of creeper, which hold moisture through most of the driest spells, and there are shoots a few inches high of more and more scrubwoods.

So now it has become a lovely ridge, because of these lovely plants. And it's a wondrous ridge, as it exposes more and more of the wild and wonderful rock towers, pillars, call them what you will, and their ever changing relations. Lot's Wife and her daughters, and even more spectacular, the views down onto Man o' War Roost, the vertical grey wall of one Asses Ear, and the black head of Frightus Rock.

This is Blue Point, 1920 feet above sea level, and the world and Sandy Bay are spread before you. Lot looks good from this direction, but small and insignificant, just another part of the Bay. His wife had become dominant, but already she too, is losing her impact. The biblical pair are civilized after a fashion, but they are fading into the background. The rock masses now taking over are decidedly pagan, more magnificently primitive, offering up an almost bestial empathy.

It was on this ridge, twenty years ago, that George Benjamin, and his brother, found the last surviving St Helena ebony. Not exactly here, not on top, but on the face of the cliff which drops a few hundred feet into the chaotic lavas and ashes.

George had been looking through his binoculars, and thought a shrub clinging to the face, part way down, looked different. In St Helenian fashion the men drove in a spike, and George sent his brother down on the rope, swinging into a different time. George shows a photo of the cliff face under Blue Point, and points to where the plant was.

The photo looks pretty frightening, but the reality is truly vertiginous. It brings to mind the verse in *Oh God our help in ages past*:

*Before the hills in order stood*
*Or earth received her frame,*

It's as though the landscape had been removed from any earthly connection, but there is a fusion of fascination with fear. And you're still only looking down at it, you're not in it, not part of it, you can still lift your eyes and see the security of the greenery, the life, of the central Peaks.

From Lot's Wife's Ponds you looked across at the majesty of this scene. You know from the map the scale of it all. It's a setting some two thousand feet in height, and individual players, the pillars and cliffs and towers, may be a few hundred, perhaps a thousand, feet high. Even here, dimensions are unreal, but what takes over is their physical presence. It sounds obvious to say that, but you are now aware of their identities, individually and collectively. The atmosphere is mystical, and yes, a little unsettling. It takes a hold on you, you can feel the enormity. You are looking into the exposed heart of the volcano, and the violent beauty of its past drags you in.

The centre of this great volcano is related to the great white dykes that cross the Bay. They aren't monster or serpent trails, but they do lead the way to the heart of the volcano, literally now at your feet. As the island volcanic pile grew, a vast chamber of molten magma formed within it, a couple of miles perhaps beneath its summit. And as it got older and older, the chemistry of the magma changed, and became a magma of phonolite. And in the dying stages of its life, the volcano injected this lighter magma into its body as in some enormous, secret, act of *harakiri.*

This was the volcano's final act. At the time, after its long history of roaring eruptions, this was the volcano going out with a visual whimper. For this final event may have barely disturbed the surface. As the forces of the magma chamber flexed the volcano, the liquid phonolite was pushed into weak spots on the flanks, and into the four major fissures which split its centre so deeply. More than seven million years have exposed its internal workings, and the final evidence of death from this massive haemorrhaging. That's what you're looking at.

I find the starkness and austerity of these savage views beautiful, but they come very close to threatening. There is no doubting the feeling that this is a special place. There is nowhere else on the island where I am so aware of Nature with a capital N, Nature raw and magnificent, if you like, too grand for man to have any impact.

Here then, saved till last, is the ultimate traverse into the volcano's ravaged entrails. Along to the end of the rim, round the Asses Ears, across to the bottom of Man o' War Roost, up and through it, past the cliff where George Benjamin found the ebony, and back onto Blue Point.

In '96 I had decided that much as I wanted to go back round the Ears, it was for a younger man, one with a bit more, or a bit less, sense, whichever way you wanted to look at it. Gary Stevens, the butcher today, the lad with the donkey thirty years ago, wanted to come out with me walking one day. He suggested the Asses Ears, he hadn't been for ten years, he said. But we only went half way round, onto their feet so's to speak, and came back. That seemed like enough. But in '99 we wanted to go again, and Gary was game for the circuit.

At the last trig. point on the rim, the beauty of the view to the west is breathtaking. A thousand feet below, at the feet of the Asses Ears, outside Sandy Bay, is the boulder spattered apron of Castle Rock Plain. Round it, off shore, scattered like a bizarre supporting cast, are a collection of islands and islets. The ocean seethes and foams round them, draping them with turquoise and white necklaces and frills. Sea level is 2000 feet below, but you can have no idea of dimensions, just of splendour.

Dominating, is the galleon of Speery Island, a huge guano covered islet, vaster than Captain Hook's ship in imagination. And there are black rocks, sharp rocks, flat rocks, vast misshapen sharks' fins, blades and statues, even one like a snail heading for the shore. They are jewels, of unknown provenance. The daunting vertical backdrops, are juxtaposed with this seascape of such brightness. It is a romantic, almost a soft view, where all the others round here are austere and harsh. It feeds a definite awareness of time into this immensely physical place.

Dropping as they do to end the rim, the Ears are magnificent, their great columns and jointed slabs fused into a vertical fall of organ-pipes 900 feet onto the little apron Plain. Tropic birds, long white tail feathers helping them balance, wheel and glide round the Ears. They rest motionless in the wind funnelled between the two towers, and plunge screaming away out of sight to their cliff homes. We go the other way, scambling and slithering down the dust and grit and boulders onto the apron. So far so good.

The boulders that looked like pebbles from the top, are the size of concrete bunkers, the tufts of grass are in fact small bushes, the 'dust' is chips and gravel with coatings of creeper and traces of samphire, lantana and prickly pear and sudden pink dots of periwinkles called Venus roses. Speery Island and all the other islets are bigger, more radiant, but their beauty is now somehow irrelevant.

Close to where the fishermens' track drops off the Plain, into the seared rubble that takes them to the sea, are the bare footprints of a woman. They say that if you scuff out the footprints on your way down, when you return they are there again. Who she was, nobody knows. I never saw them, but I did wonder how they knew they had been made by a woman, but down here you don't ask.

Suddenly the Plain is no more, the shelter of the Asses Ears has gone, and the wind is blasting round their corner. You cross a steep slope of massive white boulders spalled from the Ears, angular, lichen crusted. You can't see the top of this one Ear, you just look amazed at the sheet of rock rearing out of sight above you, occasional scrubwoods clinging to crevices and resting on small ledges.

The clean grey rock of the Ears stops, and the ground plunges away. It's only as we reach it that I realise we are travelling just behind the back of the gorilla head of Frightus Rock. Sit awhile.

Frightus is one of a kind. Not only is the gorilla face from the other direction almost perfect, but the back of the head has rolls of fat onto its shoulders. Why it's called Frightus nobody knows, but from most vantage points you only see the great black face, and you might just say, "Well it fright us."

Quarter of a mile above, the Ears hold up the rim of the ampitheatre. Here it falls, in scourged red and yellow contortions, down past us, past Frightus, to cascade into the ocean. Opposite where we sit, is the several hundred feet end-wall of Man o' War Roost. The cliff looks black, rising from waves of crumpled and corrugated little ridges and valleys.

It's easier to describe the broad features of Sandy Bay from the rim than from close to the floor of the ampitheatre. Closer to the heart of the volcano, unless you have seen it, or seen photos, however powerful your descriptive writing might be, it can only fall short. Even photos fall short. The heat, the difficulty of movement, the stark emotional awe of the setting, can't come through.

When you are in there, the intensity is modified by the tiny details of every footstep. Every hold to steady yourself, is different in some way, in many ways. Maybe that's one reason why Saints travel so easily. They only need to cross it, for fish or rabbits or lost sheep. I'm so busy stopping to look at some miniscule fragment of volcano, that concentration on my feet slips, and so do I

Now it is not only the surroundings that are awesome, for Gary heads off, to cross the tortured serrations. He's a big man, but he covers these impossible surfaces like a rabbit, he doesn't even slip on the steep gritty surfaces, on which in places I can't move at all. I know if I do it's tens of feet of slithering, on a hot cheese grater, before I stop.

I'm not sure if it 'fright us', but it's making me think a lot more than twice. This is seriously scarey. But Gary's help with a length of rope gets me over the worst. It's so bad, not only can I hardly stop to take in the scenery, but I forget to explain to Gary that Man o' War Roost is literally the centre of the volcano, that it is a dyke several hundred feet thick, that represents the final outpourings of life from the magma chamber. Twenty, thirty, perhaps as many as fifty times, earthquakes shook the south-west as the volcano heaved and cracked open, and liquid phonolite was injected a mile and more up into the broken shield. I must have been worried to forget that.

But we get to the foot of the cliff, and stand in fine dust, and tiny white puff balls of birds' body feathers. Although named after the frigate, the black man o' war, bird, the inhabitants today of this extraordinary rookery are white tropic birds. The cliff is a mass of caves and hollows, buttresses, walls and protruberances. There are poles in some places, which must be from a time long past, used for getting eggs, or catching young tropic birds to eat. It is illegal now, but it wasn't then, and the poles, looking more like toothpicks, in the scale of the cliff, remain. Now it's feral cats that leave the puff ball carcases behind.

We go along the bottom of the cliff, climb up through the other end, and sit on its top trying to breath normally. It's easier now to savour the wild scenery of this area, you are that much more appreciative because you've managed not to smear yourself into it. Gary shouts to two dots that are Blue Hill fishermen, climbing up the next ridge over on a residual track towards Lot's Wife.

When I'm recovered, we start up the little ridge to the rim. Clinging to the steep side there are delicate white flowers, forty or fifty of them, flowers of the endemic, Old Father Live Forever, only growing in three or four locations now. And scambling onto the rim crest I find beneath the creepers the new growth of tiny scrubwoods. A fitting end to the climb, these very living endemics, as you rest and look back.

The precipices are enormous, the rock pillars from a different world. It is isolated from the rest of the island, its entity is complete. Nowhere is as wild or as free, nowhere as untouched by man, this really is where the only values are those of nature. It is primordial, you are not even a dot. Here is the heart of the volcano, geologically the climax. This is where it rose from the ocean, boiling, exploding. This is the hearth of its innermost secrets. This is where it died its hidden death. Yes, this for me could contain the island's soul.

Time and the elements have seen fit to strip it down, display its core, make it available, expose its monstrous power. Yet here too, are major components of the island's life. The ebony, so long believed extinct, was found here, and so was the boxwood. Soft white flowers on their long, oh so slender, stalks of old father live forever are here, so are the gentle daisy flowers of the scrubwoods. Yes, and baby's toes and salad plant and boneseed, all unique to the island.

They are part of the opera that you can hear, as much as the splendour, the magic, of the rocks, from towering cliffs down to single sparkling crystals. It is here that you find as much of the nature of creation, as NASA sought and found in its search for remnants of the Big Bang. They had an entire Universe to find it in, and here we have it in this glorious half-hidden corner of the south-west.

It's a monstrous setting, it's not really threatening, it's just that getting there isn't easy. It offers a very special peace, the chance of a very special relationship between you and these surroundings, atavistic, unbelievably personal. Just you and the freedom of the wind and the heat, the distant ocean and tropic birds. No wonder they scream, it's exhilarating. It's the wonder of being in the heart, in the history, of the volcano. It's the wonder too, of recognizing the gift that allows you to go there.

You don't need a T-shirt after this. You know it, and it stays with you. I've been there, it was wondrous, it was magic, even if it did scare the pants off me.

# CHAPTER 21

## LAYERS OF TIME

*To every thing there is a season, and a time to every purpose under the heaven .... a time to break down, and a time to build up .... a time to cast away stones, and a time to gather stones together ..... a time to seek, and a time to lose ..... a time to keep silence, and a time to speak ....*

Ecclesiastes, Chapter 3, verses 1-7

"Yes, they're both clear now." It was a simple statement. I put the phone down. I was in my cabin, thinking about bed. It was just after midnight, and that was the Officer of the watch, calling from the bridge. I doubt if you get that kind of attention on the cruise liners.

On deck, we got away from as much of the light as possible. Warm, almost cloudless night, soft breeze. Hear the hum of engines, swash of ocean, that ubiquitous faint smell of burnt diesel. And wall to wall stars.

"There," he pointed. One way the Pole Star, crystal clear back to the Arctic if you want.

"And there," he pointed again. The other way, the Southern Cross. All the way to the Antarctic, but just as far as the island will do nicely, thank you.

It's very special that, you can feel both hemispheres. It's a bit like crossing the date line, or standing astride the meridian in Greenwich, only they have an element of artificiality about them. The North Star and the Southern Cross, they are that much more natural. It's nothing to do directly with St Helena, but for me it is the first clear indication that there is something special afoot.

However hard you scrabble round the summit ridge of the Peaks, and however cloudless is the sky, you can never actually see unbroken sea all round the island. Very close, just a couple of short moves, spider sprints perhaps, and you get it in composite, but never all at once. It doesn't seem to matter, it's a bit like the surprise you feel sometimes in Jamestown when you go through the Archway. Good God, the sea, I'd forgotten. Good grief, I'm on an island!

But sitting somewhere or other on one of the high points, you can see lots of the island falling away around and below you, so you feel satisfied that you've got so high. Then, you're pleasantly surprised at how obvious is the curvature of the horizon. If you can see that horizon over a hundred and eighty degrees and more, I don't know how far that is in miles, but it's a long way, so it should be looking a bit bent. And it really does. That adds to the special feeling, too.

You arrive abruptly on one corner of Long Range, and the cliffs at the end surprise you. They're not much more than a thousand feet high, but they are striking. The cliffs are almost sheer, and they have a perfection you don't see anywhere else. The lavas are black, layers and layers of black lava, red and yellow breaks of ash. The impact is stark, blackness, sharpness, almost of freshness. Elsewhere the cliffs look brown, and this pristine blackness says enormity. Curvature of the Earth, and clean cut high cliffs. Where is the specialness coming from here?

How long did it take this bit of the island to build up? For the fifty or sixty individual layers that you can count? Tens of thousands of years, hundreds of thousands? And then how long to erode back this far? Their slope says they probably used to finish maybe two miles out to sea. And over what kind of time? Eight million years? They've been cut back to this. It's about a foot a millenium, give or take. That's time, serious time.

I'd had that similar feeling to time at the end of the west rim of Sandy Bay, looking at Speery Island. One way there was this white islet, half a mile out to sea, and the other way, Lot, a mile and a half inland, sitting on a ridge a thousand feet high. The two great white rocks are exactly the same age, they have identical origins as infilled feeders, pipes, of volcanic vents. Same age, same origin, very much the same position in relation to the volcano's centre originally, high on the flanks. Yet now they are so totally different, because of a physical interpretation of time.

Perhaps I'm not putting it very well. There are elements

on St Helena, about St Helena, which are perfectly natural, yet you suddenly, or maybe even slowly, see them as being special. Certainly their effect on me was, is, special. To me it's all saying more about time, than about place.

But look. Here at the cliffs of Long Range. Look carefully at these marvellous, almost threatening, cliffs, and there are scratches. Those scatches are a fisherman's path, zig-zag, hop and skip, jump, cling and slither, down to fish, and back up the stairs, fastest way to get food to feed the family. And the cliffs? The enormity? It's only a staircase, really. It's a lovely island example of the enormity of time, the enormity of the abstract concept of such time, and hands-on pragmatism.

This geological time, millions of years, is everywhere. That's about as obvious a statement as it's possible to make, but it's like the air we breathe, we don't often think about it. In places I'm suddenly very aware of it. To the fishermen it's irrelevant. Wonderful cliffs, eight million years in the making, to me. Wonderful staircase, quick way down for a spot of food, for them. They probably treat it with more respect than I do, they have to climb up and down it, I just look at it.

Take the walk to Prosperous Bay Signal Station, that bit from the flatness at the end of the Plain, across the little col and up the slope to the ruin. It's a few feet and hidden in bits of broken rocks is a line (the slip surface) dividing flows of the south-western volcano from those of the older north-eastern. One step, one single step, onto lavas of the later volcano. What's the age difference? A million years? Two million years? That's a lot of time. One small step for man, and a million years or more for the volcano.

Move your foot back, and it's shifted a million years or more. Just one small step, tick, plus a million years, tock, minus a million years. You can stand there, pretty well rocking one foot on each mass. Each is a different piece of geological time. Each mass took hundreds and hundreds of thousands of years to build. And the two were brought together by that colossal slip virtually in an instant eight and a half million years ago. This is some of the geological time that surrounds you. It certainly makes me stop and think.

I know it's not the same as the Grand Canyon, or the Andes, or the Himalayas. I've watched those, wondrous. In Mysore, the pavements are made of rocks more than two *billion* years old. Half the age of the Earth, and you walk on them. That's pretty wondrous, too. The point here, on this small island, is that these different scales of time are around you, all the time. In the silence, the solitude, they offer some strange kind of reassurance, some kind of strength to help you find, if not understand, some kind of place in it all. It doesn't intrude, it doesn't bother anybody. It helps the fishermen. But its magic is there for the finding, if you want it.

St Helena loves to play with this ambivalence, this admixture of time and place. Geological time, millions of years, is one part, but on another scale is man's history of a few hundred years and the present. That is much more obvious. So much history surrounds you, that you're hardly aware that it's any different from the present, it's interwoven. Look at the population, they are living witnesses of the interplay of its history.

And to complicate things, or enhance them, on the island, these historical time shifts are superimposed with shifts of its own special geography. You stand and look in one direction at a desert, its rock pinnacles seared by relentless sun. Ah yes, there went Robert Jenkins. And behind you are dripping forest ferns. Oh yes, there went Joseph Banks. Half turn one way, and there are rolling pastures. Oh yes, the invading Dutch fought here. Half turn the other, and distant jagged cliff tops. Yes indeed, those are Darwin's cliff tops.

One morning, sitting in the garden of Bishop's Rooms, I looked up and saw clouds going in opposite directions. Puffs of cloud coming down the valley, and windy wisps of cloud going up the valley. It was a sort of climatic equivalent of seeing pink elephants, looking up at the clouds and seeing them blowing in opposite directions at the same time. It could be a terrible way to start the day if you had a hangover. My meteorological informant explained the existence of a wind shear at about five thousand feet. Fine, but again, aren't clouds that do that a bit special?

And that evening, I had the chance to watch in its entirety, a total lunar eclipse. It was due to begin at 22.21, I'd been told. So I'd eaten, and put my chair and table on the little patio. It was a wonderful cloud free evening, brilliant full moon, straight overhead. And more or less next door, the reception room of the Consulate Hotel was celebrating a wedding. One personal terrestrial event oblivious to the forthcoming celestial event.

The live music, yes, that's right the Brooks Brothers' Band, was loud and fun, the non-stop mix of all sorts, and the solid clumping of dancing feet. You dance to anything the band plays, goes without saying, certainly goes without hearing, it's deafening in the thick of things. It was pretty noisy on the fringes. But you couldn't get what I'd got if you paid a fortune. A total eclipse *and* live music. It wasn't Wagner, but it was special.

To start with, there were very few stars close to the moon. But once the shadow crossed three quarters of it, the sky was alive with stars. *Hang out your Washing* and *Pack up your Troubles*, as the moon seriously started disappearing.

The moon as we know it had almost gone, a final thin bright crescent and most of the dark bulk with a deep reddish tinge, looking like a foetus lit from behind, or within. When the reddish tinged disc was complete, *Run Rabbit Run*. And as the texture strengthened, *I've got sixpence* and *Bless 'em all* brought an end to the wartime nostalgia.

Amazing. You watch, and there is the primordial uncertainty that the moon will return, that life as we know it might die out, that the sun will rise again sometime. And disco music, while the band takes a break. The noise seems a far greater threat than the disappearance of the moon.

*Staying Alive*, and a deep orange sphere in an otherwise normal starry sky. And then *mariachis*! Still this unreal globe, and they're back with *Anchors Away* and a proper whistled version of *Colonel Bogie*. *Over There* and the last dance is announced, and there's still no real moon. A female country and western singer, with a throat like sandpaper, sings the evening out and the newlyweds off.

A fairy tern flies high above the valley, lit from below, like a slow pale meteorite, and the moon is silvery gold, with darker *maria* and a brighter crescent starting where that first hint of darkness began. The clatter of clearing up, laughter and shouting of the waiters quickly finishes, long, long before the crescent has moved significantly.

In peace and quiet from the hotel, but with increasing numbers of barking dogs, and the time-challenged cockerels of the Run, the moon returns. It's even more splendid than when it went away, even brighter, and whole areas of stars have disappeared once more. The moonlight is as bright as I've ever seen, you could read large print. The white buildings of town are almost glowing, and the shadows are black, as though painted. I don't know what the dogs will do when true dawn breaks, it must be very confusing.

In the sixties, the lights of town were switched off at eleven, or was it ten? I keep forgetting. They all went out, and cockerels calling all hours from the Run didn't sound right somehow. If the lights had just gone off, how could dawn conceivably be just around the corner? Very dim they are, cockerels. But it meant that in town you could see the full brilliance of the night sky.

If you were staying up country, and you got a clear night, it was even more wondrous. I've seen stars in some pretty remote places, but on St Helena the night sky has a presence like no other. The sky has a texture, there are all shades of blackness and starbright. You feel you could reach out and put your hands behind one group of stars, in front of the next, run your fingers through them like coins, they are that tangible. Your eyes begin to ache, as you try to look farther and farther into the layers of curtains. You can almost hear the stars.

All right, you can't really see these great distances into the night sky, that's just how it feels. But the stars are indeed all different distances away, and their light has taken all kinds of different times to reach the Earth. So you're looking at a kind of time collage, time map. Some light took only a few years to get here, some took millions of years, some maybe took billions. And it's all visible with the naked eye, all shining on you, arriving on your retina at the same time. It's a sort of time curtain now, as you look at it, but of course you can't see it, it's invisible. Well, time is, or at least it usually is.

So you have a sort of *aurora borealis,* or rather *aurora australis,* shimmering, flickering, dancing before you, but it's an aurora of time, invisble, all changing as you look up, tens of years and millions of years and billions of years, all jumbled before you. And yes, of course you can see this anywhere. But do you? Do you stop and look, and think just that? Or do you think it doesn't matter? Here it matters, here you have the time to stop, to see it. Oh but it's invisible, I'm forgetting, all right so you don't see it, but you feel it.

This then, is the last great element of time reaching the island, the invisible aurora. And part of it was the lunar eclipse, mixed with the more recent fabric of musical times from the Brooks Brothers. These different elements of time, even more obscure than Dickens' ghosts in *A Christmas Carol*, bathe the island, and you move in them all. It's not just that you have more chance to think, more opportunity to wonder, there's something here that stirs up things in your mind that other places haven't reached.

And there is something else special, but I'm not sure where it fits in with any of these times. On very rare days there is a light, so clear that it changes your perceptions. Maybe it's not to do with time directly, or perhaps it is, for it happens so rarely, it's a bit like the special relationship of the lunar eclipse. Or then it is so rare, so special, it is independent of time. Or is that confusing? It is certainly independent of place, in that its message is of beauty, yes, even of wonder, pure and simple.

It comes upon you suddenly, an awareness that the scene is so clear. The clarity brings an intensity that you would expect only with a telephoto lens or binoculars. The complete texture of a scene changes. Looking at a wooded slope across the valley, every tree stands out, individually. Or a slope covered in flax, and you can see, at least you imagine you can, not just the individual rows, and plants, but each blade. Some of it may be imagination, but only a little because it's upon you so quickly that the first thing you notice is the surprise with which it takes you over.

There are cattle in a pasture across the valley, and you feel you can pick them up, one at a time. And their shadows are so soft, if you were over there, you would be able to feel the shadow settling on you, like a dark shawl. Colours come alive. The island is double blessed anyway, with the range of colours you see every day, in every direction. But in this light, every colour stands out, as though softer, as though harder, sharper. And every colour has a new range of shades, new dimensions if you like.

It's like seeing not just every shade of the rainbow, but as though each of the rainbow colours was a rainbow in itself. There are shades and nuances of colour you couldn't believe. A bit like in a really good northern autumn, when that incredible range of yellows, golds, reds, bronzes, seems overwhelming. Well, in this light the same happens with all the colours.

On days like this the light can change back almost as suddenly as it started. Days like this are inscribed onto your memory. I had only three in the eight months I was on the island in the nineties. One of them was the afternoon when Stedson Stroud took Basil and me across Sandy Bay, down below Lot's Wife to see the newly discovered boxwood. The colours of the entire Bay were alive, from red to violet. If you stopped to watch, it was so beautiful it was an effort to move again, even with the prospect of seeing a plant believed to have been extinct for nearly two centuries. That is the intensity of the light.

It's as though the visible spectrum is falling on your eyes like the invisible spectrum of time, from the different stars at night. It is a sensation that something very different is washing over you, through you. It's like a drug that lifts you into some other dimension, while keeping your mind clear. I don't mind if such days have anything to do with the island's layers of time or not, I accept them as being outside any normal run of experience.

In the heart of the volcano, as much as anywhere, perhaps more than anywhere, it is the concept of time that permeates all the senses. The island today has been shaped by the elements over however many million years. In some places this enormity is more prominent. In Turk's Cap Bay it is primitive, hard to grasp, a little harsh because the scenery is austere. In Sandy Bay with the magnificence from tree-fern Peaks to wave cut flat shorelines, it is less obtrusive. The landscape is so beautiful, that time, however great, is secondary, it doesn't impinge, doesn't really enter your head.

But at the end of the rim, before the Asses Ears, looking down on the stunning and bizarre accumulation of savage and gentle beauty, time is very present. And living time is here too, the endemic flora saved ten million years ago, as its origins were shifted and destroyed. Or twenty years ago when George Benjamin saved the ebony from extinction, even a couple of years ago when Stedson Stroud found the boxwood. You walk through that feeling on the Peaks, millions of years of time, where there is only vegetation. You walk through that here in the heart of the volcano, the ebony, the boxwood, the scrubwoods, proud in their awesome landscape of convoluted rocks.

St Helena is a bit like that aurora of the night sky, when all the different ages of the stars arrive at once. The views, and the atmosphere all around, are a mosaic of all its history, all its bits and pieces of people and places coming together in what appears to us a single scene. And particularly in its wild places, its private places, there is with it the enormity of peace. This is what the island's fabric of different times is about. When you can feel it, feel the layers of time playing with you, feel yourself trying to play with them, then you know, not that the island has taken, but that you have given the island, a part of your soul.

# EPILOGUE

*You cannot reasonably hope to change the nature of a community at one fell swoop. It must take time. Again, that sine qua non to progress, namely capital, is almost entirely conspicuous by its absence in St Helena. Handicapped as they are, it is not surprising that the St Helenians find it up-hill work in their efforts to work out their own salvation. Time alone will solve the problem. In the meantime I, like many other "birds of passage," will continue to watch St Helena's progress with the deepest interest and concern.*

Governor Lieutenant-Colonel H. L. Gallwey, Plantation House, 1908

Whenever the RMS was in, preparing to sail, I usually stayed in town, at least for the morning, for the last minute rush to get letters away. There is something different about 'boat day'. Half the island seems to be there, the town is busy, lots of vehicles bringing and fetching people and all their stuff. And the seaside is alive, people watching, waiting, seeing off, receiving, people in their working clothes, everyday clothes, people in their leaving clothes.

St Helenians are not particularly emotional, not outwardly, and certainly not the men. But when the time approaches for passengers to get the bus at the wharf gate, to take them those last few yards to the steps, and the waiting boats, there is a change in the atmosphere, the laughter is that bit more forced, and there are damp eyes, wet eyes, even faces folding in grief. I wondered about this. They're an island people. Ships, and people, are always on the move. How is this different?

It's the finality, real or imagined. Friends, family, loved ones, leaving, and it may be the last time you see them for years, or for some it will indeed be the last time. It's something to do with the remoteness of the island, it's something to do with ships and the sea. Airports seem so much easier, to many of us I think they really are a little unreal. Big, brash, bright, piped faceless orders and instructions, lists of destinations like an index, check in, check out, wave it off, and straight away they'll be where they're going, or they're back, almost before you get home and get the kettle on.

Ships are different, and the ocean is different. And the reason they are going is different. The older they are, the more people they've seen leave, and the more they've not seen again. You can see that finality in people's faces. You can feel the finality long before the bay is empty, and then there's just the slosh slosh slosh of the water.

For 'birds of passage' it's different. They can come back again, or they might not want to come again. Another day, another place, the ship's another means to an end, not the end itself. And now it was my turn. I was leaving again, after four more wonderful months. Maybe I'd now had enough. Man and boy I'd been all over this island, legged it, loved it, it was time to move on, wasn't it?

Seale, pragmatic son of the island, writing in 1834 said understanding the island could throw light on understanding the structure of the globe. St Helena reveals so much of its wild and fiery history it is wonderful, but it hides so much, even of its geology. More than a century and a half ago Seale could write that. And you could write it today. And you could wait as long again and find the island still preserving some of its mystery, some of its magic.

This is the strength of the island, the top of a volcanic pile more than three miles above the floor of the ocean, and sculpted into scenery like the other side of the moon. This is the mystery, and these are the rocks of mystery. No, Seale's prophecy must wait a few more centuries, and in the meantime I'm happy just relishing the wonder of this place.

I'd had my last walk, out towards the Asses Ears, and dropped down through Man o' War Roost to Sharks Bench, right through the volcano. And Basil had taken me for a last drive round the island, so I'd remember all its bits, and for a last dinner at his home, with Barbara and whoever in the family was around The RMS had been sitting in the Road all night, brightly lit, welcoming. I was packed, if not sorted out.

The logistics of leaving are simple, close your savings account at The Castle, pay your bills, get your clearance at the Police Station, and you're all set. All those days, weeks, of preparing for it, consciously or otherwise, and it's all over so quickly. One minute on the wharf with friends, people you know, sights and sounds that have become your background, and the next you're in the bus, getting out at the steps, getting into a boat, onto the RMS, and she's sailing. And the wharf and Jamestown are barely distinguishable.

It's late afternoon, and the ship is heading almost into the brilliant light left behind by the sun when it sank out of sight. We're far enough away to see the island as an entity, and that late light has turned it bronze. It's impossible to see details, just make out individual valleys etched into it. It's like a polished sepia print, and it's etched on me. The sea is ocean now, not James Bay from the seaside, not the white scars you saw from the hills, but broad swells, and the ship is steady.

As it gets darker, the island is a smudge, and it fades, thought by thought, as piece by piece memories are locked away, like treasures closed in museum drawers. I can't see anything any more, I don't know that I can actually think. The sea is invisible, the stars are brilliant, and silent, and the island is no more.

This was '99, and I was returning via Ascension. Just two nights and a day, you hardly notice, you're hardly on board before you're off again. It was not something I had particularly wanted to do. But I'm glad I did. As a volcano it's not as interesting as St Helena, and as an island for walking it isn't in the same class. But it's fascinating for a short time nonetheless, and there are winds of change. Better technology can reduce the numbers of people needed to run the high tech equipment, so why not promote the wonder of the turtles that choose Ascension to lay their eggs? At the right time of year, January to April or thereabouts, turtle watching is a bizarre and magical pastime.

At the moment Ascension is a bit like a transit camp, room here, food there in the canteen, set hours, set menu, friendly enough Saints moving you on your inevitable way. I walked up and round the top of Green Mountain, which was fun. A kind lady opened the museum for me, that was fun. And I went to a lecture by a specialist followed by a guided tour, turtle watching. That was unforgettable.

At night, great Krakens dragging up the beach, digging pits

you could lose buses in, and laying eggs. In the golden dawn, the beach is scarred with their caterpillar tracks. The higher beach is like photos of Paschendaele, obliterated with craters, and the slower mothers are making their way to the water. Frigate birds, truly pirates these, patrol looking for any tardy youngsters, or the eggs of earlier layers disturbed by the bomb-burst tunnelling of the later. Wondrous.

Then in the evening I was taken for dinner in The Volcano Club. What a name! But no T-shirt, how sad. And to the airport. Floodlights, plastic, people, and in roars the DC10 from the Falklands, more people. The transit lounge in the transit camp island.

Roaring again, and out goes the DC10, several hundred servicemen and women, they're serious birds of passage, and a few of us amateurs, into the night sky and the firework display, off left, port is it? Incoming multiple warheads test-fired from Florida, just to miss the island. The turtles on the other hand, coming from more or less the same direction, and without all that hard and software, have to hit it.

What a day. Silent dawn, breaking on those turtles, and midnight aircraft racket and intercontinental ballistic fireworks. Strange world, isn't it? At least the South Atlantic is.

Eight hours, lovely and comfortable, bit of sleep, decent breakfast, happy service people going home. Into Brize Norton, bus to Swindon, all so organized. And stand on the train all the way to Paddington. Welcome to the rest of the world.

It can't be long till St Helena has its airstrip, though God knows who'll pay for it. And Prosperous Bay Plain will lose its silence, revert to a different racket to replace its ancient bird rookery. Even so, the strip would probably not be big enough for long haul aircraft, and they would be looking for a feeder service in and out of Ascension. It will be useful to the islanders. With their proper citizenship restored, they'll need to travel more, medical emergencies come to mind, and the island will need easier access for visitors.

It was Governor Gallwey who started the golf course at Longwood, and his words above are still of interest. But time won't sort out the islanders' future, *they* will. Fishing and fish licenses aren't enough, and there's no off shore oil or gas. Tourism is perhaps the only source of a financial future. It will employ constructively a lot of islanders, currently un- or under-employed. It might bring back some of the offshore workers, reduce the number of separated families.

It will never be a bumper tourist destination, no beaches, too quiet, too much hard work walking. It's got so many special attractions, but they aren't, luckily, to everyone's liking. So people will come for the quiet, the peace, the staggering scenery, the endemics, and the different world. They'll come for the memories of Napoleon, of Dinizulu, of the Boer prisoners, of the East India Company, and so much more of the history. Maybe they'll even come for the layers of time. Keep it as St Helena plc, so the earnings, as far as that is possible, come to and stay on the island.

As a holiday island, it could have everything a rather special type of visitor wanted. Get the numbers right, local flights twice a week or whatever from Ascension. If there wasn't an expensive airstrip then a dedicated fast ocean catamaran might be an attractive enough alternative. But the right number of visitors through most months of the year would constitute packages with a tailor-made difference.

They need a lot of services and support. Drivers, guides, hotel and catering staff. A lot of people with traditional skills, for restoration work, for building work, masons, carpenters, plumbers, electricians, higher tech ones. Down to earth ones for local produce, all those fruits and veg that once were grown, it should bring a renaissance to the island's agriculture

But the airstrip will change the island instantly, in one way. It will remove its isolation. It may not bring it too far into line with the mainstream islands. But it will erode its unique characters, in time, slowly and steadily. And will that be for the worse? Nobody today would question the changes from the squalor and the slums of the 1840s, the 1890s, or the 1930s. How many changes and improvements in so many ways, have I seen since the 1960s?

The island will still have its special places, still have its silence. And with the inhabitants, it will retain the special characters they derived from history and isolation. But it must protect the extraordinary fragilty of its ambience, its plants and scenery. Those desert areas may look rough and tough, but they and their framework are fragile. Too many feet traipsing over the Peaks could erode too, the wonder of the endemics. How much more might the effects be on the desert places, and the isolated boneseed, or some other unique plant thought to have been long extinct?

To preserve the integrity of the island and her people, all aspects of development must progress in step. How many times in the past, and not too distant at that, has one step forward led to two steps back? Much of the world outside lurches forward, if that is the word, with little or no consideration for all its parts. St Helena can't afford to do that. Its special character, the serendipitous overlying its ancient nature, is too sensitive. If you lose that, then in effect, you lose this special island.

And then there was to be another postscript. After 1999 I hadn't intended to go back, but within months I had booked again for another four months on the island from November 2003 to March 2004.

And it was another marvellous visit, wetter, cooler than earlier summers, but great walking, great company. I cleared up a lot of problems with the geology, and found a lot more. I was shown aspects of the social problems: of migration now of families not just the workforce, dwindling numbers of skilled and trained people, of uncertainty of a future with an airport. But the future must await other writers, other 'birds of passage', and I'll read with great interest about developments, in all their aspects.

But now it's time for Ecclesiastes: there is a time to gather stones, and I have gathered; there is a time to seek, and I have sought; there is a time to speak, and I have spoken; and a time to keep silence - now it is time for that.

# BIBLIOGRAPHY

**Ashmole, Philip and Myrtle** : *St Helena and Ascension Island : a natural history*, Anthony Nelson, Oswestry, 2000.

**Beatson, Alexander** : *Tracts relative to the Island of St Helena; written during a residence of five years,* W. Bulmer and Co., London, 1816.

**Bellasis, G.H.** : *Views of St Helena*, George Hutchins, London 1815.

**Bishop of St. Helena's Commission on Citizenship** : *St. Helena The lost county of England*, Government Printer, St Helena, 1996.

**Brooke, T.H.** : *A History of the island of St Helena*, Black, Parry and Kingsbury, London, 1808.

**Brookes, Dame Mabel** : *St Helena Story*, Heinemann 1960.

**Carter, Edward** : *The Dovetons of St Helena*, Privately printed, Cape Town 1973.

**Castell, Robin** : *St Helena*, Wensley Brown 1979.

**Cleverly, Les** : *W.J.Burchell, Special Agent or Naturalist. A Short Biography*, Vereiniging, South Africa 1989.

**Crallan, Hugh P.** : *Island of St Helena. Report on the history and Preservation of Buildings of Special Architectural or Historic Interest*, Private, London May 1974.

**Cronk, Q.C.B.,** : *The endemic flora of St Helena*, Anthony Nelson, Oswestry, 2000.

**Darwin, Charles** : *The Voyage of The Beagle*, Natural History Society Edition, 1962.

**Forsyth, William** : *History of the captivity of Napoleon at St Helena : from the letters and journals of the late Lieut.-General Sir Hudson Lowe*, 3 vols, John Murray, London 1853.

**George, Barbara B.** : *Jacob's Ladder*, Printsetters, Bristol 1995.

— : *Napoleon arrives on St Helena*, Printsetters Bristol 1995.

— : *St Helena - The Chinese Connection*, Printsetters, Bristol, 2002

**Gosse, Philip** : *St Helena 1502-1938*, Cassell and Co, London, 1938

**Gourgaud, Baron Gaspard** : *The St Helena Journal of General Baron Gourgaud*, translated by Sydney Gillard, John Lane, The Bodley Head, London, 1932.

**Hooker, Joseph Dalton** : *The Botany : The Antarctic Voyage of HM Discovery ships Erebus and Terror in the years 1839 - 1843*, Reeve Bros, London 1847.

**Jackson, E.L.** : *St. Helena: the historic island*, Ward Lock, London, 1903.

**Janisch, H.R.** : *Extracts from the St Helena Records, and chronicles of Cape Commanders, compiled by the late Hudson Ralph Janisch CMG, Governor of St Helena*, Benjamin Grant, St Helena, reprinted by P.L.Teale, W.A. Thorpe and Sons, 1980.

**Kemble, James** : *St Helena : During Napoleon's Exile : Gorrequer's Diary*, Heinemann, London 1969.

**Kerr, Robert** (Translator) : *Voyages and Travels* Vol II: from original Portuguese of Hermen Lopez de Castenada *History of the discovery and conquest of India by the Portuguese, between the years 1497 and 1505*, George Ramsay and Co, Edinburgh, 1811.

**Kitching, G.C.** : *A handbook and Gazeteer of the Island of St Helena including a short history of the Island under the Crown 1834 - 1902*, Draft MS to Government of St Helena 1937 and 1947.

**Martineau, Gilbert** : *Napoleon's St Helena*, Translated from the French by Frances Partridge, John Murray, London 1968.

— : *Napoleon Surrenders*, Translated from the French by Frances Partridge, John Murray, London 1971.

**Mathieson, Ian, and Carter, Lawrence** : *Exploring St Helena: A Walker's Guide*, Anthony Nelson, Oswestry, undated.

**Mayer, Erich** : *On St Helena - Full of Heartache* [*Op St Helena - Vol Van Hartpeyn*] in Afrikaans, Protea Boekhuis, Pretoria, 2000.

**Melliss, John Charles** : *St. Helena : a physical, historical, and topographical description of the Island, including its geology, fauna, flora and meteorology,* L.Reeve and Co, Ashford, Kent, 1875.

**Oliver, S.P.** : *On board a Union steamer*, WH Allen and Co, London, 1881.

**O'Meara, Barry E. :** *Napoleon in exile; or a Voice from St Helena,* Printed for W.Simpkin and R. Marshall, London 1822.
**Ransford, Oliver** : *The slave trade*, John Murray, 1971.
**Seale, R.F.** : *Geognosy of the Island of St Helena*, Jamestown, 1834.
**Shine, Ian** : *Serendipity in Saint Helena*, Pergamon Press, Oxford, 1970.
**Teale, P.L.** : *Saint Helena : A History of the Development of the Island*, 2 vols M.Arch. Thesis, University of Natal, 1972.
**Valentia, George, Viscount**: *Voyages and travels to India, Ceylon .....1802 - 1806*, 4 vols, Rivington, London 1811.
**Williams, R.O.** : *Plants on St Helena,* Report, Department of Agriculture and Forestry, St Helena 1989.